Resistance, Space and Political Identities

CW01091514

RGS-IBG Book Series

Resistance, Space and Political Identities

The Making of Counter-Global Networks

David Featherstone

WILEY-BLACKWELL

A John Wiley & Sons, Ltd., Publication

This edition first published 2008
© 2008 David Featherstone

Blackwell Publishing was acquired by John Wiley & Sons in February 2007. Blackwell's publishing program has been merged with Wiley's global Scientific, Technical, and Medical business to form Wiley-Blackwell.

Registered Office
John Wiley & Sons Ltd, The Atrium, Southern Gate, Chichester, West Sussex, PO19 8SQ, United Kingdom

Editorial Offices
350 Main Street, Malden, MA 02148-5020, USA
9600 Garsington Road, Oxford, OX4 2DQ, UK
The Atrium, Southern Gate, Chichester, West Sussex, PO19 8SQ, UK

For details of our global editorial offices, for customer services, and for information about how to apply for permission to reuse the copyright material in this book please see our website at www.wiley.com/wiley-blackwell.

Library of Congress Cataloging-in-Publication Data

Featherstone, David, 1974–
    Resistance, space and political identities : the making of counter-global networks / David Featherstone.
        p. cm.—(RGS-IBG book series)
    Includes bibliographical references and index.
    ISBN 978-1-4051-5808-4 (hardcover : alk. paper)—ISBN 978-1-4051-5809-1 (pbk. : alk. paper)   1. Anti-globalization movement.   2. Globalization—Political aspects.   3. International relations.   4. Power (Social sciences).   5. Geopolitics.   I. Title.
    JZ1318.F43 2008
    303.48'2—dc22

                                                                2008006981

A catalogue record for this book is available from the British Library.

Set in 10 on 12pt Plantin by SNP Best-set Typesetter Ltd, Hong Kong
Printed in Singapore by C.O.S. Printers Pte Ltd

1   2008

To my parents

Contents

Series Editors' Preface

The RGS-IBG Book Series only publishes work of the highest international standing. Its emphasis is on distinctive new developments in human and physical geography, although it is also open to contributions from cognate disciplines whose interests overlap with those of geographers. The Series places strong emphasis on theoretically informed and empirically strong texts. Reflecting the vibrant and diverse theoretical and empirical agendas that characterize the contemporary discipline, contributions are expected to inform, challenge and stimulate the reader. Overall, the RGS-IBG Book Series seeks to promote scholarly publications that leave an intellectual mark and change the way readers think about particular issues, methods or theories.

For details on how to submit a proposal please visit:
www.rgsbookseries.com

Kevin Ward
University of Manchester, UK

Joanna Bullard
Loughborough University, UK

RGS-IBG Book Series Editors

Acknowledgements

Writing a book, as Billy Bragg has remarked, is not like writing a song. Along the way I have incurred many debts and received much help, support and encouragement. Parts of this book started out life in my Ph.D. thesis that was supervised by Doreen Massey and Steve Hinchliffe. The work here owes a vast amount to their intellectual engagement and support over many years.

The Department of Geography at the University of Liverpool has been an engaging environment in which to be based during the writing of this book. In particular my fellow travellers in the Globalization, Development and Place research group have been the source of much comradeship, insight and humour. Pete North's relentless enthusiasm for all things spatial has been a constant source of inspiration. Richard Phillips has been strongly supportive of this project since its inception, has commented on drafts of various chapters and has supplied many helpful mugs of proper tea. I have benefited from discussion with Benedikt Korf in the 'space of exception' that is the Albert in Lark Lane. I would also like to thank Bethan Evans, Richard Powell, David Sadler and Jo Waters. Andy Davies's insights into networked forms of political activity have been very useful.

The students who have taken my third year course 'Space, Place and the Making of Political Identities' have been subjected to these arguments at length. Their engagement, discussion and criticisms have helped me to clarify the arguments presented here. Not all, I hope, have found the course 'frankly bloody irritating'.

I am glad that despite the increasingly neo-liberal environment in universities it is still possible to do some activities that are not subject to funding! Nonetheless I would like to acknowledge the ESRC grant that supported my Ph.D. The work on the London Corresponding Society was supported by a Liverpool University Research Development Fund grant and thanks go also to the research assistance of Andy Jobling that it helped support. The British Academy funded my attendance at the 'Middle Passages' conference at the Western Australia Maritime Museum, which was very useful for chapter 5.

Thanks to the networks and many helpful individuals of the Inter-Continental Caravan for allowing me to participate in discussions and events. Thanks are also due to the many helpful archivists who have assisted with this research. The ideas in this book have benefited from discussion in many seminars and conferences. I would like to thank the many helpful engagements and criticisms that have helped me to develop these arguments.

Many people have encouraged the work here. I would like in particular to thank John Allen, Alan Lester, Miles Ogborn, Marcus Rediker and Jane Wills. At Blackwell/RGS-IBG book series Nick Henry was very encouraging in the early days of developing the proposal. Jacqueline Scott's editorial help and guidance has been indispensable and I would also like to thank Jack Messenger, Hannah Morrell and Kevin Ward. The generous and insightful comments of two anonymous readers were very helpful. Working with Noel Castree and Andy Herod was very useful in terms of sharpening my understandings of the debates over scales and networks, though they won't necessarily agree with the position outlined here. Clive Barnett generously commented on chapter 4, though likewise will not necessarily agree with it. In Glasgow, Andy Cumbers and Paul Routledge have provided indispensable support, discussion and engagement.

Cian O'Driscoll, Kelly Kollman, Karen Wright, Ana Langer and Orian Brook have all contributed in different ways. The support and engagement of Harriet Fletcher, Jon Hallé and William Mortada goes way back and is much appreciated. Occasional forays to 'the Nook' with Tim Bunnell have helped the process even if my pool technique remains unimproved. Thank also to Bev Bishop and Polly North for their hospitality. Many thanks are due to my brother and sister for their support.

I would like to thank the generous support and engagement of all the Humes, especially John and Pat. Their hospitality, discussion, humour and warmth are much appreciated.

My parents Mike and Tess Featherstone have been a constant source of encouragement, support and love. I would also like to thank them for keeping some sense of progressive values alive in the border hills in the dark years of Thatcherism.

Two people have made writing this book a much more enjoyable experience than it otherwise would have been. My daughter Marni has been a great mate. Hanging out together has brought my life much joy. She has also been a useful source of scepticism about my arguments, reminding me, for example, that despite my concern with mutinous sailors, Nelson was the bravest man ever and that pirates were just sea robbers.

Finally, my debt to my partner Mo Hume is immeasurable! She has supported the book in more ways than is reasonable. Her love, irreverent humour, support and intellectual companionship have made this a better book. She has also tolerated the frequent interjection of conversations with random remarks about the relationships between different chapters and arcane aspects of eighteenth-century radicalism. Her insights, discussion and engagement have sharpened the arguments in many ways. More importantly, she has made the process of writing it a much happier one.

David Featherstone
Glasgow and Liverpool, November, 2007

The editor and publisher gratefully acknowledge the permission granted to reproduce the copyright material in this book:

Extracts from the Newfoundland missionaries' letters used in chapter 3. Reprinted by permission of the United Society for the Propagation of the Gospel. Extracts from the Shelburne papers. Reprinted by permission of William L. Clements Library, University of Michigan. Parts of chapters 2 and 7 were previously published in Featherstone, D. J. (2003), 'Spatialities of transnational resistance to globalization: the maps of grievance of the Inter-Continental Caravan', *Transactions of the Institute of British Geographers* vol. 28, issue 4, pp. 404–21. Reprinted by permission of Wiley-Blackwell. Parts of chapter 3 was previously published in Featherstone, D. J. (2005), 'Skills for heterogeneous associations: the Whiteboys, collective experimentation and subaltern political ecologies', first published in *Environment and Planning D: Society and Space*, 2007, 25, pp. 284–306; reprinted by permission of Pion Limited, London. Parts of chapters 1 and 4 were previously published in Featherstone, D. J. (2007), 'The spatial politics of the past unbound: transnational networks and the making of political identities', *Global Networks* vol. 7, issue 4, pp. 430–52. Reprinted by permission of Wiley-Blackwell. Thanks to the South Wales Miners' Library at the University of Swansea for permission to reproduce the illustration of the banner of the Abercrave Lodge of the NUM (figure 1.1).

Every effort has been made to trace copyright holders and to obtain their permission for the use of copyright material. The publisher apologizes for any errors or omissions in the above list and would be grateful if notified of any corrections that should be incorporated in future reprints or editions of this book.

Introduction

Space, Contestation and the Political

In Glasgow in June 2007 a delegation of activists from trade unions and social movements in Colombia presented evidence of British Petroleum's 'corporate crimes'. They gave testimonies of BP's poor environmental record in Colombia, particularly in Casanare. They also demonstrated what was at the very least complicity between BP and assassinations of leaders and activists of the Colombian Oilworkers Union USO. Since 1988 USO has suffered '105 assassinations of its members, 2 members "disappeared", 6 kidnapped, 35 wounded in assassination attempts, 400 internal refugees, 4 members in exile, 300 members have experienced death threats, 30 have been detained, 900 are undergoing criminal proceedings and 55 have been subject to "mobbing".'[1] The Colombian speakers related this to the broader context of assassination and intimidation of trade unionists and to the impunity of multinationals in Colombia.

This event was part of a transnational set of mobilizations instigated by the People's Permanent Tribunal (PPT), a non-governmental tribunal set up to investigate and challenge the role of multinationals in Colombia. The PPT uses 'exemplary cases' 'to show how the Colombian state has facilitated and contributed to the exploitation of our natural resources by these companies, by committing crimes and permanently violating the rights of the individual citizens and their organizations' (PPT, 2007). The Glasgow event was one of seven preliminary public hearings being held in relation to the oil industry. There were four hearings in Colombia in Saravena, Barrancabermeja, El Tarra–Northern Santander and Cartagena. The PPT also 'invited supporting organizations in the home countries of the three biggest corporations Occidental (USA); Repsol YPF (Spain) and BP (UK) to hold preliminary public hearings in the run up to the full tribunal' (Colombia Solidarity Campaign, 2007). The evidence presented at these preliminary hearings fed into a formal public hearing of these three oil corporations in Bogotá in August 2007.

These events produced a networked opposition constructed through connections between activists in different places and through bringing together different groups mobilising around oil politics and the political situation in Colombia. This book is about the forms of political identity and agency crafted through such 'unruly alliances and flows'.[2] The book explores the geographies of connection that have shaped forms of opposition to dominant forms of globalised practices. I argue that there are significant histories and geographies of networked forms of subaltern political activity that have frequently been omitted from both more totalising and nation-centred accounts of resistance. Further, the importance of these forms of political activity has been marginalized in debates on globalisation. This has had significant effects in both theoretical and political terms.

It is my contention that these histories and geographies of subaltern political activity profoundly unsettle accounts that construct globalisation as a contemporary process without history and uneven geographies and as solely the product of neo-liberal actors. In contrast I position globalisation as a set of unfinished processes with multiple and contested histories and geographies (see Massey, 2005, Slater, 2004). The book situates past as well as present forms of resistance as constituted through engaging with the unequal geographies shaped by dominant processes of globalisation. To engage with the dynamic and productive subaltern spaces of politics produced through such struggles I use the term 'counter global networks'. This refers to networks of resistance to dominant forms of globalisation that are transnational in reach. I contend that telling stories about the geographies of connection formed through such struggles, and the forms of political identity and agency they have shaped can animate contemporary political imaginaries.

When the opposition to neo-liberal globalization first became internationally prominent and visible during the Seattle protests in 1999, these resistances were quickly labelled 'anti-globalization' movements. They were seen as representing an atavistic desire to return to bounded forms of the local or national. These debates have moved on. This is partly because movement activists and intellectuals refused the terms on which this debate was posed (see Bové and Dufour, 2001: 159; Graeber, 2002: 203; Klein, 2002a, 2002b: 76–84). They have shifted the terrain of debate from being pro- or anti-globalization to being about what kind of globalizations are produced. Their indictment of the current forms of neo-liberal globalization has been a condition of possibility for the discussion of the construction of alternative globalizations. As Boaventura De Sousa Santos has argued, what is at stake here are struggles for counter-hegemonic forms of globalization (De Sousa Santos, 2006: x). These movements have produced diverse alternatives to neo-liberal globalization, the *World Social Forum* being foremost among these.

That these debates have moved on to being about what kinds of globalization are produced is a testament to the generative, productive forms of political activity shaped through counter-global networks. This book seeks to engage with a number of intellectual challenges thrown up by these forms of spatially stretched resistance to globalization. Firstly, what kinds of political identities and agency are formed through these counter-global networks and how can they be theorized? Secondly, how are these networks constituted, what forms of alliances and solidarities do they generate and what is the productive character of their activity? Thirdly, what are the histories and geographies of counter-global networks? Finally, there is a set of questions about the political significance of these networks and movements. To engage with these challenges I outline a relational account of space, place and political activity. The next section of this introductory chapter outlines the key elements of this approach. I then discuss the political positionality that structures the book and justify its use of both past and present struggles. I then outline the structure and content of the book.

Theorizing Networked Resistances

This book develops an explicitly relational approach to the political. It does this to engage with the challenges posed by networked forms of resistance to neo-liberal globalization. Central to this project is the assertion that there are both histories and geographies of subaltern political activity that are not bounded.[3] They have been constituted through, and have constituted, various relations that stretch beyond particular places and sites. Understanding the connections that they have produced, articulated and crafted opens up important questions about the forms of political identity and agency generated through their activity. Such a set of concerns, however, is dissonant with many central assumptions about the geographies of resistance and subaltern political activity.

One of the central arguments of this book is that dominant ways of thinking about the geographies of political activity and resistance have been complicit with the construction of resistance movements as bounded. The dynamism of neo-liberal globalization has frequently been counterposed to the settled, bounded spaces of subaltern political activity (see Castells, 1997; Escobar, 2001; Harvey, 1989, 1996; Swyngedouw, 2004). This position has been most dramatically posed in David Harvey's aphorism that 'working-class movements are . . . generally better at organizing in and dominating place than they are at commanding space' (Harvey, 1989: 236). This way of thinking about the geographies of subaltern politics is not innocent. It has had severe effects on attempts to engage with the forms of identity and agency generated through subaltern political activity. One of the key aims of this book is to counter the dispossession of agency that flows from these understandings of the spaces of subaltern political activity. To do this I outline a theoretical vocabulary that engages directly with networked forms of resistance. The aim of this is to foreground the dynamism of subaltern spaces of politics rather than to make them the settled, bounded 'other' of neo-liberal globalization. This involves the following key theoretical interventions.

Firstly, I situate place-based politics, even those struggles designated 'militant particularisms', as the products of relations. Long-standing traditions in geographical theorising have treated place and space as constitutively separate (Cox, 1998, Harvey, 1996, Tuan, 1979). This counter-position of space and place structures the dispossession of subaltern agency in accounts of the constitution of spatial relations. The position developed here disrupts from the outset this counter-position of space and place (see Massey, 2005: 177–195). Rejecting this bifurcated view of space and place permits a focus on the ways in which place-based politics is produced out of negotiations with translocal connections and routes of subaltern activity rather than being 'fixed, local places' or as the 'origins' of political struggles (Mitchell, 2002: 69, Harvey, 2000: 241). This account of place-based politics has consequences. It opens up possibilities for accounting for the dynamic formation of subaltern identities and agency. Rather than viewing struggles as formed in particular places, then networked, this allows more ongoing, contested, recursive and generative relationships to be posed between place-based political activity and networked relations.

Secondly, this account is based on a particular account of networks. I define networks as the overlapping and contested material, cultural and political flows and circuits that bind different places together through differentiated relations of power. This draws on theoretical work that disrupts ways of theorising networks, and the social more generally, as the sole product of intentional, human-centred action (Law, 1986, 1994, Latour, 1993). In line with such work I position networks as 'materially heterogeneous'. By this I understand networks to be the connections and relational effects generated through associations of humans and other diverse entities which are constituted through multiple and contested relations. I do not see networks, as some have, as a privileged alternative form of spatial organisation of politics which is necessarily non-hierarchical. I contend, rather, that this ontology of the political can bring significant theoretical resources to bear on the fissiparous, contested and uneven spatialities generated through political activity.

Thirdly, I adopt a networked account of the geographies of solidarities. The formation of solidarities has often been reduced to the constitution of linkages between discrete bounded actors in different places or nations. Here I develop a processual account of solidarities and connections as networked, ongoing, contested and productive. This evokes the productive character of articulations and solidarities as part of the ongoing constitution of social and material relations (Braun and Disch, 2002: 507). Thus, rather than solidarities being seen as fixed interests formed around a static object, they can be reconfigured as ongoing interventions in the orderings of networks. This also permits a focus on the different relations of power through which transnational political networks are generated, formatted and shaped.

Finally, I position the geographies of contestation and the formation of antagonisms as dynamic, generative in process. Networked accounts of political activity have often evaded the significance of contestation to the political (see Braun and Disch, 2002; Featherstone, 2007; Lee and Brown, 1994). I argue, in contrast, that developing networked ontologies of the political offers resources for theorizing political agency and identities. I thus reject an account of antagonisms as bearing on disembodied values or fixed interests that pre-exist the conduct of political activity. Rather, I situate the formation of antagonisms as ongoing contestations over the orderings of associations of humans and non-humans. I develop a focus on the explicitly spatial practices through which antagonisms are constituted through using the term 'maps of grievance'. This term is used to foreground the diverse spatial practices through which geographies of power are brought into contestation through political activity.[4]

These theoretical interventions have implications for the accounts of political identities and practices developed throughout the book. I draw on the distinction between politics as an 'institutionalized arena of the political system' and the political 'as a type of conflictual relation that can develop in any area of the social' (Slater, 2004: 22). The book engages with different forms of resistance to dominant globalizing practices which in many ways are outside of, though certainly not autonomous from, institutionalized politics. I am concerned with the disruptive, generative geographies of political contestation they produce. In this regard, though the book is fundamentally concerned with forms of 'resistance', I find it useful to go beyond the concerns with the relations between resistance and domination that have structured debates in geography (see especially Pile and Keith, 1997; Sharp et al., 2000). Instead, I take as my focus the diverse forms of identity and agency constituted through subaltern political activity. This position refuses to view 'resistance' politics as the mirror of domination. It foregrounds the dynamic trajectories of resistance politics, while not evading the forms of contested geographies of power that are constructed through resistance politics.

To do this the book draws on Ernesto Laclau and Chantal Mouffe's relational account of political identities (Laclau and Mouffe, 1985). Their work views political identities as produced through political activity, rather than seeing the political as an arena defined by negotiations between actors with already constituted identities or interests. Their work is also significant through positioning political identities as formed through the ongoing negotiation of power relations and through the negotiation of multiple antagonisms (see Laclau and Mouffe, 1985; Mouffe, 1993, 2000). I dislocate their understanding of the formation of political identities however, in three key ways through combining insights drawn from spatial thinking and actor network theory.

Firstly, I challenge the human-centred account of the political adopted by Laclau and Mouffe. Their radical democratic project remains embedded within the terms of what Latour has described as the 'modern constitution', where the social and natural are viewed as constitutively separate and purified domains (Braun and Disch, 2002; see Latour, 1993, 1999a, 2004). Their account of the political views the political as bearing merely on the 'organization of human coexistence' (Mouffe, 1998: 16; see also Laclau, 2005a; Mouffe, 2005). There are, thus, important limits to their attempts to think the political in 'relational' terms. In their relational account of the political it is the purified human subject that remains central (Featherstone, 2004; Whatmore, 2002). In contrast I am concerned with understanding the formation of political identities as ongoing interventions in social and material relations. This is an account of the political that bears on the negotiation of heterogeneous associations, associations that bring together humans and non-humans through different strategic arrangements (Latour, 1998). This opens up important ways of accounting for the forms of agency and identity constituted through subaltern political activity.

Secondly, I contest Laclau and Mouffe's tendency to view political identities as always constituted negatively in relation to a 'constitutive outside' (Laclau and Mouffe, 1985; Laclau, 1996). I also question Chantal Mouffe's tendency to reify conflict as *the* foundational characteristic of the political (Mouffe, 1999a, 1999b, 2005). I think her assertion of the importance of antagonism and conflict to the political is significant. I argue, however, that it is necessary to see the spaces of the political as defined by a radical openness. I assert that the political can be productive of diverse and multiple outcomes, and that theorizing the political in explicitly spatial ways can help foreground such outcomes. Rather than negativity being the deciding factor in the constitution of political identities, this stresses the generative character of other attributes such as friendship, solidarity and association in shaping the formation of political identities (see also Massey, 2005; Hinchliffe et al., 2005).

Finally, in opposition to Laclau's stress on the radical emptiness of political activity (Laclau, 1996: 36–46), I insist on the significance of the 'relational contexts' of political activity (Thrift, 1996: 2). Laclau's stress on radical emptiness positions political activity as in process and becoming, but obscures the constitutive character of particular histories and geographies on political activity. It is paradoxical that one of the consequences of the lack of attention to these histories and geographies of political activity is an unproblematized nation-state framing of politics in Laclau and Mouffe's work (see Sparke, 2005: 176). My concern is not to argue that such relational contexts determine the character of political identities. Rather, it is to recognize that histories and geographies exert pressure, set limits and constitute possibilities for the construction of political identities (Williams, 1977: 85).

This final point is central to the account of subaltern political agency developed here. It is necessary to situate political activity in relation to spatial and temporal relations to understand how subaltern political activity brings into contestation, reworks and generates geographies of power. In *Justice Nature and the Geography of Difference* David Harvey argues that 'anti-capitalist agency is everywhere and in everyone' (Harvey, 1996: 430). These comments about agency 'lack specificity even at the theoretical, never mind empirical level' (Castree, 2006: 264). Further, Harvey quickly circumscribes this agency and views it as restrictively localized. For Harvey, it is capital that is dynamic and 'anti-capitalist agency', 'though militant, often remains particularist (sometimes extremely so), often unable to see beyond its own particular form of uneven geographical development' (Harvey, 1996: 430). One of the key aims of this book is to provide a different set of cartographies of subaltern agency and identities.

To generate accounts of subaltern political agency, which are both more situated and more generous, I mobilize the relational account of the political outlined above. This permits an account of agency that is ongoing and in process. I view agency as constructed through the ongoing negotiation of cross-cutting relations of power (see Moore, 1998). Subaltern groups construct agency through specific negotiations of power relations and through reconstituting spatial relations. This position draws on accounts of agency as the 'relational effects' generated between different human and non-human actors (see Law, 1986, 1994, Latour, 1993, 2004). I also argue, however, that one of the central ways in which agency is constituted is through the construction of geographies of power in antagonistic ways.

Refusing to see subaltern political activity as the settled other of (neoliberal) globalization allows a more generous assessment of subaltern political agency. I foreground such forms of agency through interrogating various forms of spatially stretched resistances. These have generated agency through specific and dynamic spatial practices, including mobility, the translation of repertoires of activity between different struggles, the constitution of solidarities and bringing networked power relations into contestation. They have also generated particular forms of political subjectivity, such as subaltern cosmopolitanism (see de Sousa Santos, 2002: 465–467.

Tracing these spatial practices is fundamental to delineating dynamic cartographies of subaltern forms of agency.

This does not necessarily construct the 'big' globalized forms of political agency prescribed by Harvey or Hardt and Negri; indeed, it unsettles them (see Woodward et al., 2007: 1–2). Neither does it necessarily produce restrictively localized accounts of agency. Rather, it situates forms of subaltern agency as generated through ongoing negotiations in the constitution of particular networked social relations and relations between places. That these forms of agency are situated and partial does not mean that they should be ignored, marginalized or dismissed. One of the central arguments of the book is that there are important histories of spatially stretched forms of resistance to dominant globalizing practices that have been ignored and downplayed. The next section justifies the engagement with both historical and contemporary counter-global networks here and sets out the political and theoretical project which structures this choice.

Spatial Politics of Past and Present

Debates about globalization have been structured by a remorseless presentism. There has been a pervasive tendency to position current forms of transnational political activity as a radical break with past forms of political practice (see Amin, 2002, 2004; Harvey, 1996; Vertovec and Cohen, 2002). Thus Byron Miller has argued that there has been a 'fundamental shift away from place-based forms of political organizing and towards transnational mobilization networks' (Miller, 2004: 224). This counterposition of the spatial politics of the past and present contributes to the dispossession of subaltern agency. In contrast I explore what is at stake in both political and theoretical terms in asserting that the spatial politics of past struggles were the products of various relations. Recovering the relationships between past subaltern political identities and practices and spatially stretched relations can foreground forms of subaltern identity and agency which have often been marginalized. Further, asserting that there have been spatially stretched forms of resistance to globalizing processes in the past has the potential to revitalize contemporary political imaginaries. These past forms of resistance can resonate in interesting, unexpected and provocative ways with the forms of political activity being crafted through transnational opposition to neo-liberal globalization The book seeks also to be alive to the specific identities and articulations crafted in different circumstances, conditions and space-time contexts.

These concerns are related to a particular political positionality and trajectory. They emerge from an engagement with the construction of 'usable pasts' shaped particularly by the historians associated with the New

Left (see esp. Thompson, 1968). My participation in attempts to use the past in explicitly politicized ways have also shaped this project. Central here was being involved in the land occupations associated with The Land is Ours in the mid-to-late 1990s (see Land is Ours, 1999).[5] I was impressed and inspired by the inventive ways in which these occupations mobilized aspects of England's radical past such as the Diggers and the postwar squatting movement. I was slightly troubled, however, by the cultural nationalisms that framed these events. They were structured by the kinds of cultural nationalism which Paul Gilroy has argued structured the work of E. P. Thompson and Raymond Williams (see Gilroy, 1987, 1993b: 10–11; see also Schwarz, 1982). The result was to reproduce a rather bounded, homogeneous tradition of English dissent that was shorn of links to imperial contexts, connections and struggles.

A very different usable past emerges from the work of Peter Linebaugh and Marcus Rediker. Their work is profoundly influenced by the historians like E.P.Thompson, but it engages precisely with the questions ignored by the New Left. They counter the bounded, national traditions that shaped the historians of the New Left, with a focus on the diverse interconnected multi-ethnic resistances that traversed the Atlantic world in the seventeenth and eighteenth centuries (Linebaugh and Rediker, 2000). They argue that these connections were productive of 'multi-ethnic conceptions of humanity' (Linebaugh and Rediker, 2000: 352). What I find particularly inspiring about some of these networked subaltern movements in the past, then, is not only that they brought unequal geographies of power into contestation. It is also that in particular contexts they generated multi-ethnic forms of political activity through doing so.

One of the key tensions of resistance to neo-liberal globalization is that exclusionary chauvinistic forms of opposition have coexisted with resistances which have shaped solidarities between different struggles. The 'usable past' developed through this book then has two key aims. Firstly, it asserts the significance and continuities of the ways in which forms of subaltern political activity have contested globalizing practices in both past and present. This is not to suggest a singular body of resistance which is timeless or spaceless. Rather the book seeks to foreground the articulations and solidarities constituted through different struggles and the diverse forms of identity and agency crafted through such struggles. Secondly, I assert the significance of past struggles that constituted plural, cosmopolitan identities and solidarities. This engagement is shaped by attempts to construct open, plural forms of resistance to neo-liberal globalization in opposition to those which mobilize closed, particularist and exclusionary forms of identity.

These engagements with both past and present forms of political activity are shaped by a particular style of political and theoretical intervention.

Recent debates in political geography have developed rather polarized delineations of their political commitments. Thus Matthew Sparke has valorized the importance of 'persistent critique' (Sparke, 2005: 312). Clive Barnett, by contrast, has argued that 'it is important to keep open a space for reflection on normative principles that is easily closed down by the certainties of radical denunciation' (Barnett, 2003: 197; see also Agnew, 2003). This choice between critique and reflection on normative principles forecloses the possibility of more generous and productive forms of engagement with political practices (see Massey, 2007b). Here I seek to refuse the certainties and forms of closure offered by 'persistent critique' and normative judgements in favour of attending to the inventive forms of identity, agency and solidarities constituted through political activity. This is not about being uncritical, or evading political commitments. Rather, it is out of a conviction that developing more generous forms of engagement with political activity allows us to be more alive to the inventiveness, vitality and significance of such activity.

To facilitate this engagement with these relations between space, political identities and resistance in the past and present, this book is structured in three parts. Part I outlines the relational construction of the political developed through the book. I then apply this perspective to five key themes that have been central to debates around geographies of resistance: geographies of labour, spaces of democracy, subaltern nationalisms, geographies of power and the making of transnational political networks. The first three themes – labour, democracy and subaltern nationalisms – are used to explore different aspects of the 'geographies of connection and contestation'. They are developed through discussion of subaltern politics formed in relation to Atlantic networks of trade, labour and political activity in the eighteenth century. The second set of themes – geographies of power and transnational political networks – are developed through discussion of the spaces of politics of the contemporary counter-globalization movement.

Chapter 1 intervenes in debates around the relations between place-based politics and spatially stretched social relations. The chapter interrogates the relations of place-based political activity to geographies of connection. To do this I engage with the insurgent imaginative geographies of resistance developed in C. L. R. James's *Black Jacobins*. I then outline a relational way of theorizing place-based political identities. Chapter 2 develops this account of the relational construction of political identities. I interrogate the spatial practices through which solidarities and antagonisms are constituted, arguing that solidarities and antagonisms are co-produced through political activity. This draws on a critical account of the contributions of radical democracy and actor network theory. It outlines how solidarities are active in bringing together and reshaping place-based political struggles and in constituting materially heterogeneous networks.

It positions the construction of antagonisms as constitutive of political identities and alliances. The chapter argues for a focus on the diverse and contested maps of grievance constituted through political activity.

Chapter 3 demonstrates how subaltern politics in the eighteenth century was formed through dynamic ways of negotiating mercantile networks with an Atlantic reach. It explores the trajectories of the Whiteboys, an Irish agrarian secret society, showing how their political activity linked Ireland, Newfoundland and London and shaped dynamic labour geographies. Chapter 4 makes a distinctive contribution to debates on the relations between democracy and spatial practices. It discusses the experiments of the London Corresponding Society with forms of organizational democracy, arguing that particular forms of spatial practices were key to its experiments with democracy. It explores the geographies of connection that shaped these democratic identities through relating them to transnational democratic political networks. Chapter 5 challenges pervasive assumptions that the territorial configurations of nations and nationalisms are fixed and given. It interrogates the relations between heterogeneous, multi-ethnic subaltern cultures, shipboard spaces and emerging forms of Irish 'nationalist' political activity in various mutinous events and conspiracies in the 1790s. This opens up possibilities for understanding the relations between subaltern nationalisms and geographies of connection.

Chapter 6 explores the geographies of power contested and shaped through contemporary counter-globalization networks. It critically engages with Hardt and Negri's arguments concerning the diffuse nature of power that characterizes contemporary neo-liberalism and the need for a totalizing opposition to Empire (Hardt and Negri, 2001, 2004). The chapter argues that this position evades the key tensions generated through the activity of these counter-global networks. It outlines a position drawing on Ernesto Laclau's account of populist logics that seeks to foreground these tensions (Laclau, 2005a). Chapter 7 then intervenes in debates about the constitution and effects of transnational political networks. It demonstrates how counter-global networks bring together political movements with different trajectories and identities through a discussion of the Inter-Continental Caravan, an alliance of Indian farmers and West European green and social justice activists against genetically modified seeds. It examines the tensions generated through such networks by examining the pressures exerted by nationalisms and exclusionary gendered organizing practices on the conduct of these solidarities. The chapter concludes that these movements face a choice between constructing exclusionary oppositions to globalization based around bounded, chauvinist versions of the local and national or constructing alliances between political movements from different places.

The conclusion draws out the key theoretical and political implications of the book. I revisit the arguments about the making of usable pasts that structure the book. It asserts the importance of mobilising usable pasts in ways which are attentive to the geographies of connection that made up past struggles. I then draw out the implications of the argument of the book for debates around the relations between space, neo-liberalism and contestation. I then outline the key political implications of the arguments and material presented in this book. It considers their significance for attempts to reject chauvinistic, narrow forms of opposition to globalisation. I contend that crafting connections between different place-located struggles is crucial to opposing exclusionary nationalist oppositions to globalisation and to constructing open, transnational political networks defined by solidaristic identities. I argue that such networks have the potential to shape collectives in ways which are more equal, less riven by unequal geographies of power, and less ecologically wasteful and damaging than the collective experiments of neo-liberal globalisation.

Part One

Networking the Political

Chapter One

Place and the Relational Construction of Political Identities

On 8 March 1792, Thomas Hardy, a Scottish shoemaker who was the first secretary of the London Corresponding Society, wrote to a prominent Sheffield abolitionist, Reverend Bryant. He addressed Bryant as follows:

> Hearing from my friend, Gustavus Vassa, the African, who is now writing memoirs of his life in my house, that you are a zealous friend to the abolition of that cursed traffic, the Slave Trade, I infer from that circumstance, that you are a zealous friend to freedom on the broad basis of the Rights of Man. I am fully persuaded that there is no man, who is, from principle an advocate for the liberty of the black man, but will zealously support the rights of the white man, and vice versa. (Hardy, 1976: 45–6)

The LCS was the 'most controversial and most famous' of the various reform movements that emerged in Britain in the 1790s (Thale, 1983: xv). It has been understood as part of a distinctively English tradition of radical dissent. E. P. Thompson located the LCS as part of an 'English agitation, of impressive dimensions, for an English democracy' (Thompson, 1968: 111). This first piece of correspondence of the LCS gives a markedly different sense of the constitution of the political identities and practices of the LCS. This letter can also be used to question many dominant assumptions about the relations between space, place and political activity.

The letter demonstrates that contacts between the LCS and reform societies in Sheffield were facilitated by Gustavus Vassa. He is better known today as Olaudah Equiano, the ex-slave, free black and anti-slavery activist whose memoirs *The Interesting Life of Gustavus Vassa* became a key abolitionist text (Equiano, 1995). Equiano's life traversed the Atlantic. He is a prominent example of what Ira Berlin has defined as an Atlantic creole (Berlin, 1998; Carretta, 2005: 367).[6] Berlin defines Atlantic creoles as having 'by their experiences and sometimes by their person . . . become part of the three worlds that came together in the Atlantic littoral. Familiar with the commerce of the Atlantic, fluent in its new languages, and intimate with its trade and cultures, they were cosmopolitan in the fullest sense' (Berlin, 1998: 17). Equiano explicitly embraced a cosmopolitan identity, defining himself as a 'citizen of the world' (Carretta, 2005: 367).

The relationships between Hardy and Equiano, and between activists in London and Sheffield, emphasize that from its formation the London Corresponding Society was produced through negotiating connections that stretched beyond London. They locate the formation of the LCS as part of the 'irreducible social heterogeneity and transnationalism of the cultures of anti-slavery' (Fischer, 2004: 226; see also Gilroy, 1993b: 10–11). Further, it emphasizes that these connections shaped the notions of political community, practice and identity adopted by the LCS in significant ways. This opens up a more generous, recursive sense of the ongoing relations between place-based political activity and geographies of connection. This chapter seeks to make an intervention in the understandings of subaltern spaces of politics through engaging with these dynamic relations. I argue that adopting a relational account of place-based political activity as always already intervening in the ongoing construction of flows and routes of political activity, opens up important possibilities for understanding political identity and agency. These implications have not been fully worked through. In particular, such a relational account of place opens up important resources for understanding the dynamism of subaltern spaces of politics, which continue to be theorized as less geographically networked and dynamic than capital flows and elites (Cox, 1998; Escobar, 2001; Harvey, 1989, 1996, 2000; Harvey and Swyngedouw, 1993; Swyngedouw, 2004).

The first section contests accounts which construct resistance politics as localized and working within limits circumscribed by capitalist social relations (see Harvey, 1996: 380; Escobar, 2001; Miller, 2000). It argues that there are important histories and geographies of dynamic networked subaltern spaces of politics and uses the term 'counter-global networks' to foreground these forms of networked subaltern political activity. I then explore the insurgent spatial imaginaries of C. L. R. James's *Black Jacobins*, arguing that it is a neglected intervention in the relations between space and politics. The chapter draws on this work to construct a contested, dynamic and ongoing account of the relations between geographies of connection and subaltern political identities. The final section of the chapter draws out the implications of this approach for place-based political activity. It argues that adopting a relational account of place-based politics can foreground the 'inventiveness' of subaltern political activity. The chapter concludes by outlining key aspects of the relational construction of the militant forms of place-based political activity, which Raymond Williams termed 'militant particularisms'.

Spaces of Subaltern Politics and the Making of Counter-Global Networks

In his book *Justice, Nature and the Geography of Difference* David Harvey makes a key historical claim regarding the geographies and histories of radical struggles in Britain. He argues that socialism in Britain has always been 'powered by the sort of militant particularisms' that Raymond Williams discussed in his writings about Wales and that Harvey encountered in relation to the struggles over the Cowley car plant in East Oxford (Harvey, 1996: 39). Harvey characterizes these socialisms as being rooted and cemented primarily through 'local bonds' (Harvey, 1996: 23, 33). Williams used the term 'militant particularisms' to describe precisely the militant 'place-bound politics arising out of the experience of class solidarities and gender relations' formed through particular struggles in particular places (Harvey, 2001: 176). These concerns were shaped by his engagement with the militant politics of areas like the mining valleys of South Wales. For Williams, there was a 'decisive difference between militant particularism and militant socialism'. He argued that militant socialism 'necessarily' depended on having 'a political movement at the centre, a broad strategic aim to transform society' (Williams, 1979: 380). He celebrated this move as the 'unique and extraordinary character of working-class self-organization' through which militant particularist struggles and identities were connected 'to a general struggle' (Williams, 1989: 115).

Harvey and Williams construct place-based struggles as the products of 'fixed, local places' or the bounded 'origins' of political struggles (Mitchell, 2002: 69; Harvey, 2000: 241). Harvey follows Williams in seeking to examine how 'ideals forged out of the affirmative experience of solidarities in one place get generalized and universalized as a working model of a new form of society that will benefit all of humanity' (Harvey, 1996: 32). In this way his account is structured by a constitutive separation between 'the militant particularisms of lived lives' and the 'struggle to achieve sufficient critical distance and detachment to form global ambitions' (Harvey, 1996: 44). Militant particularisms, here, become the already constituted building blocks needed to form a universal global ambition (Harvey, 1996: 44). This position conflates two very different binaries: local–global and particular–universal. It produces topographies of political engagement where the local is elided with the particular. The result is that universalism becomes defined against the practices of local struggles. This makes it impossible for local political activity to break out of this prison-house of particularism in ways which shape political imaginaries. This becomes left to those 'intellectuals' capable of abstraction and who are positioned 'outside' of the practice of local struggles.[7]

This counter-position of space and place, and their association with the 'universal' and the 'local', serves to marginalize the agency and dynamism of subaltern forms of political activity (see Gibson-Graham, 2002; Massey, 1999, 2005). As I argued in the introduction, this counter-position has powerfully structured David Harvey's work (Harvey, 1989: 236; see also Harvey and Swyngedouw, 1993; Smith, 1993). Thus Castree has commented such a position counterposes 'the seemingly irresistible gales of capital's creative destruction to the limited means that place-based workers have at their disposal to make their own history and geography' (Castree, 2000: 275). The spaces of politics of subaltern activity, then, have been defined negatively as the settled opposite of the dynamism and networked spatialities of capital.

The contention of this book is that this way of constructing the spatialities of subaltern politics, both in the present and the past, is deeply damaging to radical political imaginaries. Positioning forms of place-based politics as 'always already' negotiating flows and routes of political activity challenges rigid counter-positions of place-based political activity and national or global political ambition. This opens up more generous possibilities for accounts of place-based political activity. As the example of Equiano and Hardy's friendship suggests, their intersection through place-based political organizing in London contributed to explicit notions of multi-ethnic 'political community', though these were framed by exclusionary gendered constructions of politics (see chapter 4). The formation of the LCS was shaped by practices where it makes little sense to make such a rigid distinction between the 'local' and the 'universal'. The routes of political activity that came together through the place-based political activity of the LCS contributed to multi-ethnic notions of political community, and linked struggles for political liberty in Britain, with anti-slavery politics (though see chapter 4 for the fragmentary and contested character of these associations). This permits an account of militant particularist action, not as the product of a bounded politics of place, but as the product of sets of relations and as productive of 'multi-ethnic conceptions of humanity' (Linebaugh and Rediker, 2000: 352).

These resources for understanding the dynamic generative forms of place-based political activity are undermined through the counter-positions of local and global, particularism and universal, that structure Harvey's work. They are further undermined by the pervasive tendency to counterpose the spatial politics of the past and present. Conceptions of the spaces of the political as the products of flows and networks have become increasingly influential both in geography and across the broader social sciences (see Amin, 2002, 2004; Connolly, 1995; Hardt and Negri, 2001, 2004; Latour, 2004; Marston et al., 2005; Massey, 2004, 2005, 2007). The prominence of vibrant forms of transnational opposition to neo-liberal globalization has also emphasized the redundancy of bounded understandings of political activity. These bodies of work have forged a number of significant insights through moving beyond bounded and nation-centred geographies of the political. They have positioned places as products of diverse forms of connection and relations. They have challenged scalar accounts of spatial relations which have emphasized boundaries between different spatial scales, marginalized the flows which constitute subaltern spaces of politics, and counterposed space and place in problematic ways (see Featherstone, 2003; Marston et al., 2005). Finally, they have situated political activity as part of the ongoing constitution of networks (Braun and Disch, 2002).

There is a tension, however, in the ways that these relations between space, politics and transnational networks have been conceptualized. The constitution of the spaces of the political through flows and networks is often figured as something that is an 'entirely' new development. A networked and transnational present is frequently counterposed with a spatially more settled, and simpler, past (see Cohen and Rai, 2000). Hence, Rogers and colleagues argue, 'the once clear-cut separation between the domestic sphere of national life and the external or international sphere has largely broken down' (Rogers et al., 2001: 1–2). Ash Amin has argued that the rise of transnational flows and networks 'no longer' allows 'a conceptualization of place politics in terms of spatially bound processes and institutions' (Amin, 2004: 33). These accounts, then, suggest an ontological disjuncture between contemporary forms of political activity that need to be theorized in terms of networks and flows and past forms of politics that can be adequately understood in terms of 'spatially bound processes and institutions'.

Such ontological disjunctures structure the iconoclastic political theorizing of Hardt and Negri in *Empire* and *Multitude*. Hardt and Negri use the term 'multitude' to suggest new forms of radical political collectives. (see also chapter 6 below) They argue that the multitude is constituted through smooth space, in contrast to the forms of 'traditional social organizations' such as labour unions (Hardt and Negri, 2004: 136–7). This disjuncture between past and present forms of organizing temporalizes different forms of spatial politics. Thus, for Hardt and Negri, the multitude forms not a situated politics in particular places, which can connect up to become part of broader networks or cycles of struggles, but a total resistance to Empire, where different forms of global sovereignty are pitted against each other (Allen, 2003: 89). This account of the multitude is dependent on a notion of 'smooth space'. This produces a reductive account of the spatial politics of the past through ignoring the diverse connections that have made up past struggles. This in turn produces a limited account of the spatial politics of emerging resistances to neo-liberal globalization. Thus they argue that place-based movements like the Zapatistas are specific and 'based on immediate regional concerns in such a way as they could in no respect be linked together as a globally expanding chain of revolt' (Hardt and Negri, 2001: 54). This ignores the generative relations between place-based struggles and transnational networks. The solidarity networks inspired by the Zapatistas, for example, were a key formative influence in the emergence of counter-global networks of resistance to neo-liberalism (Olesen, 2005). These were also related to histories and geographies of international solidarity in the region, such as the coffee brigades to support the Sandinistas in Nicaragua.

Placing ontological distinctions between the spatial politics of past and present struggles does work, then, in both theoretical and political terms. Theoretically, it sets restrictive limits on resources for what Amin has described as the project of developing a networked vocabulary of the political (Amin, 2004: 38). It closes down a focus on the different legacies of past political cultures on the spatial politics of the present, such as the important traditions, subjectivities and repertoires of solidarity associated with internationalisms. It makes it harder to recover and account for dynamic subaltern spaces of politics. In political terms this marginalization of subaltern agency in the past risks feeding a sense of dispossession of subaltern agency in the present. This is one of the effects of constructions of globalization as solely the product of networked neo-liberal actors able to outwit subaltern resistances trapped in the confines of particular places (see Castells, 1997: 354; Harvey, 1989: 236; Peck and Tickell, 2002). Asserting that there have been spatially stretched forms of resistance to globalizing processes in the past can counter this dispossession of subaltern agency.

Diverse bodies of work have challenged this tendency to counterpose the spatial politics of the past and present and offer resources for foregrounding forms of subaltern agency constituted through spatially stretched forms of resistance. Post-colonial theorizing, for example, has challenged dominant understandings of key terms of debate such as cosmopolitanism (Appiah, 1998). Cosmopolitanism has often been theorized as a bounded product of 'Western liberal democratic universalism' (Holton, 2002: 153). Recent scholarship, however, has emphasized how such forms of universalism are often merely forms of particularism which generalize Western experiences and give the pretence that they are universal (Chakrabarty, 2000; Hall, 2002) and has interrogated the particular exclusionary gender and class relations constituted through cosmopolitan practices (Anderson,

1998, Waters, 2007). These exclusionary ways of framing cosmopolitanism have marginalised the ways in which forms of internationalism and democracy emerged at the intersections of west/non-west actors such as the connections between Hardy and Equiano (see Slater, 2002). Through discussion of 'The Universal Races Congress' held in London in 1911, Holton has drawn attention to the existence of a 'plurality of forms of cosmopolitanisms' which he argues are 'an important conceptual extension to our understanding of intercultural encounters and conflicts within the global arena' (Holton, 2002: 167). This exposes 'the Eurocentricity of the older unitary Western cosmopolitanisms' and foregrounds the multiple geographies through which different forms of cosmopolitanism are constituted.

Holton's work dislocates the 'awkward elitism' frequently associated with cosmopolitanism (Anderson, 1998: 268). As Vertovec and Cohen note, a 'frequent attack on cosmopolites is that cosmopolitanism is only available to an elite – those who have the resources necessary to absorb other cultures' (Vertovec and Cohen, 2002: 5; see also Calhoun, 2002). In a temporalizing move, however, they argue that this has 'historically, been true', with the majority of the population living 'their lives within the cultural space of their nation or ethnicity'. This temporalization of difference serves to marginalize important forms and traditions of what might be termed subaltern cosmopolitanism (see also Gidwani, 2006; Pollack, forthcoming). It leaves little space for the cosmopolitan forms of identity produced by 'Atlantic creoles' like Equiano. It marginalizes forms of subaltern cosmopolitanism produced in cities like London in the eighteenth century which were an important context to the multi-ethnic political cultures of the LCS. Further, it ignores the kinds of unruly, heterogeneous, multi-ethnic, cosmopolitan social relations produced through sites such as the ship in the early modern Atlantic (Linebaugh and Rediker, 2000: 151).

Foregrounding these multiple geographies of cosmopolitanism challenges the idea that historical forms of cosmopolitanism were solely the preserve of elite groups. This suggests the importance of powerful social and political movements like pan-Africanism, which contested globalizing processes such as colonialism through the formation of spatially stretched alliances and political networks. The geographies shaped through these movements have been foregrounded by Brent Hayes Edwards in his account of the radical black internationalisms constructed by the political activists George Padmore and Tiemoko Garan Kouyaté in the 1930s. Edwards notes that 'figures such as Padmore and Kouyaté' were 'mobile not just in their own colonial spheres, but moreover among metropolitan "centers", within each other's circuits of activity (Padmore moving from a British colony in the Caribbean to the US, and then not just to London but to

Moscow, Hamburg and Paris; Kouyaté moving from one French colony to another and then to Paris and to Moscow).' He argues that these forms of black radicalism formed counter-logics, an 'unruly pattern of flows and alliances' (Edwards, 2003: 245).

Such unruly 'flows and alliances' are central to this book. The book interrogates the geographies of these counter-logics. I use the term 'counter-global' to account for forms of subaltern politics which are constituted through 'unruly patterns of flows and alliances' and formed through antagonistic relations to dominant ways of generating 'globalization', whether these be mercantile capitalist, imperial or neo-liberal. The term evokes forms of political activity which have contested dominant forms of globalization in both past and present, but have eschewed, challenged or exceeded bounded forms of the local. It deliberately echoes Gramsci's notion of counter-hegemony which signalled forms of resistance constituted through connections and articulations between unlike actors (see Gramsci, 1971).[8] This book attempts to foreground the dynamic spatialities produced through these alternative ways of generating global networks. In contrast to Hardt and Negri and other authors who have argued for a smooth space of flows, it situates these counter-global networks as situated, partial and contested (see also Bunnell and Nah, 2004).

Edwards's work on Padmore and Kouyaté is a significant challenge to ways of thinking about the subaltern politics of the past. It emphasises the vibrant, powerful forms of subaltern cosmopolitanism which constituted movements like pan-Africanism. Paul Gilroy has argued that pan-Africanism offers a profound challenge to dominant understandings of the relations between place, space and the political 'because it overflows from the confining structures of the nation-state and comprehensively queries the priority routinely attached to those structures in historical and sociological explanations of social and cultural change' (Gilroy, 1993b: 151). Debates on cosmopolitan democracy and radical democratic theory, however, have ignored the experiments with transnational organizing and radical democratic practices constituted through pan-Africanisms (Held, 1995; Laclau and Mouffe, 1985). As James Tyner has argued, debates in political geography and on nationalism remain 'woefully ignorant of pan-African nationalism and other African diasporic movements' (Tyner, 2004: 343; see also Mckittrick, 2006). The forms of oppositional knowledge produced through pan-Africanism don't just challenge dominant, nation-centred, explanations of social and cultural change. They offer important resources for rethinking the ways in which space, politics and the geographies of connection might be understood. The next section seeks to engage with the ways in which these concerns are figured in C. L. R. James's *Black Jacobins*, one of the 'great inaugural texts of the discourse of anti-colonialism' (Scott, 2004: 9).

The Black Jacobins, Subaltern Agency and Geographies of Connection

The Black Jacobins is one of the few texts associated with pan-Africanism that has pressed on debates about space and politics. A powerful retelling of the story of the Haitian revolution, it makes a radical break with the 'Western' canon of social and political theory, and particularly with the Marxist tradition James was writing in, by centring Atlantic slavery as a key process in the constitution of world history. The book is insistent in viewing slaves as active in the making of their own history and in asserting the slaves' historical agency. This is developed through an account of Toussaint Louverture, one of the political and military leaders of the revolution in St Domingue. James wrote out of a frustration with depictions of black people as historical victims (Hall and James, 1996: 21). Instead, he sought 'to show that black people were able to make historical progress, they were able to show how a revolution was made' (James cited in Hall, 2003: 32). In this way his account was an attempt to provide a 'usable past' for the anti-colonial struggles of the mid-twentieth century.

This 'usable past' emerged from a set of dynamic, radical forms of transnational political practice. James was shaped by the work of Trinidadian intellectuals like J. J. Thomas, whose book *Froudacity*, a major critique of the Oxford historian J. A. Froude, who dismissed the capacity of the West-Indian people for self-rule, was a key intellectual influence on James (Cudjoe, 1997: 120, 124; see also Hall and Schwarz, 1998). *The Black Jacobins* was written while James was living in Nelson, Lancashire, with the West-Indian cricketer Learie Constantine, and reporting on the Lancashire League for the *Manchester Guardian*. James notes that his involvement in the culture of the Independent Labour Party in Nelson challenged the previously 'rather abstract' character of his 'labour and socialist ideals' (James, 1994: 119). His political outlook was decisively shaped by his involvement in the international Trotskyist movement. His research in the Parisian archives, where he met the Haitian military historian Colonel Nemours, was partly funded by his Nelson friends and comrades, Harry and Elizabeth Spencer, to whom the book was dedicated (James, 1989: v–vii). The book took on its own transnational trajectories, influencing various anti-colonial intellectuals and activists in different space-times (see Hall and James, 1996: 22). Finally, James produced a play out of the research for his book which was performed in London through the prestigious Stage Society in 1936. The play was written and produced in 'part as a protest against Italy's invasion of Ethiopia in 1935' (Kaplan, 1998: 56). Paul Robeson played Toussaint Louverture, and the production was significant for bringing together two of the most important black radicals of the twentieth century, as well as for casting a black lead actor (James, 1980: 256–64; see also Duberman, 1996: 196–7; Fischer, 2004: 246, 349n7).

These routes of transnational political activism shape the book's concern with the interconnections through which the Haitian revolution was made. The book does not view the slaves' agency in isolation. James foregrounds the relations of their struggles to the French revolution, famously noting how the slave revolt in St Domingue dislocated and challenged the notions of liberty formed in the French revolution. As James argues:

> The blacks were taking part in the destruction of European feudalism begun by the French revolution, and liberty and equality, the slogans of the revolution, meant far more to them than to any Frenchman. That was why in the hour of danger Toussaint, uninstructed as he was, could find the language and accent of Diderot, Rousseau, and Raynal . . . Toussaint could defend the freedom of blacks without reservation. (James, 1989: 198)

Central to James's account of the Haitian revolution, then, is a telling of how the French and Haitian revolutions were co-produced. This eschews and challenges Eurocentric geographies and histories. The geographies of connection posed in the text fundamentally dislocate the idea that the Haitian revolution was some kind of mere translation of French revolutionary ideals to the 'periphery'. This section interrogates the importance of these geographies of connection, signalling their importance by engaging with David Scott's reading of *The Black Jacobins*, which through its focus on the temporal dynamics of narrative construction obscures the insurgent, imaginative geographies which structure James's book (see also Sparke, 2008).

Scott's political and theoretical project is to develop a way of using *The Black Jacobins* to speak to the post-colonial present. He does this through a brilliant close reading of the different forms of narrative construction in the 1938 and 1963 editions of the book. The second edition of the book includes the 'inspiring' essay entitled 'From Toussaint L'Ouverture to Fidel Castro', which 'dramatizes the history of the Caribbean in its world-historical personifications, from Toussaint to Fidel' (Schwarz, 2003a: 40; James, 1989: 391–418). Scott's reading rests, however, on the significance of 'seven paragraphs' inserted in the second edition at the start of chapter 7 which form 'a very profound meditation on tragedy' (Scott, 2004: 11; James, 1989: 289–92). For Scott, the insertion of these paragraphs changes the dramatic and political structure of the book. It dislocates the 'romantic' construction of Toussaint and the history of the Haitian revolution developed in the first edition, replacing it with a construction of Toussaint as a tragic character. Through 'an explicit consideration of the tragedy of Toussaint Louverture' Scott argues these paragraphs bear on 'the larger tragedy of colonial enlightenment' (Scott, 2004: 11).

Scott's concern with the narrative structure of the book emerges from his contention that the 'relation between pasts, presents and futures is a relation constituted in narrative' (Scott, 2004: 45). Through temporalizing the construction of narrative, Scott excludes concern with how the connections between places are figured through James's work. Edward Said has written evocatively of how in *The Black Jacobins* 'events in France and in Haiti criss-cross and refer to one another like voices in a fugue'. He continues: 'James's narrative is broken up as history dispersed in geography, in archival sources, in emphases both Black and French' (Said, 1993: 338). Said's account of the book is more suggestive of the importance of geography to the text. Neither Scott nor Said, however, interrogate the significance of the geography through which the narrative is structured. This geography becomes something that the history is merely 'dispersed' through, a backdrop to the dynamic events of the book. These approaches do not allow any commentary on the significance of James's intervention in producing this particular insurgent, imaginative geography of the Haitian revolution. These dynamic geographies of connection are seen as just there to be uncovered. The significance that James gives to these forms of connection and how these connections actively shape his retelling of the story of the Haitian revolution, however, are integral to the politicized usable past this account creates. Evoking these dynamic geographies of connection allows a more generative, slightly more optimistic, if more modest politics, than that envisioned through Scott's focus on 'tragedy'.

Bill Schwarz has argued that James was exceptional 'in regarding the peoples of the Caribbean as a modern people. He understood from early on that the Middle Passage and the plantation were located at the centre of the making of the modern world' (Schwarz, 2003a: 49). Integral to this understanding of the Caribbean was James's project to 'place ourselves in history' (James, 1969: 45). For James, 'placing ourselves in history' meant decisively rupturing the geographies through which 'history' was constituted. One of the key achievements of *The Black Jacobins* is to dislocate and challenge the story of the bounded emergence of Western civilization. This was not only a challenge to imperialist historians like Froude. It also decisively challenged the 'model at the centre of the most developed parts of Marxist theory, which suggested that capitalism evolved organically from its own transformations' (Hall, 1992: 280). The political and theoretical project of *The Black Jacobins* is completely dependent on this challenge to the dominant geographies through which 'history' was constituted.

James does not merely 'place' the Haitian revolution as a key event in world history which signals the agency and revolutionary potential of black political subjects. James draws attention to the dynamic geographies of connection between the French and Haitian revolutions. His attention to these connections has been marginalized in recent debates. Thus, Homi Bhabha emphasizes Toussaint's failure to challenge and dislocate the limits of the notions of liberty forged through the French revolution: 'What do we make of the figure of Toussaint . . . at the moment when he grasps the tragic lesson that the moral, modern disposition of mankind enshrined in the sign of the Revolution, only fuels the archaic racial factor in the society of slavery?' (Bhabha, 1994: 244). For Bhabha, Toussaint becomes a 'victim' of the French revolution's failure to decisively end slavery. Scott, similarly, positions Toussaint as a 'tragic subject of a colonial modernity to which he was, by force, conscripted'. This 'tragedy inheres in the fact that inescapably modern as he is obliged by the modern conditions of his life to be, he must seek his freedom in the very technologies, conceptual languages, and institutional formations in which modernity's rationality has sought his enslavement' (Scott, 2004: 168).

'Modernity' here is constituted through a geography that seems to dispossess Toussaint of any role in constituting it. James, however, provides a more multifaceted and generative account of the connections between the slave revolt in St Domingue and the French revolution. Crucially, for James, they are *both* transformed through the political events of St Domingue. This dynamic sense of interconnection between subaltern politics in St Domingue and the French revolution is integral to the structure of the book: chapters 4 and 5 are titled 'San Domingo Masses Begin' and 'Paris Masses Complete'. This not only positions the transnational geographies of slavery as central to an account of modern politics. It also profoundly disrupts an imaginative geography whereby political activity in the 'periphery' is positioned in a subordinate way to political activity in the 'metropolis'. James's text thus offers important resources for what Slater has described as the challenge of thinking about 'relations across space' which focus 'on the mutually constitutive nature of west-non-west interactions' (Slater, 1998: 669).

James's play, based on his research for the book, foregrounds these connections. It contains the following piece of dialogue:

ORLEANS: Tell me something. How is the Revolution in France going?
MARAT: The white slaves in France heard that the black slaves in San Domingo had killed their masters and taken over the houses and the property. They heard that we did it and they follow us. (James, 1992: 74)

Marat, an aide to the Haitian general Dessalines, powerfully turns upside down the sense that the slaves in St Domingue are not active in constituting transnational connections. By asserting that it is the French that follow the black slaves, not vice versa, James creates a subversive rupturing of dominant geographical imaginations. It demonstrates that these connections were as important for French subaltern politics as they were for the constitution of Caribbean political identities. It creates an inspiring and unusual form of 'usable past' where 'black' and 'white' subaltern politics are seen as connected and part of the same struggles through shared opposition to slavery. This unsettles both dominant narratives of black nationalisms and the usable pasts created by the radical historians of the New Left, structured as they were by English cultural nationalisms (Gilroy, 1993a; Linebaugh, 1986).

For Scott, this usable past has limited 'resonance' with the present conjuncture. He argues that the future which 'constituted James's horizon of expectation (the emergence of nation-state sovereignty, the revolutionary transition to socialism)' and which he anticipated in *The Black Jacobins*, 'we live today as the bleak ruins of our postcolonial present'.

> Our generation looks back so to put it, through the remains of a present that James and his generation looked forward to (however contentiously) as the open horizon of a possible future; James's erstwhile future has elapsed in our disappearing present. But if this is so, if the longing for anti-colonial revolution, the longing for the overcoming of the colonial past that shaped James's horizon of expectation in *The Black Jacobins* is not one that we can inhabit today, then it may be part of our task to set it aside and begin another work of reimagining other futures for us to long for, for us to anticipate. (Scott, 2004: 45)

The 'problem space' that characterizes the present conjuncture is, as Scott contends, markedly different to that which shaped both editions of *The Black Jacobins*. It is a conjuncture marked both by the challenges posed by 'transnational disciplinary forms of neo-liberalism' and by often chauvinist, exclusionary, particularist forms of resistance (Sparke, 2005: 163; see also Retort Collective, 2003).

One of the key aims of this book is to assert and articulate kinds of 'usable past' which pose connections, juxtapositions and resonances between forms of spatially stretched resistance to forms of globalization in different places and at different times. It is in this respect that I contend that *The Black Jacobins* has slightly more optimistic resources for engaging with these tensions than Scott's reading allows. By centring the geographies of connection that shaped the Haitian revolution, James generates a particular kind of 'usable past'. *The Black Jacobins* can be read as a powerful story of the formation of 'unruly alliances and flows' which brought the geopolitics of Atlantic slavery into contestation. It is a story of geographies of connection which destabilize the idea of the West originating 'organically from its own transformations'. The book celebrates spatially stretched

forms of subaltern resistance to globalizing practices and their global rever-
berations. Further, it foregrounds the power of the hybrid radical political
identities formed out of this resistance, which drew on 'enlightenment'
ideas and fundamentally challenged, reworked and dislocated them. *The
Black Jacobins* is of significance to this project precisely because it assert
histories and geographies of connection that disrupt assumptions that it is
'capital' or 'colonialists' that are dynamic and mobile, and subaltern politics
that is always reactive and place-bound.

There are many tensions in *The Black Jacobins*. There is its paradoxical
marginalizing of African political cultures, which Stuart Hall has argued
'remain a kind of silence' in James's account (Hall and Schwarz, 1998: 25).
There is its fetishization of a particular relationship between violence and
masculinity as what counts in the formation of revolutionary politics. This
shapes a construction of a romantic heroism which gives 'free reign to the
imaginative possibilities and limitations of pure masculinist heroism' and
which structurally excludes female agency (Kaplan, 1998: 55). There is the
tension between its attempt to foreground the activity of black masses and
its primary focus on the leadership of Toussaint and Dessalines. The powerful imaginative geography of James's *Black Jacobins*, however, begins to
emphasize what is at stake in both theoretical and political terms in asserting that past subaltern political struggles were constituted through dynamic
geographies of connection.

Firstly, it develops a powerful sense of subaltern agency. It asserts the
ways in which these geographies of resistance were made through the
meeting up of dynamic trajectories. This results in a strong insistence
that globalizing processes cannot be reduced to linear processes of
westernization. Secondly, it positions the formation of political identities
as the outcome of various connections. An account of subaltern agency
emerges here because James foregrounds these connections, and demonstrates how subaltern political practices and identities were formed through
contesting their location in these connections. Finally, James gives a sense
of how these connections shaped particular place-based identities in
various ways. Significantly, for James, it is as much identities in France
that get reworked as those in Haiti, and these places become key sites
through which transnational networks are made and remade. This produces a contested and ongoing sense of the activity of transnational political networks in contrast to the smooth spaces that structure Hardt and
Negri's account of the multitude. This is a condition for foregrounding
the diverse and contested forms of subaltern agency in constituting these
networks and for recovering the productive and generative forms of
subaltern political practices. The next section explores the impact of this
relational construction of the political for accounts of place-based political
activity.

Place, Agency, Identity

The preceding section argued that C. L. R. James's *Black Jacobins* develops an insurgent imaginative geography of resistance through foregrounding subaltern geographies of connection. James's account has resonances with the influential relational accounts of place that have emerged in recent work in geography, especially those associated with the writings of Doreen Massey (Massey, 1999, 2005, 2007a; see also Amin, 2004). James, however, doesn't engage with the practices through which the geographies of connection that he foregrounds in his book were made and constituted. His Hegelian Marxist account of 'world history' was not sensitive to the partial, contested, situated geographies crafted through particular Atlantic connections (see Schwarz, 2004: 104). The final section of this chapter seeks to rework existing accounts of the politics of place through interrogating their relation to geographies of connection. I argue for a relational account of 'militant particularisms' which views militant place-based activity as always already part of the ongoing negotiation of connections. I then draw out the implications of this way of theorizing place-based political activity for accounts of subaltern identity and agency.

In a talk given to commemorate the fiftieth anniversary of the General Strike of 1926, Raymond Williams spoke movingly about the 'ardent' participation of his father, a railway signalman in the small Welsh border village of Pandy (Williams, 1989: 105).[9] This was part of the solidarity action with locked out miners that sparked the General Strike (see Francis and Smith, 1980: 52–73; Skelley, 1976). While emphasizing that solidarity begins 'in very local, even physical ways', Williams also gives an important sense of the role of solidarities and connections in reconfiguring identities:

> By the very fact of the railway, with the trains passing through, from the cities, from the factories, from the ports, from the collieries, and by the fact of the telephone and the telegraph, which was especially important for the signalmen, who through it had a community with other signalmen over a wide social network, talking beyond their work with men they might never actually meet but whom they knew very well through voice and opinion, and story, they were part of a modern industrial working class. (Williams, 1989: 106)

Williams's account of the General Strike foregrounds important geographies of connection. He emphasises that these connections actively shaped the solidarities, political outlook and activity of the railway workers in Pandy. He also emphasises how these connections were absolutely integral to the working lives of these railwaymen, noting how their solidarities exceeded local bonds and were produced with 'men' they knew by 'voice and opinion, and story'.

This account of the relations between place-based political activity in Pandy and the 'geographies of connection' which were produced through the General Strike opens up a more dynamic account of the constitution of militant particularisms than Williams is usually credited with. David Harvey, among others, has emphasized the ways that Williams situates 'militant particularisms' as the 'origins' of 'political struggles' (Harvey, 2000: 241). Rather than militant particularisms being the 'given', bounded origins of political struggles in particular places, here they emerge as produced through the ongoing negotiation of connections and relations. Williams's discussion of the militancy that characterized industrial South Wales, rather than focusing on narrow, bounded struggles, also situates militant particularisms as outcomes of struggle and interrelations. In *Towards 2000* he finds 'the real grounds of hope' emerging from the ways in which 'massive and diverse immigration' into the Welsh mining valleys was transformed into 'some of the most remarkably solid and mutually loyal communities of which we have record' (Williams, 1983: 196).

Williams, as Paul Gilroy has emphatically argued, grounds his arguments about militant particularisms in a notion of 'long experience' which is deeply exclusionary. Williams's concerns with 'authentic' place-based politics and with the importance of long experience reinscribe an essentially bounded notion of place. This reproduces the assumptions about 'authentic and inauthentic types of national belonging' which underpinned the racist discourses of the right (Gilroy, 1987: 49–50; see also Gilroy, 2004: 88). Williams doesn't interrogate the gender relations that such 'militant particularists' reproduced and depended on, and produced passive, unchanging representations of women in his work (see Massey, 2000: 230). Further, Williams fails really to address the significance of his insights that these politicized communities were the result not merely of 'local bonds', but also of 'massive, diverse immigration'. He fails to position Welsh subaltern political identities as actively produced both through hostility to 'outsiders' in events like the riots against black sailors in Cardiff in 1919 and through positive identifications with other movements and struggles, such as the involvement of South Wales miners in the International Brigades in the Spanish Civil War or the support the South Wales NUM gave to Paul Robeson against the McCarthyite repression which denied him a passport (Evans, 1982, Francis, 1984, Francis and Smith, 1980:429, C. Williams, 2002).

This unsettles Williams's assumption that 'solidarity and engagement' are formed in discrete places and then extend beyond these local places, which has been cited approvingly in recent work on the geographies of social movements (Miller, 2004: 227). The writer and miner B. L. Coombs made clear in relation to the 'racially mixed workforce in the Neath Valley', that the organizing of communities in the South Wales coalfield was not just a case of organizing already constituted and homogeneous communities. He recalled:

> What a mixture of languages and dialects were there sometimes! Yorkshire and Durham men, Londoners, men from the Forest of Dean, north Welshmen – whose language is much deeper and more pure than the others from South Wales – two Australians, four Frenchmen, and several coloured [sic] gentlemen. . . . The meetings had to be in English because most of the Welshmen could express themselves to some extent in English, while the majority of the English maintained a frightened silence whenever Welsh was spoken. (Coombs, 1939: 88)

Here there is a profound sense of the ways in which the production of 'militant particularist' activity in the coalfield was a work of interrelation and made out of difficult and ongoing negotiations between different groups. These solidarities were 'always, already', then the product of connections, connections which brought together activists with different political traditions and trajectories. Thus many of the Spanish workers brought into the Dowlais Iron Works in 1907, allegedly to undercut wages, were strongly 'republican and either socialist or anarcho-syndicalist in political outlook' (Francis and Smith, 1980: 11). They were to bring their political traditions to pit villages like Abercrave in the Upper Swansea Valley. Francis and Smith note that the 'young militant miners' leaders in Abercrave who emerged in the 1920s acknowledged that they primarily acquired much of their sharpened trade union consciousness and internationalist outlook from the presence of the Spaniards in their midst' (Francis and Smith, 1980: 13). The explicitly internationalist banner of the Abercrave lodge of the National Union of Mineworkers was influenced by these connections (see figure 1.1).

These accounts demonstrate that political struggles in particular localities bring together different routes of political activity. They do not exist merely as discrete struggles waiting to be brought together by intellectuals or broader political movements. Rather, it can be through place-based political activity that different political trajectories overlap and are brought together, often with diverse and contested outcomes. This unsettles the distinction between local, particularistic struggles and more universal, abstract politics, with 'global ambition', which structures both Williams's work and Harvey's invocation of it. Foregrounding the relations that make up place-based politics opens up more generous possibilities of the agency of place-based political activity in shaping political ideas which stretch beyond place. It also permits a focus on how place-based political activity can be constituted through engagement with the connections beyond and between places (see Massey, 2007a).

Figure 1.1   Internationalist banner of the Abercrave lodge of the National Union of Mineworkers, influenced by the Spanish community in the village, 1965.

Relational accounts of the formation of place-based political identities have tended to understand connections in restrictively human-centred ways, focusing on the circulation of ideas and cultures (see Murdoch, 1997, 1998). Recent work in geography, however, has emphasized the importance of 'allow[ing] non-human worlds some of the action in making connections' (Hinchliffe et al., 2005: 651; see also Braun and Disch, 2002). This has resources for understanding place-based politics as produced through the ongoing negotiation of processes and connections that are materially heterogeneous (see Law, 1994; Law and Mol, 2008). Situating place-based politics as co-produced through the fibrous, fissiparous and contested materialities which shape geographies of connection is significant. This opens up new ways of understanding the agency of place-based political activity. It permits a focus on how place-based political activity bears on particular strategic arrangements of humans and non-humans.

Williams's account of the General Strike, for example, emphasizes how solidarities were co-produced with, and delegated through, the various technologies that constituted the railway network (Williams, 1989). He argues that because 'signalmen had long times of inactivity between trains, they talked for hours to each other on the telephone – to boxes as far away as Swindon or Crewe. They weren't supposed to, of course, but they did it all the time. So they were getting news directly from industrial South Wales, for example. They were in touch with a much wider social network, and were bringing modern politics into the village' (Williams, 2003: 48). As Dai Smith (2005) has commented, these solidarities were made through his [Williams's father's] levers. These geographies of connection, then, are actively produced through particular configurations of relations between technologies and social activity. Chapter 2 develops the implications of these arguments for the geographies of solidarities, but here I develop their significance for the forms of agency and identity produced through place-based political activity.

My interest here is not to dissolve subaltern political activity into a diffuse morass of materially heterogeneous networks (see Thompson, 2004). Rather, interrogating how place-based political activity is constituted through intervening in 'strategic arrangements of humans and non-humans' opens up possibilities for foregrounding the inventiveness of subaltern political activity (Latour, 1998: 229). Andrew Barry uses the term 'inventiveness' in his account of the relations between politics and technologies as an 'index of the degree to which an object or practice is associated with opening up possibilities'. He argues that what is inventive is not 'the novelty of artefacts and devices in themselves, but the novelty of the arrangements with other objects and activities within which artefacts and instruments are situated, and might be situated in the future' (Barry, 2001: 212). Subaltern political activity in this regard produces forms of agency, forms of inventiveness through the way it generates, or attempts to generate, new forms of relations between different associations of humans and non-humans.

This can be illustrated by the strikes of Newcastle dockside workers or keelmen in the eighteenth century. Their strikes contested corrupt practices of measurement in the coal trade. Through doing so they produced new possibilities for the ordering of relations between labour, coal and the keels used to transport the coal from the dockside to the collier ships which would take the coal down the east coast to London (see Featherstone, 2004). The political agency and identities of this place-based political activity were produced through engaging with the ways connections were generated. It generated inventiveness through the way it brought into contestation particular ways of ordering social and material relations. Since the spatial relations that were produced through the coal trade were unfinished (cf. Massey, 2005), there was the possibility that the social/material relations produced through the conduct of the trade could be shaped, contested and produced in different ways. Such a materially heterogeneous account of place-based political activity can be productive through foregrounding the agency of place-based political activity in shaping how connections between and beyond places are constructed.

Conclusions: Towards the Relational Construction of Militant Particularisms

This chapter has contested accounts which have counterposed a dynamic, powerful, networked capital with bounded, local forms of subaltern resistance. It has foregrounded the diverse forms of geographies of connection which have shaped subaltern politics in both the past and present. Through doing so it has set up two of the key concerns of this book. Firstly, it has emphasized forms of agency and identity constituted through spatially stretched forms of resistance, or counter-global networks as I have defined them here. Secondly, it has emphasized the resonances between spatially stretched forms of resistance in the past and present. It has argued that this can energize contemporary political imaginaries.

The chapter has also contested the counterposition of 'militant particularisms' and 'global ambition' which treats place-based political struggles merely as building blocks of wider struggles to be networked by left intellectual elites. I have argued that adopting a relational construction of place-located political activity challenges this reductive distinction and have insisted on viewing struggles as always already constituted through various forms of connection. This produces accounts of the way militant particularisms can recombine networks of activity through distinctive political practices. This can foreground forms of subaltern agency and identity that tend to be marginalized, erased or ignored. There are four key implications of this relational reconstruction of the practices of militant particularism that I want to draw out here.

Firstly, it situates militant particularisms as performed and constituted through the way they 'bring together' different routes of activity and negotiate cross-cutting skeins of power. Rather than being the already constituted building blocks of wider struggles, place-based political identities can be reconfigured and intensified through these political activities. The formation of militant working-class communities in South Wales was not, as is so often assumed, something that emerged out of bounded communities, but was something that was the product of connections which brought together different experiences of activity and assertive political identities. The formation of subaltern political agency and identity through place-based political struggles was directly related to the ongoing and productive negotiation of such connections.

Secondly, this relational construction of local political activity suggests dynamic topographies of relations between place-based political activities and political imaginaries. It challenges the separation of 'local' political activity and the formation of universal political ambitions, suggesting how place-based political activity can decisively shape connections. The example of the formation of the LCS suggests how place-based political activity can be formed out of ongoing and plural relations. Thus, this was a specific society in a specific site, but it was articulated in ways which spoke to the formation of political imaginaries and identities and was productive of explicitly multi-ethnic conceptions of political community. The meeting up of claims and equivalences between struggles can both reconfigure local political identities and shape distinctive political imaginaries. In this sense, 'universal' political imaginaries become the ongoing product of an 'indefinite chain of equivalent demands' between different struggles (Laclau, 1996: 34). This positions such imaginaries, then, as the productive effect of the meeting up of diverse trajectories and routes of political activity.

Thirdly, this networked account positions militant particularisms as part of the ongoing negotiation of multiple spatial relations. The relational construction of militant particularisms can have multiple outcomes, producing both open political identities and exclusionary spaces of political identities. Attention to the relational construction of militant particularisms can explode the binary that suggests a separation between the politics of bounded places and those 'most obviously multi-ethnic cosmopolitan places' which it is assumed are the only places that can be thought about 'progressively' (Nash, 1998: 3). Rather, it points to the importance of examining the different outcomes that the coming together of multiple routes of political activity can produce. There are no guarantees here. The coming together of routes of such activity can produce both exclusionary spaces of politics through the ways they negotiate relations, as well as more open and plural forms of identity (see Amin, 2002: 396–7).

Fourthly, this networked account of militant particularisms emphasizes how place-based political practices intervene in the formation of materially heterogeneous processes and connections. This opens up possibilities for accounting for the dynamic forms of identity and agency constituted through subaltern political activity. It challenges accounts which have constructed subaltern political activity as just trying to 'defend' existing relations. It opens up accounts of the ways in which place-based political activity intervenes in the ongoing construction of strategic arrangements of humans and non-humans. This has resources for foregrounding the 'inventiveness' of subaltern political activity. This concern with the inventiveness of subaltern political activity is developed in depth in the next chapter through outlining networked accounts of the formation of solidarities and antagonisms.

Chapter Two

Geographies of Solidarities and Antagonisms

In her book *On the Political* (2005) Chantal Mouffe argues that the move away from a notion of the political centred on conflict and contestation has had devastating consequences for both understandings and practices of politics. Her target is the rise of a consensual approach to the political where challenging unequal power relations and neo-liberalism have frequently become placed off limits. As a result, the role for politics has been reimagined by theorists like Anthony Giddens, as to 'pilot citizens' through the challenges of transformations such as globalization (Giddens, 1998: 64). For Mouffe, such a 'post-political' vision denies the role of conflict in the political, and is based on an inadequate understanding of the constitution, and persistence of, collective political identities. She argues that the key challenge facing contemporary politics is not to move beyond conflict, but to find ways of dealing with conflict in democratic terms.

Mouffe's reassertion of the significance of contestation and the 'ever present possibility' of antagonism for the political is significant and animates the project of this book in important ways. This chapter, however, seeks to engage with some key tensions in Mouffe's theorization of the political. These tensions, I argue, produce a rather reductive account of the practices and geographies of contestation which has effects. Firstly, Mouffe comes close to reifying conflict as the foundational characteristic of the political (see Barnett, 2004a: 505). This edges out important concerns with the formation of friendships, solidarities and alliances and makes them secondary to conflict. Secondly, her account of contestation is structured by the assumption that antagonisms and solidarities will be constituted within the confines of the nation-state. Thirdly, Mouffe's distinction between agonism and antagonism produces a reductive account of the geography of contestation and elides the insistence on the diversity of forms of antagonism that was so central to Mouffe's earlier work (see

Mouffe, 1988). Finally, Mouffe's lack of attention to the practices of the political closes down a sense of the dynamic, ongoing processes through which antagonisms are constituted. This is a particular issue in relation to the restrictively human-centred account of the political which she adopts.

This chapter turns to work on the political from the traditions of actor network theory and spatial thinking to offer a more generative, ongoing and entangled account of the constitution of antagonisms and solidarities. I argue in turn, however, that Mouffe's stress on the ever present possibility of antagonism usefully unsettles some of the forms of political pluralism which structure the work of theorists like Latour (see also Featherstone, 2004, 2007). The first section of the chapter outlines a networked account of the constitution of solidarities and internationalisms. It develops a concern with the dynamic, contested and networked constitution of solidarities, and begins to relate these to the multiple geographies through which antagonisms are constituted. The second section offers a relational, dynamic account of the formation of antagonisms, stressing the co-production of antagonisms and solidarities. The final section of the chapter concludes by outlining a focus on the constitution of 'maps of grievance'. This term is used to foreground the diverse spatial practices through which geographies of power are brought into contestation through political activity. The chapter concludes by arguing that the conduct of solidarities can have significant impacts on the ways maps of grievance are constituted, and vice versa.

Networking Solidarities

In many different interventions Paul Gilroy has trenchantly critiqued the pernicious consequences of cultural nationalisms for different forms of oppositional politics (Gilroy, 1987, 1992, 1993a, 1993b, 2004). In a discussion of the legacies of left political traditions, Gilroy emphasizes how the 'loyalties' generated through internationalism involved a dislocation of the 'patriotism of national states' (Gilroy, 2004: 5). He argues of the 'dissenting social movements' that have constituted the Left that they

> pursued forms of internationalism that went beyond any simple commitment to the interlocking system of national states and markets. Socialism and Feminism, for example, came into conflict with a merely national focus because they understood political solidarity to require trans-local connections. In order for those movements to *move* they had to break down the obviousness of the national state as a principle of political culture. (Gilroy, 2004: 5)

Gilroy demonstrates here that to make sense of the spatial practices that have shaped solidarities and internationalisms it is necessary to follow such trans-local connections and the different sites through which they were made. This inevitably decentres the nation in relation to political activity. It challenges accounts that have reduced the geographies of internationalism to accounts of the relationship between internationalisms and different national traditions. Such accounts ignore the ways in which internationalisms and solidarities were, and are, constituted through particular networks and particular sites of activity that stretch both beyond and within the nation. This section argues that foregrounding the networks and sites through which solidarities and internationalisms are constituted opens up different ways of thinking about the geographies of connection and political identities they generate.

Gilroy's assessment of traditions of internationalism challenges influential accounts of internationalism by theorists associated with the New Left which were framed in nation-centred ways. Perry Anderson, for example, argues that 'the meaning of internationalism logically depends on some prior conception of nationalism, since it only has currency as a back-construction referring to its opposite' (Anderson, 2002: 5; see also Anderson, 1980: 131–56). His account is useful in asserting that internationalism is not built out of nowhere. But it too quickly centres the nation as the key building block, or at least territorial referent, of internationalism. This produces a reductive geography where internationalism is viewed primarily as the coming together of already constituted socialist traditions in different nations. This formulation is influential and is shared by many theorists on the left such as E. P. Thompson, Anderson's oft-times adversary.

Thompson's political interventions, especially post-1956 in the wake of the Soviet invasion of Hungary and the mass resignations of Thompson and others from the Communist Party, shaped a political geography of left internationalism which decisively broke with an unconditional relationship with official communism as represented by the Soviet Union (Thompson, 1978: 1–34, 1991a; Palmer, 1994: 69–86; see also Anderson, 2002: 21). For Thompson, this had implications for internationalist practices. 'Internationalism', he averred, 'ought to consist, not only in listening attentively to an international discourse, but in contributing to it on our own account. . . . It should be a concourse, an exchange. Argument is its true sign' (Thompson, 1978: iv). Thompson envisions such an exchange, however, as taking place between already constituted left traditions in different countries. 'The 'adoption' of other traditions . . . can very often mean no more than the evacuation of the real places of conflict within our own intellectual culture, as well as the loss of real political relations with our own people' (Thompson, 1978: iv). This account of the relations between national left 'traditions' and the constitution of internationalisms is marked by a singular and bounded notion of those traditions (see Nairn, 1977: 303–4). It suggests that 'English' or other left traditions are not already made out of transnational connections and flows of ideas, forms of organization and relations of power (see Gilroy, 1993b: 11–12). Further, it makes it hard to see the ways in which such transnational connections can reconfigure place-based political identities.

Centring the nation as the key territorial referent of internationalism is not inevitable and has consequences. Foregrounding the contested, multifarious geographies of internationalisms and solidarities opens up resources for understanding the dynamic spaces of subaltern politics. This involves challenging the impoverished sense of the geographies through which articulations are made and remade. It also challenges a tendency to appeal to languages of solidarity and internationalism as if they were simple uncontentious repertoires of activity (see, for example, Watts, 2005: 651). Here I outline a networked account of the constitution of solidarities to challenge nation-centred accounts of internationalisms. This draws on Latour's suggestive redefinition of 'fraternity' as 'the obligation to work with all the others, to build a single common world' (Latour, 2004: 227). This dislocates key ways in which articulations/solidarities have been conceptualized, not only in key Marxist texts and practice, but also in radical democratic theory. Adopting a networked account of the formation of solidarities, then, seeks to account for the dynamic spatial practices through which they are formed, while being alive to the ways in which they exceed and unsettle nation-centred geographies.

This position challenges work on the geographies of solidarities which has adopted scalar accounts of the relations between space and political and which has tended to adopt both fixed interests accounts of the political and static ways of theorizing antagonism (Castree, 2000; Glassman, 2001; Herod, 2001). Thus, Noel Castree's account of the Liverpool dock strikes between 1995 and 1998 usefully draws attention to internationalist geographical strategies employed by the dockers through their disputes and contests the assumption that 'the "bigger" the scale of labour struggle the greater its capacity to affect the course of events' (Castree, 2000: 273–4). Castree evaluates the dockers' strategies only in reductive terms: whether they helped particular narrowly defined 'interests' of the dockers, which remain static through the dispute. Further, his multi-scalar account of the strikes treats the local, national and international aspects of the dockers' politics as discretely different strategies, rather than enmeshed and interconnected.

This closes down a focus on the productiveness of these connections and solidarities. Arguably, the solidarities opened up through the dispute also reconfigured the grounds on which antagonisms were generated. The antagonisms became dislocated from a particular focus on the practices of the Merseyside Docks and Harbour Company to be about broader processes of global restructuring in docks and maritime labour. Further, the involvement in these internationalist connections led to the formation of different geographies of connection catalysed by the dockers' activism. The dockers have also been involved in coordinating global solidarities between international dock workers, both through internet exchanges and websites and conferences, and have offered advice to those in other disputes, such as the Irish Ferries dispute in the autumn of 2005. They set up a bar/social centre in Liverpool called the Casa and were involved, for example, in a solidarity brigade to El Salvador in 2002.[10] This demonstrates the necessity of developing dynamic accounts of the relations between political identities, spatial relations and the formation of solidarities and antagonisms.

One of the key contributions of Laclau and Mouffe in *Hegemony and Socialist Strategy*, and elsewhere, has been to challenge accounts of the political which were defined by fixed interests and identities (Laclau and Mouffe, 1985: 65–71). They destabilize these understandings of identity through developing a focus on the diversity of forms of antagonisms generated through political activity (Laclau and Mouffe, 1985: 122–7; see also Mouffe, 1988). Rather than focusing on a fixed antagonism between 'capital' and 'labour', formed before the conduct of political practices, they argued that it was in the process of political activity, or through hegemonic struggle, that identities and antagonisms were constituted (see also Laclau, 1990). This has significant implications for the formation of solidarities. For Laclau and Mouffe, solidarities became not just articulations between different groups who have 'common interests'. Rather, they argue that through the formation of chains of equivalence between different struggles, different antagonisms can be articulated to form 'collective political wills' (Mouffe, 1988: 99; Laclau and Mouffe, 1985: 152–9). These are practices of solidarity which unsettle fixed and particularistic identities to produce new and open political identities.

This account of solidarities as bearing on the ongoing constitution of political identities opens up possibilities for different accounts of the geographies of solidarities. In this respect Laclau and Mouffe have celebrated Gramsci's work for making a decisive break with orthodox Marxist accounts of solidarities and alliances which were based around deeply essentialist understandings of identity (Laclau and Mouffe, 1985: 65–71). Laclau argues that, for Gramsci, hegemony becomes a 'contingent process of political articulation in an open ensemble whose elements had purely relational identities' (Laclau, 1996: 117; see also Gramsci, 1971: 229–38). Gramsci's conception of alliances becomes more productive, I would argue, partly because it envisions a different geography from the account of hegemony developed by Lenin. Gramsci's engagement with questions of how to construct alliances between peasants in the South and the countryside and workers in the towns and the North contributed to this rupture. He saw these connections as mutually constitutive, arguing that 'the economic and political regeneration of the peasants should not be sought in a division of uncultivated or poorly cultivated lands, but in the solidarity of the industrial proletariat. This in turn needs the solidarity of the peasantry' (Gramsci, 1978: 440). He argued that such connections would have effects such as the reconfiguring of 'craft particularisms' (Gramsci, 1978: 448). This conception of solidarity situates solidarities as ongoing practices which generate new identities and new experiments with relations between workers, land and technologies (see also Wainwright, 2005).

As Laclau and Mouffe insist, an 'inner essentialist core' structures Gramsci's writings (Laclau and Mouffe, 1985: 69). Gramsci clearly privileges class as the key node around which solidarities are to be constituted. In displacing class as the core axis around which solidarities are constituted, Laclau and Mouffe's radical democratic theory opens up possibilities for theorizing the ongoing constitution of articulations. There are two key tensions, however, in the ways that these chains of equivalences are formed. Firstly, Laclau and Mouffe do not dislocate a nation-centred account of the political. Although their work develops a dynamic and plural sense of the formation of antagonisms and solidarities, these remain inscribed within the given space of the nation-state. This has restrictive effects for their accounts of agency and identity in shaping, and being shaped by, translocal connections. As Sparke argues, the effect of this 'built-in territorialization of the political' is to enclose 'sites of radical and plural democracy . . . within the larger space of differences that is the nation-state' (Sparke, 2005: 183).

Secondly, they replace Gramsci's 'inner essentialist core' of class with an insistence that chains of equivalence have to be formed through the construction of a discursive frontier. Their account of articulations between struggles falls 'back on the notion that one struggle provides the "discursive exterior" from which to interpret relations of subordination in another context' (Braun and Disch, 2002: 509). For Laclau and Mouffe, 'articulation remains the work of words alone' (Braun and Disch, 2002: 509; see also Haraway, 1992). Dislocating the making of solidarities from the 'construction of a discursive frontier', whether this be anti-state, anti-imperial or anti-capitalist, opens up possibilities. This evokes the productive character of articulations and solidarities as part of the ongoing constitution of the world (Braun and Disch, 2002: 507). Following these articulations suggests how solidarities become constituted through ongoing, contested and multiple practices that are engaged in actively shaping the world (see Mol, 1999). Thus, rather than solidarities being seen as fixed interests formed around a static object, they can be reconfigured as ongoing interventions in the orderings of networks.

This has significant implications for theorizing solidarities. Firstly, thinking about the situated transnational networks constituted through left internationalisms can foreground some of the practices in which these transnational networks were constituted, formatted and policed. The forms of political activity constituted through left internationalisms have been marked by exclusions and contestation in many different space-time contexts. Central here would be the extremely fraught and frequently exclusionary relations between left internationalisms and questions of gender and race. Feminist historians like Anna Clark and Barbara Taylor have powerfully demonstrated the exclusionary gender relations that structured early forms of trade unions and labour combination. Clark, for example, has demonstrated that they were associated with forms of gendered violence and cemented by exclusionary notions of skill as a 'masculine quality of honour' (Clark, 1996: 119; see also Taylor, 1983). This position was always contested and different forms of relations between gender and left politics articulated (see Midgley, 1992; Taylor, 1983).

Contested and extremely problematic relations between gender and solidarities continue to structure radical political activity. Before the 2007 World Social Forum was held in Nairobi, a paper was circulated which brought the gender relations of the WSF into contestation (Daniel, 2007). The paper argued that the WSF process was failing to integrate gender equality into its practices in different and linked ways. It noted that panels were routinely structured by gender inequality, that the 'feminist struggle still seems something by women for women' and that 'gender/feminist issues' were not integrated into all the themes. It also noted evidence of sexual harassment, physical violence and rape against women delegates. Where feminist organizing has challenged existing forms of labour organization, this has been productive. The network Women Working Worldwide, for example, has developed pioneering forms of organizing through engaging with informal labour practices which have traditionally been marginalized by male-dominated trade-union cultures (see Hale and Wills, 2005).

Feminist theorists like Chandra Mohanty have also pervasively brought into question the unequal relations between gender and race formed through the global women's movement (see Mohanty, 2003). Further, Mohanty has brought into question the continuing inequalities over gender and race that shape the solidarities and forms of political activity being crafted through the global opposition to neo-liberalism (Mohanty, 2003: 221–51; see also Sharp, 2003, 2007). This relates to exclusionary histories around the relations between left politics and race. Black political activists in the US, UK and beyond had to engage in bitter struggles to articulate left politics where race was not subordinated to questions of class (see Carter, 1986; Hall, 1996; James, 1998; Sivanandan, 1990; Tyner, 2004;

Yates, 1989). Caribbean political activists, for example, have been a sig-nificant, but still often marginalized, presence in the histories of the left in both the US and Britain, facing persistent exclusion and prejudice (see James, 1998; Schwarz, 2003b). In London in the 1950s a sizeable West Indian branch of the Communist Party of Great Britain was set up in response to the 'difficulties faced by many black members in working within the ordinary party framework' (see Carter, 1986: 56). Concerns such as racism and colonialism were predominantly dealt with dismissively by official left politics, generating particular exclusionary versions of interna-tionalism. The Trinidadian activist George Padmore who worked with the Comintern in the 1920s and 1930s and headed the Profintern, left Russia in 1935 because his position of organizing anti-colonial struggles became untenable when it became subordinated to the geopolitical interests of the Soviet Union. He was instructed to 'show sympathy and understanding of Britain, France and the United States', despite the fact that his political work had been concerned with attacking the colonial policies of Britain and France and working against the deeply ingrained racism in the US (Hall and James, 1996: 23–4).

Secondly, foregrounding the networks, sites and practices through which internationalisms are constituted can open up accounts of less hier-archical forms of solidarities than those that characterized the socialist internationals. This permits a focus on more networked, routed and pro-ductive practices of solidarity which tend to work against the formation of fixed, organizational hierarchies. These forms of equivalences and alliances between unlike actors refuse what Spivak has termed 'a homo-geneous internationalism' (Spivak, 1985: 350). Their activity is produc-tive, continually formed and can unsettle fixed identities. Tracing the routes and connections through which such solidarities are constituted also enables a more generative role for place-based political activity to emerge in the constitution of solidarities. Rather than thinking about internationalism as 'jumping scales', it is possible to think about the dif-ferent sites through which internationalisms are constituted. Gibson-Graham has noted the 'incredible power of discussions around kitchen tables and village wells that formed much of the political practice of a women's "movement" of global proportions' (Gibson-Graham, 2002: 35). Or there are sites such as the club for 'colored [*sic*] soldiers' in a basement in Drury Lane in London frequented by the 'black Bolshevik', novelist, poet and political activist Claude McKay in 1919/20 to which he brought copies of radical black American magazines and newspapers such as *Crisis* and *Negro World* (McKay, 1985: 67–8; see also James, 2003: 79–80). Developing the argument of chapter 1, this emphasizes the co-production of place-based political activity and solidarities, rather than their counter-position.

Finally, following from the insights of theorists like Latour, it is possible to see solidarities and internationalisms as ongoing interventions in the constitution of networks. This allows solidarities and the constitution of networks and materialities to be rethought as co-produced rather than being conceived as constitutively separate. Solidarities are not produced on a smooth surface between discretely bounded struggles, but rather are part of ongoing connections, relations and articulations between places. Further, they are interventions in the social and material relations between places. This opens up possibilities for different accounts of subaltern agency and internationalisms. The refusal of Rolls-Royce workers in East Kilbride in the 1970s to work on eight Avon 207 jet engines belonging to Chilean Hawker Hunters, which had been used in the coup against Allende, is a good illustration of the way the formation of solidarities can directly engage in the constitution of connections between places.

In 1974 the engines were sent from Chile to East Kilbride for mainte-nance, but they were 'blacked' by militant shop stewards who had earlier protested against the 'takeover of the democratically elected Chilean Gov-ernment' by Pinochet (Beckett, 2002: 148; see also Somerville, 2003). On 22 March 1974,

> the union committee spread the word across the shop floor that work on them was to cease. For the next four and a half years, despite threats from Rolls-Royce and fury from Chile, court rulings and interventions by successive Prime Ministers, half the engines . . . slowly rusted in their crates in a small yard towards the back of the East Kilbride plant. (Beckett, 2002: 148)

Through disrupting the routinized maintenance operation on the engines the workers at the plant cut into the connections between Britain and Chile. This attempted to put pressure on the Pinochet regime. Their solidarities were produced through directly intervening in these connections and dis-abling them through refusing to work on the engines, leaving them to rust, even refusing to allow them to be taken 'out of their containers so they could be sprayed with preserving fluids' (Beckett, 2002: 152). These acts of solidarity in turn generated different forms of connection with Chile. Allende's widow travelled to Glasgow to 'give thanks in person' and told them that their action had been a 'symbol to my people' (Beckett, 2002: 154).

Latour, and other theorists associated with actor network theory, have tended to reduce questions of the political to the technical. These solidari-ties, however, demonstrate how the political and technical can be co-pro-duced and articulated in passionate and 'more than rational' ways (see Barry, 2001; Laurier and Philo, 1999). Thus the effect of the action of mi-litant workers in East Kilbride was not only to cause a diplomatic crisis in relations between Britain and Chile. It was also to 'circulate hope' (see

Anderson, 2006). This shaped what might be termed 'affective geographies of connection' between the workers in East Kilbride and those resisting Pinochet in Chile. I use the term 'affective geographies of connection' to refer to the 'more than rational' forms of identification, exchange and articulation produced through political spatial practices. Positioning solidarities as ongoing interventions in the constitution of networks, then, does not mean that those solidarities are understood in 'merely technical' ways. Rather, it permits a focus on the ways in which the relations between materialities and connections can be articulated in distinctive ways through political activity. This is disruptive of dominant accounts of labour geographies that are framed around strictly rationalist accounts of political activity (see especially Herod, 2001; see also Wills, 1998). This is consistent with the attempt to develop a sense of solidarities as networked, ongoing, contested and productive, which this section has outlined. The next section engages with the implications of this position for the theorizing of antagonisms.

Space, the Political and the Construction of Antagonisms

The previous section outlined a networked account of the geographies of solidarities. I have argued that to account for the construction of geographies of solidarities it is necessary to challenge fixed-interest accounts of the relations between space and politics and to see antagonisms as formed through the conduct of political activity. This section intervenes in debates on the relations between antagonisms and spatial relations through drawing together the insights of actor network theory on the materially heterogeneous construction of the social, together with radical democratic theories' insistence on the constitutive role of conflict in the political. It uses an engagement between these two bodies of theory and spatial thinking to construct a dynamic, relational and processual account of the formation of antagonisms.

In his book *Politics of Nature* Bruno Latour engages with the work of Carl Schmitt to clarify the distinctive 'skills' that 'politicians' add to a reworked notion of the political, whereby the social and natural are brought together, rather than held apart. He draws on Schmitt's argument that the specificity of the political is located in the formation of friend-enemy relations (Latour, 2004: 207; Schmitt, 1976). He goes on to argue that Schmitt 'makes the error of completely forgetting non-humans and confusing politics in general with just one of the functions (that of institution of exteriority) in which political skill plays a role' (Latour, 2004: 282n27). It is this institution of exteriority which Latour takes as Schmitt's central contribution. He reconfigures the 'exterior' not as 'a nature, but an otherness capable of doing us harm and even of doing us in' (Latour, 2004: 282n27).

For Latour, this permits a redefinition of the 'enemy'. He usefully dislocates Schmitt's purified construction of the political as a solely human achievement and unsettles the centrality of the fixed container of the nation-state to Schmitt's political theory. Thus he argues that the enemy

> will no longer be used to designate human neighbours gathering troops along a border; nor will it be used to incriminate beings so unassimilable that one would have the right to deny them even existence itself, by eliminating them once and for all as irrational. No, the enemy, human and non-human, is the one who is rejected, but who will come back the next day to put the collective at risk: today's enemy is tomorrow's ally. (Latour, 2004: 207)

Here the 'enemy' usefully becomes dynamic and constructed through relations. The political becomes defined through the ongoing constitution of friend-enemy relations and through the negotiation of materially heterogeneous relations, rather than through fixed already-constituted notions of the enemy. This dislocates some of the key terms of Schmitt's construction of the political. I think that it is useful to dislocate further aspects of Schmitt's construction of the political to clarify the role of conflict in the ongoing constitution of social and spatial relations.

Schmitt's critique of liberal accounts of politics permits a focus on the collective formation of political identities and procedures. His stress on the formation of friend-enemy groupings emphasizes that conflict cannot be simply eroded or transcended, but constitutes an ongoing challenge to political institutions and procedures. These insights challenge political theories and practices which focus solely on the role of atomistic individuals and which see the construction of adversaries as a political relation which can be eliminated or transcended. Schmitt, however, deals inadequately with questions of how the political collectives signified by friend-enemy groupings are constituted. In his account, friend-enemy relations are constituted through the formation of a homogeneous 'people' (Schmitt, 1976: 53). The 'people's' identity is constituted purely negatively against 'enemies' outside their 'territory' (see Barnett, 2004a). Hence Latour critiques Schmitt's conception of the 'enemy' as 'human neighbours gathering troops along a border'.

There is a particular geography of antagonism imagined here. Schmitt exteriorizes conflict from the people/nation through his concept of 'friend-enemy relations'.[11] It is not only political pluralism that becomes impossible in Schmitt's political theory (see Mouffe, 1999a, 199b). It is also a plurality of antagonisms. It becomes impossible to see the diverse antagonisms constituted through political practices if (as Schmitt does) friend-enemy relations are conceived in ways which exteriorize antagonisms from particular spaces such as the nation. If political activity is followed, however, it can

be seen that it often exceeds, spills over, circumvents or refuses the confining spatialities of the nation-state (see Gilroy, 1993b). Following the spatialities through which antagonisms are constituted opens up important
resources for accounting for the dynamic, ongoing constitution of practices
of contestation.

Interrogating these spatialities can help transcend some of the tensions
in Laclau and Mouffe's influential theorization of antagonisms and the
political. Clive Barnett has contended that Laclau and Mouffe's stress on
antagonism is symptomatic of a 'spatialization of key concepts of political
theory' in their work (Barnett, 2004a: 506). Barnett argues that radical
democracy is defined by an 'interminable hostility' (Barnett, 2004a: 505).
Further, he 'affirms an infinite and unconditional hospitality as the condition of political community' (Barnett, 2004a: 524). Here, I argue in contrast that it is precisely a limited sense of the geography of antagonisms
that closes down a sense of the constitution of antagonisms as an ongoing
process in Laclau and Mouffe's work, with important consequences.

In *Hegemony and Socialist Strategy* Laclau and Mouffe theorize antagonisms as social relations which prevent the formation of 'full identities'.
They contend that the 'relation arises not from full totalities, but from the
impossibility of their constitution'. Using the example of peasant-landlord
relations, they suggest that it is 'because a peasant cannot be a peasant that
an antagonism exists with the landowner expelling him from his land'
(Laclau and Mouffe, 1985: 125; see also Norris, 2002). This account suggests that there are full identities to be produced that relations of antagonism make impossible. As Laclau argues elsewhere, antagonisms arise
because they prevent the formation of an 'absent fullness' (Laclau, 1996:
36–46). This formulation of antagonism closes down a sense of the relationality through which antagonisms are constituted. Antagonisms become
produced not through the ongoing negotiation of multiple social and spatial
relations, but rather through isolated and purified identities being constituted against what they are not. This produces a limited sense of the relations through which antagonisms are constituted. Further, it prevents a
focus on the generative character of antagonisms in constituting political
identities. To situate practices of contestation as dynamic, mobile, in
process and bearing on the ongoing formation of heterogeneous associations it is necessary to think antagonisms in more explicitly spatial ways.

These tensions in Laclau and Mouffe's account of the construction of
antagonisms are related to a particular framing of the geographies of contestation. Laclau and Mouffe usefully position antagonisms as multiple and
in process. This move transcends the tendency, outlined in the previous
section, to position antagonisms such as between capital and labour as
fully formed before political activity. But their account of the constitution
of antagonisms remains framed, like their account of solidarities and

equivalences, within a nation-centred account of the political. Their implicit territorialization of the political, which treats the nation as the given space of political activity, has implications for the ways in which they construct the relations between antagonisms and political identities. My concern here is not that the nation-state isn't a significant actor. I don't follow the position of those who claim that transnational practices necessarily mean that there is an erosion of the importance of place or the nation (see Castells, 1997; Smith, 2003). It is necessary, however, to move beyond accounts which see the nation-state as a fixed container that isn't the ongoing product of spatially stretched relations (see Sparke, 2005).

The effects of this implicit territorialization of political activity can be demonstrated through Mouffe's mobilization of the distinction between antagonism and agonism (Mouffe, 1993, 2000, 2005). This powerfully inscribes an in-built nation-centred account of contestation. Mouffe argues it is necessary to find ways of transforming antagonistic articulations of conflict to agonistic ones where 'enemies' are reconfigured as 'adversaries'. She contends:

> While antagonism is a we/they relation in which the two sides are enemies who do not share any common ground, agonism is a we/they relation where the conflicting parties, although acknowledging that there is no rational solution to their conflict, nevertheless recognize the legitimacy of their opponents. They are 'adversaries' not enemies. This means that, while in conflict, they see themselves as belonging to the same political association, as sharing a common symbolic space within which the conflict takes place. We could say that the task of democracy is to transform antagonism into agonism. (Mouffe, 2005: 20)

This distinction between agonism and antagonism produces a reductive account of political practices of contestation. It produces a distinction between violent conflict between enemies that want to destroy each other, and agonistic exchange between adversaries through formal political activity. Her account confines agonistic politics to 'legitimate political channels' (Mouffe, 2005: 21). This assumes that such agonistic politics will be practised at the level of the nation-state through forms of parliamentary representation. Further, it is implicit, here, that the 'common symbolic space' within which conflict takes place will be the nation-state. This distinction elides the insistence on the diversity of forms of antagonism, which was central to Mouffe's earlier work (see Mouffe, 1988). This reductive geography of contestation closes down a sense of the plurality of political practices.

Locating antagonisms as the product of engagements with multiple spatial relations positions permits a focus on the generative and diverse practices of contestation. The geographies of power that are brought into contestation through political activity are not limited to neat containers such as the nation-state. Rather, political identities can be constituted through the ongoing ways in which they bring into contestation networked geographies of power (see also Dikeç, 2005). These often exceed the confining spaces of the nation-state. The diverse forms of resistance to neo-liberal globalization are significant here. These neither produce particularly 'violent' responses, nor seek to contain their political activity through agonistic political practices within the nation-state. Rather, these movements have constructed political agency and identities through bringing into contestation the spatially stretched power relations that constitute neo-liberal globalization and construct solidarities that stretch beyond the nation-state through doing so. This underlines the necessity for engaging with the diverse and generative political geographies of contestation and their implications for ways of theorizing antagonisms. These arguments are developed in more depth in chapter 6.

Following the spatialities through which antagonisms are constituted through political activity dislocates Laclau and Mouffe's human-centred account of the political. Such human-centred accounts of the political have been persuasively challenged by the work of theorists associated with actor network theory (ANT) (see Barry, 2001; Latour, 2004; Mol, 1999). One of the persistent critiques of ANT, however, has been its failure to differentiate between associations and ways of generating associations. Laurier and Philo have argued that ANT has tended to obscure differences 'between kinds of humans and between kinds of machines' (Laurier and Philo, 1999: 703; see also Lee and Brown, 1994; Thrift, 1999: 313). Accounts of the hybrid geographies of human and non-human associations have also tended not to account for the ways in which these associations might be configured in antagonistic ways (see Whatmore, 2002: 125–33). ANT offers significant, if under-utilized, resources for reconfiguring conflict as bearing on the ongoing constitution of materially heterogeneous relations.

Latour's critique of the 'modern constitution' permits a redefinition of the political as bearing on the entire set of tasks that allow the 'progressive composition of the world' (Latour, 2004: 53). Challenging the separation between 'politics' and 'nature' enables us to engage with the progressive composition of the world without the 'ever present possibility' that politics will be foreclosed by appeals to the judgements of the social or the facts of nature. As Latour suggests, a recourse to nature 'as already composed, already totalized, already instituted' is frequently a way to 'neutralize politics' (Latour, 2004: 3). This allows 'political ecology' to be recast as bearing on the strategic arrangements of humans and non-humans, on 'the complicated forms of association between beings' (Latour, 1998: 229).

Latour, however, is ambiguous about the status of conflict in this reworked account of the political.

In *Politics of Nature* Latour 'exteriorizes' conflict from the constitution of collectives. He reconfigures the 'outside' as 'dangerous others' which threaten the collective. This exterior 'will gradually fill up with excluded entities, beings that the collectivity has decided to do without, for which it has refused to take responsibility' (Latour, 2004: 124). As the discussion in chapter 3 of the Irish peasant movement the Whiteboys will demonstrate, however, their activity didn't just attempt to exclude particular 'things' or 'entities' from collectives. Rather, they sought to contest the way these 'entities' generated associations through generating particular contested relations of power. This positions the formation of antagonisms as ongoing interventions in 'world-building activities'. It produces an account of the formation of antagonisms as constituted through intervening in 'the strategic arrangement of collectives', rather than being merely posed between different human actors.

This section has argued that engaging with the generative and dynamic spatial practices through which contestation is produced opens up possibilities for accounting for the diverse and productive forms of subaltern identity and agency. I have argued that to do this it is necessary to foreground three aspects of the formation of antagonisms. Firstly, I have argued that antagonisms are produced through the ongoing negotiation of cross-cutting and multiple spatial relations. The formation of antagonisms cannot be reduced or contained within particular spatialities, such as the nation-state. Secondly, I have argued that foregrounding the multiple spatialities through which practices of contestation are formed allows a sense of the plurality of such practices. Following the spatial practices through which contestation is produced exceeds and unsettles Mouffe's attempt to foreground prescriptive normative categories through her distinction between antagonism and agonism. Thirdly, I have argued that antagonisms can be produced through bringing into contestation the strategic arrangements of humans and non-humans. The following section develops these arguments by exploring how the conduct of political activity produces distinctive maps of grievance through negotiating and bringing into contestation spatially stretched relations of power.

Geographies of Resistance and Maps of Grievance

The dynamic trajectories of resistance produced through opposition to neo-liberal globalization have demonstrated the generative and plural practices through which spatially stretched power relations are brought into contestation. Making sense of these practices involves interrogating the ways in which the different geographies of power reconstituting places can be contested. Imagining spatial relations in this way becomes a condition for thinking about the political as the site of multiple conflicts and antagonisms. For actors craft their political identities through the ways they engage with geographies of power relations. As I have argued in this chapter, they do not have fixed interests constituted in relation to already existing spatial configurations of power. Rather, the practices through which spatial configurations of power are brought into contestation are productive.

To explore how the political identities of movements are shaped through specific engagements with geographies of power, this section develops the term 'maps of grievance' (see also Featherstone, 2003). The term bears on the spatial practices through which power relations are constructed as antagonisms. More specifically, it bears on the practices through which power relations become known, generated and brought into contestation through political activity. Following these practices allows some sensitivity to the diversity of forms of contestation and their dynamic and generative spatialities. For the construction of grievances has both a distinctive spatiality and is constitutive of political identities. In other words the practices through which grievances are constructed both differ and matter. These constructions of maps of grievance are part of the creative, dynamic trajectories of oppositional political movements. They are not 'merely resistance', for they are not just defined in opposition to practices of domination (see Thrift, 2000: 273–4). I argue that the practices through which maps of grievances are constructed have effects on the conduct of solidarities. For the terms on which geographies of power are brought into contestation have effects on the kinds of political identities produced through political activity.

This dynamic way of thinking the relations between space and the political is significant. For existing accounts of domination and resistance in geography tend not to see resistances as the products of multiple interrelations. The politics of scale literature, for example, sees resistances as primarily local unless movements actively 'jump scales' 'from local to regional, national or international' through their activity (Glassman, 2001: 524; Smith, 1993; for critiques, see Amin, 2002; Cox, 1998: 2–3; Jones et al., 2005, 2007). This view of political activity fails to situate resistances as always already the product of different trajectories. Examining the different trajectories that constitute political activity is a key way of dynamizing subaltern spaces of politics. This does not involve viewing subaltern spaces of politics as somehow authentic or autonomous (see Moore, 1997, 1998). It does, however, demand attention to the ways in which political activity both negotiates and generates cross-cutting relations of power.

Such a position has been powerfully articulated through Foucauldian accounts of geographies of resistance. Sharp and colleagues, for example, argue that resistance needs to be viewed as 'unremittingly entangled' with relations of power and domination (Sharp et al., 2000: 31). They insist that resistance and domination need to be viewed as intertwined rather than as defined against each other, since 'resistance turns up in domination' and 'domination turns up in resistance' (Sharp et al., 2000: 20). Their rejection of spatial metaphors of autonomy is a condition for avoiding an authentic space of resistance outside of power relations. There is a key tension in Sharp et al.'s account. This is the extent to which they do not dislocate Foucault's argument that since 'there are no relations of power without resistances; the latter are all the more real and effective because they are formed right at the point where relations of power are exercised' (Foucault, 1980: 142).

Through arguing that resistances are formed 'right at the point' where relations of power are exercised, this position subordinates the spatialities of resistance to the prior spatialities of domination. Further, Sharp et al. accept Foucault's binary counterposition of domination and resistance. They dynamize this binary through suggesting that 'there will be no complete separation between two seemingly opposed practices [domination and resistance], in that the one will always contain at least the seed of the other' (Sharp et al., 2000: 20). This binary structure makes it hard to see practices of resistance as always multiple and differentiated, and thus begins to close down a sense of the multiple spatialities of resistance. This is exacerbated by their rejection of Pile's claim that 'geographies of resistance do not necessarily (or even ever) mirror geographies of domination, as an upside down, or back to front or face-down map of the world' (Pile and Keith, 1997: 2). Here, I reject the binary between resistance and domination, to focus on the ongoing formation of subaltern political identities through the negotiation of multiple relations of power. Rejecting this position permits a focus on how forms of subaltern political activity construct distinctive, contested and diverse 'maps of power' (see Haraway, 1991: 180).

It is possible to see resistances as both productive of, and 'unremittingly entangled' in, geographies of power without seeing their trajectories as being determined by spatialities of domination. Sharp et al.'s position closes down an understanding of one of the creative and generative aspects of oppositional politics. These are the practices through which adversaries are defined, constructed and brought into contestation through political activity. As Mouffe has argued, one of the basic tenets of radical politics is 'the definition of an adversary' (Mouffe, 1998: 13). She has insisted that conflict and antagonism are constitutive of the very identities negotiated through political practices (Mouffe, 2000: 21; see also Mouffe, 1993; Schmitt, 1976; Patton, 2000). The implication is that instead of 'trying to erase the traces of power and exclusion', democratic politics requires 'us to bring them to the fore, to make them visible so that they can enter the terrain of contestation' (Mouffe, 2000: 33–4). In this analysis the practices through which adversaries are isolated and defined become central to any understanding of how movements create political agency. For the presence or absence of grievances is not enough to explain political activity. It is simply not adequate to conclude that particular conflicts are the inevitable product of 'real grievances over real issues' (Martinez-Alier, 2002: 70), nor is it adequate to view the targets of political activity as merely arbitrary (see Girard, 1987: 131). Rather, it is necessary to consider how grievances are addressed, interpreted and constructed (Snow et al., 1986; Tarrow, 1994).

As I have argued in the previous section, the process of making power relations visible and part of the terrain of contestation is the product of distinctive spatial practices. These engagements with the ongoing formation of geographies of power are part of the generative, productive practices of political activity (Braun and Disch, 2002). Political activity rarely engages with static or fixed 'maps of power', for topographies of political activity are more varied and generative than this. The constitutive role of conflict in the political clearly needs to be thought in spatial terms, but this is an underdeveloped theme in accounts of the co-constitution of space and politics. Massey's influential account of the spaces of politics, for example, while drawing on Mouffe's elaboration of the constitutive role of conflict, does not examine in depth the spatial practices through which antagonisms are constituted (Massey, 2005). The term 'maps of grievance' is an explicit attempt to theorize how the construction of grievances has both a distinctive spatiality and is constitutive of political identities. It draws on the term 'maps of power', but adopts the old word grievance to signify the practices through which geographies of power are constructed, known and brought into contestation through political activity. Further, it directly addresses the diverse spatial practices through which social and political movements construct geographies of power in antagonistic ways. In this sense it seeks to go beyond the reductive binary framing of practices of contestation which is the result of Mouffe's distinction between antagonism and agonism. The term 'map' is used to suggest the location of political activity as part of dynamic and emergent, networked geographies of power relations. Examining the construction of maps of grievance can help foreground the following key aspects of political activity.

Firstly, the activity of making geographies of power part of the terrain of contestation is productive. The practices through which 'traces of power and exclusion' are made part of the terrain of contestation have effects. This is an aspect of political activity which Mouffe's work neglects through its lack of engagement with the practices of the political (see Braun and

Disch, 2002; Whatmore, 2002: 150). These practices also refuse the confining spatialities implicit in scalar or nation-centred accounts of the political. For, as the counter-globalization movement has demonstrated, geographies of power need to be dragged into the terrain of contestation. It is through these processes that what Shotter calls 'practical-moral knowledges' about the world, how it is generated and ordered, are constructed (Shotter, 1993: 6–8). These practical-moral knowledges can bear on the power relations generated through particular strategic arrangements of humans and non-humans. The construction of such knowledges is a constitutive part of political activity.

Secondly, the practices through which geographies of power are contested have effects on the identities formed through political struggles. Since grievances are constructed there is space for political activity to articulate contestation of geographies of power in different ways. The practices through which unequal geographies of power are brought into contestation matter. They are also constitutive of different political identities. Thus, which institutions or groups are brought into contestation, and the terms on which they are constructed as adversaries, are significant. A different politics flows from constructing the World Trade Organization as an adversary on the grounds that it is a key neo-liberal institution, than contesting it because it is 'foreign'. The formation of maps of grievance is not arbitrary. The terms and spatial practices through which grievances are constructed can be powerfully shaped by place-based political cultures and the particular histories and geographies of political cultures.

Thirdly, these different ways of engaging with geographies of power can have significant impacts on the conduct of solidarities. As I argued in the first section of this chapter, there are strong relations between ways of theorizing antagonisms, solidarities and the formation of identities. The ways in which geographies of power are constructed through activity has effects on these solidarities. Maps of grievance that produce exclusionary nationalisms or localisms can exert pressure on the formation of open and relational solidarities. One of the key interventions this book seeks to make is to find ways of experimenting with geographies of power and practices of solidarity that make alliances between different struggles against neo-liberal globalization more rather than less possible and productive.

Finally, following the construction of maps of grievance unsettles the counterposition of friendship and hostility that has marked debates about the political. Thus, as I have argued, Mouffe comes close to asserting conflict as *the* foundational characteristic of the political, while Barnett presents hospitality as 'the condition of political community' (Barnett, 2004a: 525). These positions rest on privileging either hospitality or antagonism as somehow foundational to the 'political' and are ultimately reductive. Rather than seeing the political as open, ongoing and productive, these positions close down definitions of the political around one key characteristic, rather than being alive to the diversity of modes of political engagement and practice. Challenging this counterposition of hostility and friendship opens up different cartographies of the political. It opens up accounts of how the formation of solidarities, and the production of connections between different sites of political activity, can change the terms on which maps of grievance, and political identities, are constructed. The solidarities constructed between East Kilbride and Chile through the 'blacking' of Hawker Hunter engines gives a sense of the dynamic maps of grievance constructed through negotiating geographies of power. They also emphasize how particular friendships and solidarities can be generated in relation to such maps of grievance.

Conclusions

This chapter has outlined an approach to the formation of solidarities and antagonisms which is alive to the dynamic and shifting geographies of contestation and connection. I have mobilized a networked ontology of the political to develop relational, dynamic and processual accounts of the formation of antagonisms and solidarities. I have foregrounded the spatial practices through which solidarities and antagonisms are constituted and have contended that this can do significant work in theoretical terms. I have done this in a way that demonstrates how such solidarities and antagonisms are constituted through particular networks and sites. Finally, I have sought through the concept of maps of grievance to articulate a dynamic way of theorizing the relations between spatial practices and the formation of antagonisms, solidarities. This has involved the rejection of the counterposition of friendship and hostility. I have argued that rejecting this counterposition opens up different possibilities for cartographies of the political. Part II of this book develops these theoretical arguments through a detailed engagement with the politics of spatially stretched forms of subaltern politics/resistances in the early modern Atlantic. It uses this to demonstrate these arguments about the dynamic formation of geographies of connection and contestation. This further asserts powerful forms of networked subaltern political agency in contesting the unequal geographies shaped by mercantile trade networks.

Part Two

Geographies of Connection
and Contestation

Chapter Three

Labourers' Politics and Mercantile Networks

Through the spring and early summer of 1768, labour disputes among sailors and in many dockside trades brought the London waterfront to a stop. A prosecution brief for the trial of eight coal heavers, dockside workers, accused of the murder of a sailor, James Beattie, during the strikes noted that:

> All these prisoners . . . are by trade coal heavers – Irishmen by Birth and papists – and several of them are, as they have bragg'd and given it out themselves, of the gangs of Whiteboys in Ireland, driven out from thence for the most Enormous Crimes. There are about 670 persons in all who follow this trade of coal heaving – two thirds are Irishmen and those in general Roman Catholicks but few of these are quiet laborious men, the rest are of a riotous disposition and ready to join in any kind of disorders.[12]

Assertions of links between Irish coal heavers and the Whiteboys were common in accounts of the strikes of May 1768.[13] The Whiteboys were an agrarian 'secret society'. They were active in the counties of Limerick, Cork, Tipperary, Kilkenny and Waterford in the 1760s in contesting unequal social and environmental relations such as enclosure of common land. There were continuities between the forms of organization and repertoires of activity deployed by the coal heavers and the Whiteboys. This suggests that the assertion of connections between them were plausible. They situate the strikes in relation to exchanges of subaltern political activity and forms of organisation between Ireland and London.

Miles Ogborn's discussion of the commercial expansionism that transformed London's geographies of connection in the eighteenth century has emphasized the 'problems of coordination and control' faced by merchants 'who dealt in and created this new geography' (Ogborn, 1998: 206–8). This new geography involved challenges associated with enrolling heterogeneous materials into trade networks and disciplining often unruly forms of labour. The materially heterogeneous practices through which merchants sought to combine different places through trade are defined here as 'mercantile networks'. These practices and geographies embodied mercantile assumptions and conventions about the importance of trade, its relationship to the formation of a national economy and about the ideal conduct and regulation of trade.

This chapter explores how different forms of subaltern political activity configured identities and agency in relation to these mercantile networks. It asserts the importance of spatially stretched forms of labourers' politics in the mid to late eighteenth-century. The first part of the chapter critically introduces work on subaltern politics in the Atlantic world in the seventeenth and eighteenth centuries that has challenged the tendency to characterize labour and resistance politics as settled and bounded. I then discuss three aspects of the Whiteboys' spatial politics. I explore the way they generated the constitution of social and environmental relations in antagonistic ways. I explore the way their activity was related to seasonal migration to Newfoundland and attempts to bring the power relations that structured this migration into contestation. Finally, I explore the relations between the Whiteboys and the struggles of dockside workers in London in 1768. This section develops the argument of chapter 2 that located solidarities in the ongoing formation of networks.

Atlantic Networks and Subaltern Political Identities

Chapter 1 argued that diverse bodies of work have challenged the tendency to counterpose the spatial politics of the past and present and to theorize historical subaltern movements as bounded. One of the most significant interventions in this regard has been recent work on the histories and geographies of the Atlantic world. This has profoundly challenged dominant ways of understanding politics, resistance and cultures. These perspectives, from a range of disciplinary backgrounds including geography, cultural studies and history, have challenged the centrality of the nation-state in understandings of space, place and politics (Fischer, 2004; Gilroy, 1993b; Linebaugh and Rediker, 2000; Ogborn, 2005; Roach, 1996). They have emphasized the mobility of political and cultural practices and the connections and exchanges between different subaltern groups. These concerns have strong resonances with recent work in geography which has challenged bounded ways of thinking about politics and resistance.

The work of Peter Linebaugh and Marcus Rediker, in particular, has recovered powerful traditions of multi-ethnic Atlantic resistances, riots and rebellions in the early modern era (Linebaugh and Rediker, 1990, 2000; see also Rediker, 1988a, 1988b, 2004; Linebaugh, 1988, 1992). By foregrounding circuits and networks of multi-ethnic cooperation, Linebaugh and Rediker have sought to liberate radicalisms from the confining spaces of the nation-state. Their work provides an inspiring corrective to the stifling 'categories of merely national history' which have buried the 'vitality of political movements in so many ethnically and economistically arranged cemetery plots' (Gilroy 1993a: 71; see also Linebaugh, 1988: 216). Rejecting these confining spatialities opens up rich imaginative geographies of resistance. Linebaugh and Rediker stress the connections, interrelations and circulations that made up the many riots, mutinies and rebellions which were produced alongside, within and against the formation of Atlantic trade networks (Linebaugh and Rediker 2000; see also Linebaugh 1992; Rediker 1988a). They situate these connections as productive, arguing that they generated 'egalitarian, multiethnic conceptions of humanity' (Linebaugh and Rediker 2000: 352).

These connections challenge the construction of subaltern political cultures which invoked the moral economy as restrictively 'local' or 'particular' (Thompson, 1991b: 185–258). E. P. Thompson defined the 'moral economy' as 'a popular consensus as to what were legitimate and what were illegitimate practices in marketing, milling, baking' which framed crowd actions such as English food riots in the eighteenth century. This consensus was grounded upon 'a consistent traditional view of social norms and obligations' (Thompson, 1991b: 188). Thompson's formulation of the term sets up an association between the moral economy and local and bounded activity. He argued, for example, that food riots were mobilized to contest power relations 'within the community' (Thompson, 1991b: 188; see also Tilly, 1995: 33; Bohstedt, 2000). This construction of the moral economy has had legacies. It structures the arguments of theorists like Craig Calhoun who counter-poses transnational political networks with 'the old home feeling' and 'sense of mutual obligation' he associates with the 'moral economy' (Calhoun, 2002: 88). This is symptomatic of the enduring tendency to associate such interventions with bounded versions of the local.

Linebaugh and Rediker challenge this pervasive tendency to associate politics that invoked the moral economy with bounded versions of the local. They demonstrate how subaltern political cultures could intervene in the constitution of transnational networks of labour and materials that produced and reproduced Atlantic trading networks. This opens up important possibilities for recovering the dynamic geographies of labour in the eighteenth-century Atlantic world. I develop these arguments through stressing three key themes: the multiple and contested subaltern identities generated through negotiating Atlantic networks; the multiple outcomes of geographies of connection; and the way that subaltern activity negotiated the constitution of such networks.

One of the central contributions of work on Atlantic subaltern political cultures has been to signal the role of particular sites, whether they be ships, port cities, or plantations, as hubs of connection and exchange between different groups (Christopher, 2006; Linebaugh and Rediker, 2000; Scott, 1986). This has foregrounded the dynamic subaltern spaces of politics formed through geographies of connection. Recent debates over Atlantic subaltern identities, however, have developed a rather polarized sense of the political identities formed in relation to Atlantic sites. Thus Nicholas Rogers has contested Linebaugh and Rediker's account of Atlantic working-class politics defined by circulations and cooperation. Instead, he depicts a 'Hobbesian' Atlantic, 'a violent world of marchlands . . . in which relatively little space opened up for amicable relations between people of different cultures, let alone the cultivation of wider solidarities' (Rogers, 2003: 224). Rogers' account, however, treats identity as fixed and immutable, as made before interaction in Atlantic spaces. Through doing so he ignores how unstable, and heterogeneous, categories such as 'black' and 'white' were in the Atlantic world, particularly in maritime contexts (see Berlin, 1998; Bolster, 1997).

Such categories as Ira Berlin has powerfully demonstrated were ongoing, contested, in construction (Berlin, 1998: 1–14). There are counter-stories that emphasize the production of different identities, and forms of solidarities especially in shipboard spaces (see chapter 5 below). As Emma Christopher's work on the sailors who crewed slave ships has demonstrated, however, the solidarities and exchanges produced through these encounters were situated, limited and partial (Christopher, 2006). Her work has recovered important, and hitherto neglected, forms of cooperation and solidarity between sailors of markedly different ethnicities aboard slave ships. But she has also shown how these forms of exchange, solidarity and multi-ethnic cultures of resistance were limited, not extending, for example, to the slaves they transported (see Christopher, 2006: 51). Overlaps, exchanges and intersections of different groups could produce cooperation, and the formation of new identities and motley associations (see Berlin, 1996; Scott, 1986). This cooperation was not inevitable. These intersections could also produce antagonisms between and within subaltern groups. The practices through which these antagonisms were constructed and negotiated were shifting and dynamic and were crucial to the formation of subaltern political identities. A focus on these multiple political identities can foreground the diverse and contested outcomes of the meeting up of different subaltern networks and groups.

This opens up a set of concerns about how subaltern political activity was constituted through the ongoing negotiation of Atlantic networks. Atlantic networks are defined here as the multiple and overlapping material, cultural and political circuits and flows that traversed the Atlantic and bound different places together through differentiated relations of power. The chapters in this section of the book interrogate the spatial practices through which political practices, actors, ideas and repertoires of activity moved. They explore how different subaltern groups came together, often with contested results, through political activity. The spatial relations that constituted the Atlantic world, however, are not seen as a mere backdrop to these struggles. The chapters explore how the geographies of power that shaped Atlantic trade (and other) networks were brought into contestation through subaltern political activity. They also explore how different subaltern groups used the mobility afforded to them by their locations in mercantile networks to develop spatially stretched forms of resistance.

This position has important methodological implications. I have used various archival sources to reconstruct the relations between subaltern activity and Atlantic networks. I have situated texts, letters, trial records and newspaper reports not as bounded artefacts, but as parts of the production and reproduction of particular networked social relations. Following these texts and engaging with the social and spatial relations they were part of can give a sense of the ongoing constitution of identities and the connections that constituted Atlantic networks. This approach draws on Ogborn's argument that it is necessary to consider 'writings of various sorts as material objects and endeavour[ing] to understand how and why they move around the world' (Ogborn, 2002: 156). Ogborn usefully positions texts as part of networked social relations and as constitutive of world-building activities, and not just representing such activities (Ogborn, 2002: 166; see also Lambert, 2005).

The approach developed here seeks to make a significant intervention in the production of networked archival research practices by using them to foreground geographies of subaltern knowledges and practices. There are longstanding debates about the problems of recovering subaltern knowledges and experience (see, for example, Guha, 1983; Samuel, 1994; Thompson, 1968: 648). Developing networked archival research practices opens up possibilities here. Rather than assume that there is a coherent body of Atlantic working-class experience, I have sought to foreground the dynamic spatial practices through which subaltern movements constituted and negotiated geographies of connection. I have also sought to demonstrate and assert connections convincingly through triangulating between different sources. This approach has also been taken as a way of recovering the productive and generative forms of these connections. It has involved reading official testimonies against the grain to glean information about the logics and forms of subaltern political activity and identity.

This has involved drawing on testimonies such as court martials which have been viewed with increasing suspicion by some scholars. Recent debates over the conspiracy associated with Denmark Vesey have emphasized the difficulties of using such sources (Johnson, 2001). Rather than reject such evidence as inevitably unsound, however, I draw on the imaginative response of historians like John Barrell and James Epstein to such tensions. They have situated encounters such as trials as constitutive events in themselves, with their own sense of theatre, spatial practices and social relations (see Barrell, 2006: 75–102; Epstein, 2003: 59–82). I seek to develop a more networked account of these spatial practices than the rather bounded research practices of Barrell and Epstein allow, and position such events in relation to flows of ideas, actors and geographies of power.

This decision to foreground the spatially stretched forms of resistance is structured by a particular political engagement. Like longstanding traditions in social history, stretching back to the influential Communist Party Historian's Group and beyond, it is part of an attempt to construct 'usable pasts' (see Schwarz, 1982). The connections foregrounded in this section of the book challenge the tendency of New Left historians to present the histories of English dissent and radicalism as though they 'were produced spontaneously from their own internal and intrinsic dynamics' (Gilroy, 1993b: 11). The cultural nationalisms that structured the work of these New Left historians led them to isolate subaltern movements and struggles from 'pattern[s] of antagonistic relationships with the supranational and imperial world' (Gilroy, 1993b: 11). It is these relationships between histories of subaltern political activity and spatially stretched forms of resistance and power that I foreground here. This is necessary to recover the presence of networked subaltern agency, identity and solidarity.

Spatial Relations, Antagonisms, Inventiveness

In 1762 'Joanna Meskell' sent the following threatening letter to a gentleman who had called a 'county meeting' to concert measures for 'restoring order', or as Joanna expressed it 'for defeating the method I have taken to ward off an impending famine'. The letter stated:

> Your honour is sensible . . . that while of the land which their ancestors held at four or five shillings an acre they got a few acres at four pounds, to set potatoes in, they behaved peaceably and quietly. Your honour is also sensible that the laws of the land have made no impression for them, and that the customs of the country seem to have been appointed for their total destruc-

tion and desolation; upstarts supplanting my poor people on expiration of their leases, and starting their lands with bullocks. . . . I thought it incumbent on me to provide for the support of my people as inoffensively as I could, by ordering them to dig up a few fields, offering to occupiers treble rent for the same. As to the killing of cattle on a late occasion, it was intended as a scheme to owe some obstinate and uncharitable stock jobbers into compliance with the just and necessary demands of my poor afflicted people. (cited by Froude, 1881: 28)

This threatening letter introduces key aspects of the Whiteboys' political activity. It introduces an incisive sense of how they positioned 'risks' like famine as produced through particular unequal material and social practices. It signals the ways their politics engaged in the relations between different entities, and constructed particular entities such as livestock as 'enemies'. Finally, the letter illustrates how their forms of politics were articulated through particular performances of violence and threat which were sanctioned by legitimizing notions associated with the moral economy.

The Whiteboys were active in the counties of Tipperary, Limerick, Waterford and Cork in the province of Munster and in Kilkenny in the early 1760s. They were a 'secret society' known for their nocturnal gatherings where, garbed in dresses and adopting carnivalesque forms of activity, they dispensed a rough justice against those who had transgressed the norms of the moral economy. These activities earned them the name of 'midnight legislators' and they were described by one nineteenth-century observer as a 'vast trades union' for the 'protection of the Irish peasantry' (Lewis, 1836: 99). The Whiteboy movement was not undifferentiated, but it was largely an 'insurrection of . . . cottagers'.[14] Cottiers and labourers worked for middlemen and landlords, often not being paid in cash but in access to conacre, 'tiny patches of land rented for the time necessary to plant and sow a crop of potatoes' (Kenny, 1998: 19). Their signing of declarations and threatening letters with names like Queen Sive and Joanna Meskell, and adoption of female dress, allowed them to appear as an almost mythical force of judgement. Gibbons has argued that figures like Sive and Meskell 'hovered between the other world and everyday life in the imagination of the peasantry' and were associated with mythical traditions of the Kilkenny and Tipperary countryside (Gibbons, 1996: 141). They also signal how they produced particular forms of gendered violence, where male-bound secret societies enacted forms of violent justice in the guise of women.[15]

Dominant accounts of the Whiteboys, and of other Irish agrarian secret societies, have represented them as restrictively 'local', 'defensive' struggles (see Donnelly, 1978; Wall, 1973). There were, however, important relational contexts to their activity. Exploring how their activity negotiated these relational contexts can foreground the inventiveness and dynamic spaces of politics formed through their conduct. From the mid-seventeenth century, Munster became progressively integrated into an Atlantic 'provisioning' market, which was of particular importance for the French Atlantic world. By the mid-eighteenth century, Cork had become a centre of the 'most advanced meat-packing industry in the world' through using advances in beef barrelling techniques (Truxes, 1988: 154). Connections with the French Caribbean were particularly significant (see Mandelblatt, 2007). There, 'cow beef', 'an Irish specialty produced by fattening aged dairy cattle, whose carcasses were cut up into small pieces for processing', became an important source of protein in slaves' diets (Rodgers, 2000: 176–7). Control of these provisioning routes became a matter of geopolitical importance and conflict during the American War of Independence (see Bell, 1964–8, vol. 6: 64, 297–8).

The 'provisioning trade' produced particular Atlantic mercantile geographies of connection. These trade networks depended on particular changes in spatial and social relations in Munster. These practices enrolled sheep and cows through social and spatial relations which threatened and excluded commoning practices. This reconstitution of spatial relations was co-produced through changes in livestock. In the second part of the eighteenth century there was a shift away from Irish longhorns and black cattle to breeds that matured more quickly, and thus met the demands of emerging export practices (O'Shea, 1954: 8). In the mid-eighteenth century improving landlords and middlemen enrolled a range of non-humans to produce political technologies of space that threatened commons and customary rights. Enclosed orchards on the Kingston estate in South West Tipperary in the early eighteenth century, for example, were protected by 'a double ditch set with whitethorn' (Smyth, 1976: 37). The sheep and cattle used to stock pastures were used by improvers to produce profitable uses of land (see Young, 1892, vol. 1: 457).

Whiteboy activity brought the effects of Atlantic trading networks in exacerbating existing inequalities into contestation. Their forms of activity contested different grievances such as the enclosure of common land through the use of walls and ditches, tithes and the building of deer parks, and against officials such as tythe proctors as they moved across Munster.[16] Whiteboy activity also negotiated tensions between and within subaltern groups, with actions such as intimidation of 'spalpeens' or 'migrant workers' in Kilkenny in the 1770s.[17] They produced distinctive forms of subaltern organization, based around oath-bound secret societies. Their activity was characterized by audacious forms of territorialization constituted through violent forms of masculinity. They marched in sub-military forms led by pipers.[18] They stole horses which they rode into towns like Clonmel at night, marking their presence by shouting 'Huzzas' and blowing horns.[19] They dug mock graves along roadsides and attacked houses at night.[20] They tore down the official proclamations issued to stop them and replaced them with their own notices.[21] Their activity had effects. In 1762 the agent of Lord Carberry, Jeremiah Jackson, at Farningstown in Co. Limerick, noted that the outbreak of Whiteboy activity had 'put a stop to buying and selling, and if it continues, it will be very difficult to get in the rents'.[22] His letter emphasizes the legitimacy of the Whiteboys' alternative forms of justice. Although condemning their activity as 'a bad way of redressing grievances', he commented that 'there seems to be a real necessity for it, and if they go no further than their declarations, few will condemn them'.[23]

These acts were held together by shared dispositions and practices informed by notions of fair conduct and customary right. The Whiteboys' activity, however, was not a static defence of common right. Their activity was constituted through challenging dominant understandings of spatial relations. They didn't passively accept dominant definitions of what was defined as common land. Rather, definitions of common rights were reshaped through their activity. When 'disguised miscreants levelled a part of the Deer Park Wall' on Lord Grandison's estate in Dromana, Waterford, it was 'represented to these miscreants by some of their leaders to have been a Common perhaps some hundred years since' (*A Short Narrative*, 1762: 25). An aggrieved upper-class commentator noted this representation conflicted with the 'known fact' that the 'Forest on his Demesne' 'has been time immemorial the sole and separate property of his lordship and his ancestors' (ibid.). This emphasizes that Whiteboy activity was not merely a spontaneous reaction against new enclosures, but also contested spaces which had longer histories of appropriation by landlords.

The inventiveness of Whiteboy activity was constituted through dislocating the associations between invocations of customary right and the moral economy and forms of social deference. This is demonstrated through accounts of the rough forms of justice they dispensed. These produced notions of what was 'just' through practices of regulating how humans and non-humans were brought together and combined. An account of their 'unofficial forms of justice' by one contemporary commentator makes this clear:

> They established councils at Stated places . . . The council summoneth persons, Swore them to secrecy, and allegiance to the sovereign Queen Sive Oultagh, issued orders . . . for all operations where fences should be levelled, where Orchards should be torn up, rooted out and destroyed, where timber trees Should be cut down, what houses Should be burned, or thrown down, what corn mills and public Pounds Should be demolished, What persons Should be taken out of their beds at midnight, and carried to a distance from

home naked, upon thorns and briars . . . (*A Short Narrative*, 1762, in Kelly, 1989: 22)

The Whiteboys' forms of justice, then, were not a purified human achievement. They intervened in the ongoing relations between humans and non-humans. They constructed certain ways of generating relations between humans and non-humans as unjust. The practices of these 'midnight legislators' recast political activity as not about the pursuit of fixed goals or interests, but as interventions in the ways in which the relations between cottiers, land, fences, walls, ditches, middlemen, animals and potatoes were produced. That an agent like Jackson saw their attempts to regulate the price of potatoes as fair suggests the depth of communal legitimacy for their forms of regulation.

Central to these forms of regulation was the contestation of particular relations between humans, animals and spaces. They constructed the walls and ditches that constituted the enclosure of commons as 'enemies', as they did the cattle and sheep used to stock the common land and transform them into pasture. A key activity associated with the Whiteboys was 'houghing', the vicious maiming of cattle and sheep.[24] The threat of houghing is powerfully invoked in the following threatening letter:

> We Levellers and avengers for the wrongs done to the poor, have unanimously assembled to raze walls and ditches that have been made to inclose the commons. Gentlemen now of late have learned to grind the face of the poor so that it is impossible for them to live. They cannot even keep a pig or a hen at their doors. We warn them not to raise again either walls or ditches in the place of those we destroy . . . If they do, their cattle shall be houghed and their sheep laid open in the fields. (cited by Froude, 1881: 25)

It would be tempting to interpret these violent and hostile relations between the Whiteboys and animals as a form of what Stallybrass and White refer to as 'displaced abjection': the 'process whereby "low" social groups turn their figurative and actual power, *not* against those in authority, but against those who are even "lower"' (Stallybrass and White, 1986: 53 emphasis in original; for such an interpretation of the Whiteboys, see Donnelly, 1978: 24). To interpret the vicious mutilation of cattle by Whiteboys in this way, however, would be to miss the ways in which these acts were interventions in the relationships between animals, land and cottiers. These acts were not just symbolic. They were also interventions in the ways in which relations between these different human and non-human actors were constituted. The threat of violence against animals also acted as a warning against others stocking common land with cattle or sheep.

These assaults against animals contested the ways enclosure reworked the relationships between land, animals and labourers. Cattle and sheep did not only displace labourers, they were active agents in the transformation of these spaces from 'common' to 'pasture' (see Young, 1892). The animals were constructed as 'enemies' not just because they were targets onto which the Whiteboys displaced their anger, but also because they were part of social relations which Whiteboy practices 'articulated' as unjust. This is a relational account of the enemy. Here the enemy becomes located and constructed through their role in constituting relations and networks, rather than being positioned 'outside' of the formation of collectives. These forms of contestation also figure particular relations between entities as more 'just'. This stresses the relations between antagonism, spatial relations and inventiveness. Constructing particular relations as unjust allowed the possibility that different relations between these entities, land and labourers might be articulated and generated.

The threatening letter cited above, while constructing sheep and cows as enemies, also figures positive articulations with non-humans, which emphasize that the identities of Whiteboys were not only constructed in negative ways. The invocation of the importance to cottiers of keeping 'a pig or a hen at their doors' emphasizes that Whiteboy activity figured positive articulations with particular spaces and non-humans. Humphries and Neeson have noted the importance of commons and customary rights for poor English families, emphasizing that the labouring poor constructed independent identities through skills and practices associated with commoning spaces (Humphries, 1990; Neeson, 1993: 158–84). There were similarly diverse usages of commoning and smallholding spaces in Munster in the eighteenth century. Oral tradition relating to commoners in Connabery in County Waterford, for example, suggests that rushes, which were used for lighting, bedding, thatching and basket-making, were collected from commons.[25] Diverse materials were collected for fuel. Many townships had rights to 'turbary', peat from nearby bogs; furze was also collected, as were thistles, 'the hawm [stubble] of our corn fields', waste wood and cow dung (Molesworth, 1723: 36, 37; Willes, 1990: 73).

These uses of commons had effects. An advocate of agricultural improvement in Ireland, writing in 1723, complained that 'com[m]ons in general are a Grievance and Nuisance' and that the poor used practices such as gleaning to 'refuse wages' (Molesworth, 1723: 26, 31–3). These spaces were articulated as threatening due to their importance in generating assertive and independent subaltern identities (see also Willes, 1990). Through their activity, then, the Whiteboys developed and politicized these associations of custom, and the uses of particular spaces, with assertive, independent subaltern identities. This is a key way in which Whiteboy activity exceeded assumptions about the deference which many have seen to be inherent in invocations of customary right and the moral economy. These assertive identities, as the next section will suggest, were also used to negotiate labourers' positions in geographies of connection.

Subaltern Identities and the Constitution of Mercantile Networks

Whiteboy activity was the product of relations. In the early 1760s Whiteboy activity and forms of organization were translated across the counties of Munster. Their forms of political activity were mobile and easily mimicked. In the early 1760s oath-bound organizations characterized by secrecy and violence circulated across the counties of Limerick, Cork, Tipperary and Waterford. By 1763 Whiteboy activity had reached County Kilkenny.[26] Their forms of organization and unruly subaltern cultures also moved beyond Ireland. Letters of missionaries in Newfoundland in the mid-1760s suggest the importance of the Whiteboy activity as a context for the emergence and intensification of rough subaltern cultures in Newfoundland. This section explores the relations between such activity, patterns of seasonal migration and the construction of place.

A recurrent theme in the writings of missionaries of the Society for the Propagation of the Gospel stationed in Newfoundland during the 1760s is anxiety about the formation of unruly subaltern cultures. Their accounts position the formation of this 'motley' culture at the intersections of different routes of subaltern activity. In November 1766 the missionary Edward Langman based in St Johns noted that 'a greater number of poor Irishmen [were] brought here this spring from Waterford, than has been known in the years before'. He continued that it was 'strongly imagined, that many of them were of the White Boys in Ireland getting a passage privately to this island for fear of being apprehended'.[27] In 1768 his fellow missionary James Balfour noted that 'we are so incorporated with numbers of Whiteboys, that have lately come from Ireland, that the Honest and Industrious can barely live'.[28]

These letters suggest that Whiteboy activity contributed to the emergence and intensification of unruly subaltern cultures in Newfoundland; though it is unclear the extent to which 'Whiteboy' functions merely as a generic term for the 'low' Irish. The correspondence suggests these routes of action contributed to an experience of mobility, constituted through interconnections between poor English and Irish, which was profoundly ambivalent about authority. They express anxiety about their lack of authority, about Sabbath breaking and the way the common fishermen 'Irish and English in this parish marry and baptise' themselves.[29] There are also more direct suggestions that these groups of immigrants were using some of the techniques associated with Whiteboys to negotiate their subordinate position in Newfoundland. Langman commented in November 1767 that 'trade [was] depressed', which 'necessarily obliges the Irish here to mob frequently'.[30]

These unruly subaltern cultures had contested relations to the geographies of power that structured seasonal migration to the fisheries. In 1767 the governor of Newfoundland, Hugh Palliser, issued a number of memoranda and orders in relation to the labour practices of seasonal migrant labourers who worked the island's fisheries. Palliser noted that a 'great number of idle, distressed men [were] staying in the country' after the fishing season was over (Palliser, 1767a: 149). This was related to two key factors. Firstly, 'neither master of the ship carrying them out, nor the master hiring them there' thought 'themselves obliged to provide' for seasonal migrants' passsages home. The ships' masters were paying the fishermen 'in effects and liquor in advance . . . so that when their time of service is expired they [were] destitute of means to return to England/ Ireland' (Palliser, 1767a: 149). These forms of labour organization were contested. Palliser noted that 'thousands of men' had 'yearly complained of the distresses and oppression they labour under' (Palliser, 1767a: 149). Secondly, Palliser noted that 'some idle dispossessed men desert from their masters service before the end of the voyages for which they engage to serve and betake themselves to a loose, idle vagabond life' (Palliser, 1767a: 155).

These debates over the organization of labour in the fisheries of Newfoundland draw attention to the ways in which labourers were positioned in subordinate location in the networks that constituted seasonal migration. Palliser's 'orders' suggest that they experienced oppression in geographical ways, through being unable to return 'home' after the season within which according to Palliser they were defined as 'useful' or through having to sell 'themselves to the American Agents' who made a trade of 'seducing from Newfoundland such distresed seamen and fishermen' (Palliser, 1767b: 147). The debates suggest how the spatial relations through which seasonal migration and the fisheries were ordered were brought into contestation through subaltern politics. They also signal one of the key spatial practices through which mobile labourers negotiated their subordinate position in mercantile networks: practices of desertion.

Desertion was used in diverse Atlantic contexts and to negotiate different mercantile networks by labourers as diverse as Newcastle keelmen, West African boatmen and Caribbean 'masterless' sailors (see Featherstone, 2004; Gutkind, 1985; Scott, 1986). Hardt and Negri reduce desertion to refusal, arguing that desertion 'does not have a place: it is the evacuation of the places of power' (Hardt and Negri, 2001: 212). Marcus

Rediker has developed a much more productive account of desertion. He argues that workers in early modern America 'took to their feet or threatened to take to their feet, in an effort to influence the conditions of their labour. They ran, individually and collectively, in "confederacies" and after "conspiracies", from seaport to seaport, looking for better maritime wages, or from one seasonal or casual labour market to another' (Rediker, 1988b: 237). This positions desertion as a dynamic technique through which workers negotiated power relations either through exercising mobility or the threat of mobility. A discussion of practices of desertion can illuminate how spatial relations were constituted in antagonistic ways through Atlantic subaltern politics.

Desertion, and the contestation of seasonal rhythms of labour, constituted motley, unruly subaltern cultures in Newfoundland. Palliser's accounts emphasize how desertion was productive of 'loose idle vagabond' lifestyles. These 'vagabond' identities were produced through particular uses of spaces and through particular relations with the 'respectable' inhabitants of the place. He argued that they 'subsist by plunder, rapine and abandon themselves to all kinds of wicked causes and disorders . . . even to live as wild savages in the woods and so become dangerous to the lives and properties of the rest of the king's subjects' (Palliser, 1767a: 153). For Palliser, these practices threatened the very status of Newfoundland as a 'nursery of seamen' (Palliser, 1767b: 47). This construction of place was a powerful way in which marginal places defined by seafaring were articulated as integral to the imperial ambition and power of Britain (see also Brewer, 1994); that practices of desertion unsettled Palliser's sense of Newfoundland as a 'nursery of seamen' emphasizes how desertion could actively reconfigure place-based identities. The letters of missionaries like Langman and Balfour also suggest that these unruly subaltern identities were formed in relation to flows of subaltern political activity associated with the movement of 'Whiteboys' from Munster to Newfoundland.

Atlantic mercantile networks then had a paradoxical relation to subaltern political activity. They depended on and produced exploitative relations, as the account of the forms of labour organization the fisheries depended on suggests. But they also allowed the circulation of forms of subaltern political activity and organization such as those associated with the Whiteboys. The orderings of Atlantic networks, such as the geographies of power that structured seasonal migration in the fisheries of Newfoundland, were brought into contestation through different subaltern struggles and practices. The practices through which these networks were contested were productive. Desertion was constitutive of identities which exceeded the constructions of 'well-disciplined' labour associated with official Newfoundland's view of the fishery as a 'nursery of seamen' and where labourers staying on past their time of use were defined as 'out of place' and 'useless'.

These assertive constructions of identity were also located at the intersection of different routes of subaltern cultures. The next section uses this focus on the dynamic trajectories of subaltern political cultures to explore the solidarities formed through the strikes on the waterfront in London in 1768.

Connections, Solidarities, Materialities

The strikes among dockside workers, sailors and weavers in 1768 in London were formed in relation to repertoires of subaltern political activity that circulated through emerging trade networks. Thus, sailors' disputes were linked to earlier stoppages in Newcastle.[31] Disputes among weavers in Spitalfields drew on the power and forms of activity of weaver's combinations in Dublin and across Ireland.[32] There was evidence of direct communication between weavers' combinations in Dublin and London (Linebaugh, 1992: 278). It is in the context of such exchanges that the prosecution brief, cited above, asserting links between coal heavers and Whiteboys should be positioned.

Coal heavers were among the most visible and threatening of the labourers involved in the disputes of 1768. Their labour was to unload coal from ships from the Northeast to the lighters – the flat-bottomed boats which docked alongside the coal wharves. The work 'was done by gangs of sixteen (to eighteen) coal-heavers, who shovelled the coal from platform to platform in the hold, and finally into the measuring vat, from which it was tipped into the lighters' (Ashton and Sykes, 1964: 205). The work was marginal and of low status. Coal heavers described it in a 1764 petition as 'dirty and slavish' (Coal Heavers, 1764). The trade had been established when the Fellowship of Billingsgate Porters 'restricted itself to cleaner cargoes' (George, 1927: 230). It was controlled by middlemen, known as 'undertakers'. They ran the trade from dockside taverns, made a raft of deductions from coal heaver's wages and were implicated in various corrupt practices. Assertions of links between Irish coal heavers and the Whiteboys were frequent in accounts of the strikes of May 1768 and suggest the need to interrogate the relations of strikes to networks of subaltern movement and political activity (see also Linebaugh, 1992: 309–18).[33]

There were continuities between the forms of organization and repertoires of activity deployed by the coal heavers and the Whiteboys. This suggests that these forms of subaltern activity were mobilized by coal heavers to negotiate their subordinate position on the river. Distinctive modes of organization and activity emerge in the brief cited at the start of this chapter and the reports of informants. This suggests continuities between the activity of the Whiteboys and the coal heavers in the strikes of 1768. The coal heavers' action and organization were characterized by secrecy and exemplary intimidation. This secrecy, together with targeted and legitimized violent action, was instituted through the formation of oath-bound secret societies, a key organizational form associated with the Whiteboys. These secret societies met in particular riverside taverns, spaces of association which were the subject of legal repression after the strikes. After May of 1768, the licenses of nine publicans were taken away for 'encouraging and harbouring the coal heavers'.[34] An informant, George Mayhew, 'a coal heaver and an accomplice', noted that 'about 5 or 6 months ago 45 Coal heavers entered themselves into a society by the name of Bucks of which the informant was one'. There was a similar society called the Brothers.[35]

Violent forms of clandestine action were mobilized in similar ways to the actions of the Whiteboys. There were nocturnal assaults on the houses of those who had transgressed their notions of fair conduct, such as the assault by an assembly of coal heavers armed with stones, cutlasses and muskets on the Roundabout Tavern, run by John Green in April, 1768, an undertaker in the coal trade who had organized labour outside of the coal heavers' combinations.[36] Their action constituted similar audacious forms of territorialization to the Whiteboys'. Norton complained that during their disputes with sailors from the Newcastle collier ships, the coal heavers 'grew so audacious as to keep watch on the shore in gangs all day long in order to attack any of the masters of the colliers or their men who should come on shore'.[37] There were similar relations between violence, masculinity and territorialization, and commonalities in terms of the use of ritualistic forms of alternative justice sanctioned by custom. An account of the strikes notes how coal heavers enforced stoppages of work on the docks by making any one carrying out business ride the 'Wooden Horse' 'which is carrying them upon a sharp stick, and flogging them with ropes, sticks and other weapons' (St James's Chronicle, 14–17 May 1768). The Whiteboys utilised similar forms of exemplary intimidation, as did journeymen weavers in Dublin and Carrick on Suir.[38]

Accounts of the coal heavers emphasize 'customary' understandings of labour. Ralph Hodgson, an advocate of the coal heavers, noted that the labour of unloading the coal vessels might, 'by a kind of prescription of custom, be deemed the property of the Coal-heavers, whose livelihood depended on it' (Hodgson, 1768: 15). These mobilizations of practices associated with customary rights to materials were ongoing and productive interventions in the organization of mercantile networks. Coal heavers' labour practices were located within relations of power which produced coal through diverse and contested forms of property relation and measures. Their struggles brought into contestation the practices through which coal was generated and defined through mercantile networks. Through their labour, coal heavers were 'folded' into the materially heterogeneous networks of the coal trade (Latour, 1999a: 189). They developed their own techniques for negotiating these networks, such as pilfering (Linebaugh, 1992: 307).

Observers like Patrick Colquhoun who attempted to discipline dockside spaces noted that coal heavers possessed a 'disposition to pilfer' (Colquhoun, 1800: 143–4). The labouring Irish were also renowned for their pilfering. Arthur Young found the labouring poor of Ireland 'addicted to thieving' and pilfering (Young, 1892: vol. 1, esp. 60–8, 99, 109). This reputation, and assertive performances of pilfering, travelled with them. It is easy to dismiss pilfering as a mundane 'crime'. Pilfering can be positioned as a dynamic technique labourers used to negotiate the expanding volumes of materials that flowed through the port of London by situating it as part of ongoing struggles over how materials were to be generated through mercantile networks.[39] The very term 'pilfering' suggests the contested materialities at stake through the struggles and activity of riverside labourers. For labourers, taking coal for their personal use was not something they considered a crime. They considered 'sweepings' – the small, broken up pieces of coal left after they had heaved the coal out of a ship, lighter or barge – a customary right (see Linebaugh, 1992: 432–3). Coal was not a stable commodity neatly defined as the property of the merchants. Rather, how coal was defined and generated was brought into contestation through various political interventions, such as the coal heaver's actions and pamphlets which contested the systematic use of fraudulent measures by coal merchants.

Coal heavers' political activity and solidarities were formed through ongoing interventions in how the foldings of merchants, labourers and coal should be generated. These solidarities shaped ways of generating labour and coal which were instituted and shaped through the delegation of the power of subaltern actors through particular contested material practices. These forms of delegation were constituted through various different struggles. Thus the under-meters, who oversaw the unloading of coal, didn't enforce rules that the measuring vats used to measure out coal should be completely filled due to the intimidation they faced from gangs of coal heavers if they enforced such measurement.[40] Coal heavers successfully contested attempts by undertakers to monopolize the shovels used to heave out the coal. A coal heavers' petition of 1758 argued that 'by an unlawful influence of the said undertakers, the shovel makers absolutely refuse either to sell or to make any shovels for the Petitioners, or even to mend those they have made, though tendered ready money for such work'.[41] Their use of customary rights to coal, which generated part of the load of a coal barge or lighter as a customary right of coal heavers, not as the 'property' of merchants, can also be related to these subaltern relations of power. These

practices were used to generate alternative material networks which coexisted alongside the official coal trade, most visibly in a market for 'pilfered'
coal at Execution Dock (Colquhoun 1800: 142–3). These social and material practices profoundly challenged the notions of 'spatial order' and
'regular pattern of circulation of people and goods' advocated in the writings of the architect John Gwynn or Patrick Colquhoun (Ogborn 2004:
35). These forms of delegation were backed up by threats and intimidation,
as the case of the vats suggests. Reports that the coal heavers had 'bragg'd
and given it out themselves' that they were Whiteboys suggests that this
culture of threat was also produced through mobilizing subaltern geographies of connection in intimidating ways.

These cultures of threat and intimidation had effects on the negotiation
of relations between different dockside workers. Sailors and coal heavers
were located in different relationships to mercantile coal networks. In trying
to redress their own grievances, coal heavers cut into the fragile labour
practices of the collier sailors. The work of these sailors was subject to
uncertainties. Changes in tides and weather conditions meant that the time
that the collier ships took for return journeys to Newcastle was highly vari-
able. Nonetheless these sailors 'were paid a lump sum for the return voyage
from the Tyne, regardless of the time taken' (George, 1927: 239). Preventing the unloading of the coal further delayed the uncertain time of the
voyage and the coal heavers' strike action thus impacted directly on the
Newcastle sailors. Sailors became aggrieved by the actions of the coal
heavers who boarded collier vessels, obliged the men to quit their work,
and kept a picket on the shore keeping 'them indefinitely in the river by
refusing to unload their ships' (George, 1927: 239). Violent conflict between
the sailors and coal heavers resulted in the murder of a collier sailor, James
Beattie, by coal heavers on 24 May 1768. Eight coal heavers were tried for
this murder, two of whom, James Murphy and James Dogan, were con-
victed and hung.[42] Subaltern political cultures impacted on how these solidarities were produced and articulated. The links between violence and the
constitution of masculinity, coupled with the hard drinking cultures of
these dockside labourers, exerted pressure on the formation of solidarities.
They also emphasize that such solidarities were not constituted in narrow
technical ways, but could generate violent antagonisms between different
groups of labourers.

Following from Latour's insights (noted in chapter 2), the formation of
articulations/solidarities can be positioned as part of the making and remaking of networks. Solidarities and the constitution of networks and materialities, rather than being conceived as constitutively separate, can be rethought
as co-produced. Subaltern political activity in these disputes generated
agency and inventiveness through contesting the relations between labour
and coal. The contested relations formed through ways of generating soli-

darities through particular interventions in materially heterogeneous networks unsettles Latour's reframing of solidarities as bearing on the 'the obligation to work with all the others, to build a single common world' (Latour, 2004: 227). Following the different overlapping networks of labour practices as they intervened in these mercantile networks suggests how solidarities can become articulated in contested ways within and between subaltern groups, and not necessarily just subordinated to a consensual world-building project. It also suggests that the passionate, messy articulations of relations between labourers and coal produced solidarities through 'more than rational' articulations which unsettle Latour's rather rationalist construction of world-building activities (see Haraway, 1992; Laurier and Philo, 1999).

This discussion of the solidarities and interventions in the networks of the coal trade formed through the activity of the coal heavers in the disputes of 1768 has been used to illustrate why it is useful to situate solidarities as part of the ongoing constitution of networks. This account of their disputes has suggested that it is necessary to think about the power relations and geographies at stake through the process of shaping a 'common world' and through world-building activities. Solidarities are not formed through easy consensual practices, but through ongoing and contested negotiation of spatially stretched relations of power. In situating solidarities as part of the ongoing constitution of networks it is necessary to concede that the politics produced through these articulations might not allow the 'control' of the production of spatialities in the ways demanded by some (see Harvey, 1989: 236; Smith, 2000). Further, they might not be successful in developing the kind of 'total' opposition to Empire demanded by Hardt and Negri (2001: esp. 55–6; see also chapter 6). Rather, they suggest how solidarities might generate situated interventions in networks. These include forms of delegation which have effects on the constitution of networks, such as the refusal to allow coal vats to be filled, and the dynamic use of pilfering to shape alternative material geographies. These solidarities, then, were active in intervening in and shaping mercantile networks and in generating alternative ways of ordering heterogeneous associations.

Conclusions

This chapter has followed the dynamic trajectories of Whiteboy activity. It has demonstrated how the forms of activity associated with the Whiteboys were productive of mobile subaltern political cultures. These were used to negotiate mercantile networks in inventive ways. This is suggestive of the paradoxical relations between mercantile networks and subaltern forms of political activity. These mercantile networks created mobile and often multi-ethnic labouring classes. The mobility that was central to these labour practices was used by different labourers to bring the unequal geographies of power produced by mercantile networks into contestation. This also allowed the circulation of different repertoires of subaltern political activity, such as those associated with the Whiteboys. In exploring the geographies of their activity I have drawn on Linebaugh and Rediker's work, which has challenged the association of subaltern political activity that invoked customary rights and the moral economy with bounded forms of politics. I have argued that these forms of subaltern politics could have different effects.

Through these interventions the chapter has made a set of contributions to ways of theorizing geographies of resistance and labour. It has challenged assumptions about the 'inveterate localism and fixity of . . . the lowest orders' (Lloyd, 2003: 367). Through doing so it has asserted the significance and situated forms of agency generated by different labourers' politics as they negotiated their location in spatially stretched mercantile networks. It has demonstrated some of the forms of inventiveness generated through subaltern political activity as it negotiated mercantile networks and their effects. It has noted, for example, how Whiteboy activity brought into contestation dominant ways of generating social and environmental relations and constructed them in antagonistic ways. I have explored the dynamic ways in which labourers' politics negotiated their location in emerging mercantile geographies, such as through the contested forms of seasonal migration to Newfoundland. Finally, I have explored the ways through which solidarities were made through intervening in the constitution of these mercantile networks. This has demonstrated that there are important histories and geographies through which labour has produced forms of political identity and agency through negotiating spatially stretched relations of power in dynamic ways. The next chapter draws out another productive set of political activities formed in relation to Atlantic circulations of political ideas through exploring the geographies of democracy.

Chapter Four

Making Democratic Spatial Practices

William Connolly has argued that today, 'democratic politics flows, below, through and above the level of the state' (Connolly, 1995: 160). The work of Connolly and other poststructural political theorists has usefully challenged accounts that treat democracy as emerging from, and negotiating relations within, bounded spaces such as the nation. This opens up different cartographies of democracy. As David Slater has argued:

> In an era of globalization, any attempt to reconstruct our vision of the trajectories of democratic politics needs to take into account the history of West/non-West encounters. When discussing the differential nature of sovereignty and governmentality, the coloniality of power and its geopolitical effects need to be allocated a central importance in the contextualization of the analysis. Such an emphasis can help us to go beyond perspectives which frame the West as a self-contained entity, and which invest its particularities with a universal relevance. (Slater, 2002: 271)

Through foregrounding these trajectories of democratic politics, Slater situates democratic practices as emerging through geographies of connection. These practices of democratic politics transgress and exceed the confining spatialities of the nation-state and bounded notions of the 'West'. This permits a focus on the diverse forms of agency and identity that are produced through democratic politics.

This chapter is a contribution to this project of theorizing the relational spatialities of democracy. It explores the generative and contested character of democratic spatial practices through theorizing democracy as a contested and productive form of relationality. It does this through an engagement with the democratic spatial practices of the London Corresponding Society. The LCS established itself as a democratic society open to 'members unlimited', amid the political turmoil and unrest of the 1790s (see

Thompson, 1968; Thale, 1983).[43] Here I interrogate the innovative forms of democratic practice produced by the LCS and position these organizational forms and political identities in relation to transnational flows of democratic practices.

The first section of the chapter explores how particular spatial practices were central to the LCS's experiments with democracy. I argue that these practices were not just a chance by-product of the political interventions and strategies of the LCS. They shaped the organization's identities and political practices in significant ways. I then contest recent work on the relationships between geography and democracy, which has argued for a normative approach to democracy and a reassertion of the importance of the nation-state as the 'most obvious container' of democracy (Barnett and Low, 2004: 11). Instead, I outline an account of democracy as a contested and productive form of relationality, arguing that this account permits the foregrounding of the diverse subaltern identities formed in relation to democratic practices. The final section explores the relations between the LCS and transnational democratic networks. It explores how LCS activists crafted their political identities in relation to these networks, the effects of their differing relations with such transnational networks and the processes through which transnational democratic networks were constituted.

Spatial Relations, Collective Experimentation and Democracy

The LCS was formed to effect a reform in the system of government. It was 'devoted to two main goals: annual parliaments and universal manhood suffrage' (Barrell, 2006: 47). It did not, however, only campaign vigorously for parliamentary reform. Central to the LCS's activity was a concern with making democratic logics integral to alternative political practices. The LCS was itself to be a demonstration of the potential of democratic activity. The tailor and prominent reformer Francis Place argued that they attempted to assimilate 'its organization as much as possible to what we conceived was the best form of the government for the nation' (Place, 1972: 139). Central to these democratic alternatives was experimentation with particular spatial practices. These practices were not just a chance by-product of the political interventions and strategies of the LCS. They shaped the organization's identities and political practices in significant ways. This section focuses on these actually existing democratic spatial practices. It introduces the system of divisional organization of the LCS, relating this to various routes and flows of democratic political activity. I then discuss the fragile and contested character of the LCS's democratic spatial practices.

The LCS was organized through a system of divisions. These democratic 'cells' met weekly in groups of twenty to thirty men in public houses in particular areas of the city. By 1795 the secretary and assistant secretary of the LCS boasted of having 'forty one regular divisions' (LCS, vol. 2: 141). The divisions were integral to the movement of the LCS. When divisions 'collected more than a certain number of members, they divided in two, and thus had the ability, as the Attorney General put it, to "spread themselves by degrees"' (Barrell, 2003: 8). A representative from each division was delegated to the general committee of the LCS. The divisions facilitated both a democratic imaginary where each division could be represented to the organization and 'the more easy and orderly proceeding of the Society' (LCS, vol. 1: 80). This speaks to the concerns of the LCS to produce organizational forms and conduct that were conducive to political democracy and debate. These forms were defined, at least in official LCS publications, against rough, rowdy 'low' tavern political cultures. Jon Mee notes, however, that some of the 'meetings associated with the LCS had much more of the flavour of tavern free-and-easies than the civicism stressed in the official publications would suggest' (Mee, 2003: 239; see also Davis, 2005; LCS, vol. 1: 124–5). The LCS was socially heterogeneous, including both gentleman reformers like Horne Tooke and artisans like Thomas Hardy.

These forms of democracy were constituted through exclusionary gender relations. The LCS was a male-bound organization that constituted political identities around ideas of 'manly conduct' (see LCS, vol. 1: 4; vol. 5: 120–1). These forms of democratic practice constituted particularly gendered spaces of politics. As Anna Clark has argued, as 'men's organizations grew more formal, women were relegated to the discredited sphere of crowd violence' associated particularly with food riots, in which their participation was often dominant (Clark, 1996: 151; see also McDowell, 1999; Staeheli and Mitchell, 2004). There were, however, intersections between the LCS and LCS members with radicalized women. Women attended their outdoor meetings and a female citizen published in the LCS's *Moral and Political Magazine* (Thale, 1983: 87; Mee, 2003). This publication also carried notices of Mary Wollstonecraft's work. On his tour of Kent, John Gale Jones encountered politicized women who had studied Wollstonecraft's *Vindication of the Rights of Women*. He notes that he concurred with the wisdom of their views (Gale Jones, 1796: 91).

The adoption of the system of divisions situates the LCS at the intersection of routes of democratic practice and imaginaries. When Thomas Hardy wrote to the Reverend Bryant of Sheffield on the advice of Olaudah Equiano, he requested advice 'respecting our internal government'.[44] The reply he received from the Sheffield Constitutional Society detailed the internal forms of organization that the group had developed. The secretary of the

Sheffield Constitutional Society commented on the practices the movement had taken as 'our members kept increasing'. He argues that they had 'found it necessary for the sake of good order to divide ourselves into small bodies of 10 persons each and to hold a general meeting once a month'. A 'delegate or leading man' would be 'chosen and appointed to attend at their respective places' from each group of 10 persons.[45] This locates the LCS as part of networked democratic practices which produced ongoing debate and experimentation about democratic forms of organization. This emphasizes how democratic practices involving delegation and negotiation were formed through the ongoing conduct of these reform societies. It also suggests that the reform societies were generating forms of democratic practice to cope with both temporal and spatial distanciation.

The political identities and practices of the LCS were also formed in relation to various transnational networks and flows of political ideas, texts, activists and organizational forms. These networks produced a transnational democratic imaginary in the late eighteenth century (Cotlar, 2005; Koschnik, 2001; Linebaugh and Rediker, 2000). In instigating the society, Thomas Hardy drew on the inspiration of the American revolution, and on the political cultures formed in support of the American revolution in Britain (Hardy, 1976: 41–4; see also Thale, 1983: xv). He, and other members of the society, were deeply influenced by the French revolution, which Hardy saw as 'one of the greatest events that has taken place in the history of the world'.[46] One of the first proclamations of the LCS was a Congratulatory Address to the French Convention that hailed the French revolutionaries as 'fellow citizens of the world' (LCS, 2002, vol. 1: 30). The declarations and organizational experiments of the LCS also moved. Democratic societies in Philadelphia followed the proceedings of the LCS and republished them. Such publications allowed these societies 'to conceive of themselves as a part of the ongoing transatlantic and democratic revolutions, since the British societies played a leading part in the rise of reform movements and popular radicalism in response to the French Revolution' (Koschnik, 2001: 618). The publications of the LCS were also read in 'the closest dungeons of Russia' (Thale, 1983: 434).

The LCS's relation to transnational routes of democratic practices shaped a dynamic set of organizational practices and dispositions. The LCS was active in generating democratic political cultures through ongoing spatial practices, particularly through the divisions system. These democratic spatial practices were fragile and contested. The production of a network of sites where democratic debate and association were generated in late eighteenth-century London was not just a backdrop to the activity of the LCS. It was a significant if partial, differentiated and precarious achievement. As John Barrell has demonstrated, there was a particular political geography to this networked democratic culture. Barrell notes a strong discrepancy between the weak organization of the LCS 'within the city walls' and 'the large number of divisions that cluster to the West and North of the city' (Barrell, 2006: 55, 53). Reproducing the associational spaces that were constituted through these emergent democratic political cultures was an ongoing labour (see also Mitchell, 1995). Divisions faced significant difficulties in ensuring that they continued to hold weekly meetings. This was a struggle both in organizational terms and in terms of circumventing hostility from authorities. It was a constant difficulty to find taverns with amenable landlords, especially during the periods of strong repression of the LCS. These difficulties underline the significance of the LCS's achievement in producing networked democratic practices.

The formation of such democratic spatial practices was part of productive, ongoing forms of political activity and the negotiation of power relations. This situates the reproduction of such taken-for-granted aspects of democratic cultures as meeting sites as part of the productive spatial practices of the LCS. These democratic spatial practices were not just contested through the actions of the authorities in putting pressure on meeting sites and successfully infiltrating the LCS with spies.[47] These democratic spatial practices also generated antagonisms, as these new political practices struggled to cope with differences internal to divisions and differences between divisions. The contested relations between divisions and the central committee became most significant through various attempts to revise the constitution of the LCS. On 31 October 1793 the general committee of the LCS resolved to draw up 'a New Constitution for their good government' (Selections, 1983: 90). The ensuing debates over the constitution highlight significant aspects of the contested relationalities and conduct produced through the LCS's experiments with democracy.

The revised constitution presented to LCS members in early February 1794 was concerned to foster conduct that was compatible with democratic practices. It sought to stress the orderly and respectable character of the LCS in the wake of anti-Jacobin accusations that the LCS was low and disorderly (see LCS, vol. 1: 335; vol. 5: 182). Fostering forms of democratic practice and conduct was also integral to the political identities, practices and ambitions shaped by the LCS. To the LCS, 'a constitution was not only a way of establishing orderly procedures for meetings'; it also had a strong pedagogic function. It was 'a way of educating the members so that they could exercise their rights responsibly when Parliament and society were reformed and a way of showing the world a model of a just society' (Thale, 1983: xxviii). This commitment to facilitating exemplary forms of democratic conduct structures the constitutions. This also suggests, however, that despite the aims of the LCS to produce rational forms of democratic debate, these forms of practice were consistently undermined by the conduct of meetings in the divisions. These constitutions, and the debates around them, should be read then, not as direct accounts of the character of LCS meetings, but rather as ongoing interventions in the conduct of democratic practices.

These attempts to produce particular forms of democratic conduct are well illustrated by the first five points of the constitution in the section headed 'Order'.

1. That no Member ought to be interrupted while Speaking, unless for the purpose of calling him to order.
2. All noise is interruption, whether intended to express applause or censure; approbation may be expressed by holding up a hand.
3. To attribute the conduct or opinion of any member to factious combination, or other improper motive, is disorderly, as are also invectives and declamatory remarks.
4. The foregoing is not intended to curtail the power of accusation, agreeable to the XIth Section of this Constitution.
5. No member shall be allowed to speak longer than ten minutes at one time, nor more than twice to one question except to explain or retract. (LCS, vol. 1: 339)

These detailed regulations were attempts to generate good democratic citizens through particular forms of embodied behaviour. These forms of order are constituted through detailed attempts to regulate speaking, interruption and debate. Elsewhere in the constitution members are instructed to vote silently, by 'shewing one hand', as 'the practice of shewing both hands, or of calling, all! all! or other such exclamations' were deemed to be 'tumultuous, indecent and utterly unwarrantable' (LCS, vol. 1: 338). This suggests that the activity of LCS members undermined the forms of rational democratic behaviour expected of them.

To be good democratic citizens LCS members were expected to suppress their 'passions'. But it is clear from the rules in the constitutions that they didn't suppress these sufficiently. They engaged in forms of disruptive conduct. They interrupted. They talked for too long. They shouted. They lapsed into invective. They suspected others of combination. They got drunk. (This was presumably exacerbated by the fact that divisional meetings were held in taverns.) They walked around the room instead of sitting in an orderly fashion. The constitution attempted to regulate the microspatial orderings of meetings. Section 21 on the 'organization and power of a Division' states that 'the Delegates and Secretaries of Divisions so meeting shall not sit together, but dispersed as nearly as convenient at equal distances' (LCS, vol. 1: 341). There were also rules against walking around the room. The democratic identities and practices of the LCS identities, then, attempted to constitute particular relations between meeting places, power relations and democratic conduct.

The most contentious issue broached in the revised constitution, however, was around the relations between the divisions and the general committee. The debates around this are extremely useful for understanding the contested forms of democratic relationality produced through the LCS. Work by Barrell, Epstein and Karr has explored the spatial practices produced through key sites such as the courtroom (Barrell, 2000, 2006; Epstein, 2003; Karr, 2001). This work has treated such sites as rather bounded and has not interrogated how reform movements generated particular relations *between* different sites. Interrogating the contested forms of relationality produced through the LCS's forms of democratic spatial practice can be significant in at least two respects. Firstly, it can highlight the diverse and contested forms of political identity produced through the activity of the LCS. Secondly, it can foreground the inventive forms of political practices produced through these uses of space.

The LCS's experiments with democratic practices produced particular relations between the divisions and the general committee through the system of delegates. This made particular overlapping spatial and temporal rhythms constitutive of the democratic imaginaries and practices of the LCS. Delegates were elected by a division to serve on the general committee. The general committee met on Thursdays, and divisions were regulated by the constitution to meet on any day except Thursdays or Sundays (LCS, vol. 1: 339). Many divisions also met on a second evening to discuss political texts (see Barrell, 2006: 49). The revised constitution advocated reshaping the power and role of the general committee, stating that the 'duty of the Committee of Delegates is to direct the conduct of the executive power in all matters which do not require secrecy or expedition' (LCS, vol. 1: 345). This attempt to intervene in the relations between the divisions and committee of delegates was inflammatory.

In his account of the meeting of the LCS general committee on 26 June 1794, the spy John Groves stated that the report of the Committee of Constitution 'gave rise to great Jealousies and Animosities'. There was concern at the concentration of power in the general committee which would 'render the Division a Cypher' and that 'the whole management and Controul be placed in the hands of a few, and thereby their got be monarchical or something worse' (Selections, 1983: 189). These concerns were such that the divisions did not accept the constitution. A Committee of Revision was appointed, consisting of one member from each division, 'to expunge the objectional parts' of the original 1792 LCS constitution and 'to destroy every attempt at an arbitrary usurpation of Power' (Selections, 1983: 120). The outcome of this process reveals some of the tensions within the organizational structure of the LCS. For while 'the revised regulations did receive the General Committee's approbation in June 1794, protests were again registered from certain divisions of the LCS. The

Society continued to operate according to the constitution of 1792 (LCS, vol. 1: 331).

There were renewed debates over the constitution in August and October of 1795. Correspondence between the divisions and the general committee during this period demonstrates the contested relationalities, in particular spatial and temporal rhythms, produced through the LCS's experiments with democratic practices. Division 4 chided the general committee for 'the loss of time suffered from the numerous motions which have been referred to the Divisions for altering its regulations'. It complained that the time of the society was being 'wasted in Cavils and disputes upon mere punctilious and questions of form when it might be employed to greater advantage in reading political books or discussing political questions'.[48] Division 15 complained 'that a very large proportion of time is consumed in matters of very little moment'. It argued that 'affairs of great consequence' such as the 'motions from divisions' were being 'adjourned for several weeks together for want of sufficient time for the committee to enter into the discussion of them'.[49] These spatial and temporal rhythms, then, were seen to be negotiated by the general committee in ways which marginalized the concerns of divisions. The contested temporalities of these meetings need to be situated in relation to the heavy time demands of artisan labour (see Place, 1972).

The most dramatic impact of these debates over the constitutions was the secession of various divisions. Some divisions split entirely from the LCS, leading to the establishment of rival/fraternal organizations (LCS, vol. 2: 141). Division 12 seceded from the LCS in 1795 to form the London Reforming Society, arguing that the Committee of Delegates had 'assumed power which never belonged to [it]' (LCS vol. 2: 124–5). The division also argued that their delegate, the radical bookseller John Bone, had been treated 'with contempt and reproach' by the general committee (LCS, vol. 2: 124). There were further secessions by divisions who objected to the deism of the LCS (see Reid, 1800; Thale, 1983). These secessions highlight the contested relationality produced through the LCS's democratic practices. A key unintended consequence of the divisional structure was that it facilitated the splitting off of divisions from the LCS. The divisional structure generated important recursive articulations between different parts of the LCS, but it also posed challenges for holding the organization together.

This section has argued that integral to the LCS's experiments with democratic practices were particular experiments with spatial relations. I have positioned these experiments with spatial relations as constitutive of the democratic identities and practices of the LCS. I have traced the concerns of the LCS in generating forms of democratic conduct and practice. I have demonstrated that rather than producing a smooth set of articulations between the divisions and the general committee, these experiments with democratic practices produced contested forms of relationality. The next section considers the implications of these experiments with democratic spatial practices for accounts of the relations between democracy, space and political identities.

Space, Democracy and Political Identities

Clive Barnett and Murray Low have argued that democracy constitutes a 'ghostly presence' in geography, functioning as a 'veiled backdrop, but not usually a topic of explicit reflection' (Barnett and Low, 2004: 1). They have outlined an agenda for making democracy integral to debates in political and cultural geography and to the normative commitments of the discipline (see Barnett and Low, 2004; Barnett, 2003, 2004a, 2004b; Low, 2004). The key aspects of this agenda are as follows. Firstly, they argue that critical human geography has marginalized the study of democracy through its suspicion of state-centred accounts and liberalism (Barnett and Low, 2004). They contend that the focus of critical geographers on the diverse spatialities through which democracy is constituted has rendered accounts of the geography of democracy needlessly complex. In contrast, they recentre the nation-state as the 'most obvious site of democratic contention' (Barnett and Low, 2004: 11).

Secondly, they point to the importance of rehabilitating liberalism as central to debates around the political geographies of democracy. They argue that liberalism is the 'tradition of thought in which the meanings of modern democracy have been most systematically subject to normative-critical analysis' (Barnett and Low, 2004: 11). These concerns arise from an explicit commitment to normative political theory. They argue that the concern of geographers with radical political critique has obscured a concern with the 'basic criteria of political judgement underpinning democratic processes – criteria concerning what is right, what is just, what is good, and concerning how best to bring good, just, rightful outcomes about' (Barnett and Low, 2004: 3). Thirdly, this liberal approach leads them to contest associations of democracy and the political with conflict and contestation. Thus Barnett, as I noted in chapter 2, has critiqued Laclau and Mouffe's concerns that antagonism and power relations are constitutive of democratic identities.

Barnett and Low's interrogation of the 'ghostly presence' of democracy in geography is significant. It signals a serious engagement with the geographies of democracy that is long overdue (though see Robinson, 1998; Massey, 1995; Slater, 2002). While they engage in a rigorous scrutiny of various theoretical concerns that bear on democracy, a rather limited geography structures their account. This is related to their assessment of work on the spatialities of the political. They argue that relational geographies of the political have been structured by 'an automatic presumption against national-level forms of political practice' (Barnett and Low, 2004: 9). The consequences of this, they argue, are an 'unexamined prejudice against some of the most mundane elements of liberal representative democracy and a lack of engagement by critical gegographers with the broad terms of democratic political theory' (ibid).

I would contend, however, that problematizing the given spaces of the nation-state is a condition of possibility for engagements with the diverse forms of identity and agency constituted in relation to democratic practices. This permits a focus on the multiple ways in which democratic forms are produced and mobilized, and the diverse spatial relations they generate (see Chatterjee, 2004). The LCS's experiments with democratic spatial practices, for example, demonstrate the role of such practices in constructing relations between and within particular sites. This emphasizes the diversity of political actors and groups who have mobilized and shaped democratic practices. Attending to this diversity of democratic practices, and the spaces of democracy they constitute, is essential for theorizing the different forms of agency and identity generated in relation to democratic practices. To engage with such practices, however, it is necessary to decentre the nation-state and to consider how even nation-level democratic practices are made of relations constructed between different sites. Foregrounding the spatialities constituted through democratic practices, then, can have important consequences.

Following these democratic spatial practices also unsettles the relational geographies envisioned through Barnett and Low's account. Barnett usefully points to the ways in which forms of distanciation, representation and delegation are constitutive of democracy (Barnett, 2003, 2004b: 187–8). This has resources for engaging with the relational construction of democratic practices. This potential is closed down, however, by his counterposition of spatial and temporal logics. He critiques Massey's contention that space is 'the medium in which multiplicity and plurality can be acknowledged', arguing that the 'constitutive relationship between democracy, difference, and conflict finds its clearest practical resolution in the weaving together of overlapping temporal rhythms' (Barnett, 2004b: 188). Barnett's counterposing of space and time here renders the temporal as dynamic and the spatial as fixed and static and closes down a sense of how democracy is produced through the ongoing and productive negotiation of *both* spatial and temporal relations. The accounts of the democratic conduct of the LCS have sought to demonstrate that these were democratic practices where spatial and temporal dynamics were intertwined. It makes little sense to purify spatial and temporal aspects from each other. Rather, it is crucial to follow their co-production. Thus the LCS was constituted through overlapping rhythms that brought together different sites through a delegated committee. This produced networked democratic practices through various temporal and spatial relations.

Foregrounding the contested and productive relationalities through which democratic practices are constituted involves dislocating key aspects of the liberal political tradition that Barnett and Low invoke. The marginal role ascribed to liberal political theorists in political geography is arguably related to the sub-discipline's more generally limited engagement with political theory (see Agnew, 2003). Barnett and Low's work, however, tends to reproduce rather than challenge some of the problems that have been associated with the liberal tradition. Key among these tensions are its problematic treatment of the relations between power and democracy, a problematic construction of the autonomous subject and a failure to see democratic practices as generative. These theoretical elisions are some of the reasons why this tradition has been viewed with legitimate suspicion both by critical geographers and others (see Sharp, 2003; Slater, 2002; Young, 1990).

One of Mouffe's key contributions in her critiques of liberal political thinkers like John Rawls has been to argue that power relations are constitutive of the very identities negotiated through democratic political practices (Mouffe, 2000: 21). The implications of this are that power relations are constitutive of democratic practices and identities and not something that should be excluded from democratic practices. The LCS's activity suggests the extent to which relations of power are both productive and contested through democratic practices. There were the ongoing struggles to maintain a set of networked meeting places across the city. There were the power relations produced between divisions and general committee, which were the subject of ongoing negotiation and debate. There were also significant forms of exclusion that were produced through the democratic practices of the LCS, particularly around issues of gender, and the ambivalent relations to forms of subaltern political activity, which will be explored in more depth below. It is impossible to theorize the forms of political identity constituted through these democratic practices without situating them as part of cross-cutting and multiple relations of power. This also dislocates the centrality of autonomous political subjects to liberal political theory.

Barnett and Low assert that one of the key goals of democratic theory is to provide accounts of autonomous action (Barnett and Low, 2004). Barnett argues for 'an account of how free and autonomous actors are formed and maintained' (Barnett, 2003: 83). Adopting a relational approach to the theorizing of democracy, however, fundamentally unsettles this concern with autonomous spaces and free, autonomous activity (see

Whatmore, 2002: 146–67). It is impossible to engage with the formation of democratic identities, for example, outside of the relations produced through the conduct of democratic practices. Engaging with these relations challenges the construction of free and autonomous action that structures liberal political theory. This might be seen as a move that is threatening to accounts of subaltern identity and agency. Moving beyond notions of the autonomous subject and autonomous spaces, however, can be decisive in allowing stories to be told about how subaltern political identities and agency are formed through intervening in multiple and cross-cutting relations of power (Moore, 1998).

Positioning political activity as part of ongoing interventions in cross-cutting relations of power highlights the productive character of democratic practices. This generative character of political activity has been persistently marginalized in liberal accounts of democracy that have often reduced democratic practices to the negotiation of already constituted fixed interests. The generative character of democratic political activity is also foreclosed through reducing it to particular normative principles. I have theorized the engagements of the LCS with democracy as a form of 'collective experimentation' to draw attention to the ongoing, productive, open and contested character of these engagements (see Latour, 2004). Through locating practices of democracy in relation to diverse geographies of connection and contestation different stories about democratic practices can be told. In particular this can foreground significant forms of subaltern identity and agency constituted through the following aspects of democratic practices.

Firstly, I have positioned democratic practices as constituted through contested and productive forms of relationality. Following Barnett, I have situated democratic practices as constituted through distanciation and delegation. I have situated these practices of representation as constitutive and generative, rather than practices which undermine the constitution of democratic practices. These forms of relationality are generated through the intertwining of both spatial and temporal relations. Secondly, I have argued that it is necessary to examine the way that democratic practices are constituted through the proliferation of multiple sites. Sites such as the divisions of the LCS were not produced in isolation, but in relation to transnational flows and circulations of democratic identities and practices. The relations that linked such sites were also significant. This ruptures attempts to neatly confine democratic practices, and the political more generally, within national spaces (see Sparke, 2005). Again, this is a productive move. In terms of the LCS, it can position the emergence of democratic practices in England, as the products of various multi-ethnic political cultures, not just white, free-born Englishmen. This opens up accounts of the agency of those traditionally excluded from state-level politics in constituting democratic practices.

Thirdly, I have argued that geographies of power need to be seen as integral to the production of democratic identities. The relations between space, democratic politics and power, then, are productive. This matters in terms of the exclusionary forms of politics constituted through democratic activity; the practices through which democratic politics can bring power relations into contestation and the generative character of democratic political activity. Finally, this relational account of democracy has resources for foregrounding the diverse political identities generated through democratic practices. I have argued that the LCS's experiments with democratic practice were formed out of various geographies of connection and that these geographies of connection shaped the political identities of the LCS in significant ways. The next section explores the ways in which LCS activists' democratic political identities were configured in relation to transnational political networks.

The Contested Geographies of Transnational Democratic Networks

The LCS brought together both elite and subaltern activists and was a site of coexistence of diverse and overlapping political networks. These diverse networks didn't coalesce in easy, 'smooth' ways. They formed collective identities only through shifting, contested articulations between different activists constituted through overlapping friendships, networks and associations. These reform networks were precarious achievements. They were produced not through 'underlying and spontaneous' forms of immanence, but through ongoing and partial articulations (see Laclau, 2005a: 240). This section develops the concern with theorizing democracy as a form of contested and productive relationality through an account of the LCS's relations to transnational democratic networks. It explores how LCS activists configured diverse democratic political identities in relation to these networks. It also foregrounds the processes through which transnational democratic networks were formatted, policed and constituted.

In February 1794 John Thelwall, the poet, lecturer and political theorist, who became a key LCS activist in the mid-1790s, drafted a letter to an 'American friend'. The letter gives a clear sense of how he functioned as a constitutive part of transnational democratic political networks.[50] The letter justifies Thelwall's role in the LCS against accusations made by his American correspondent that he had become allied with the moderate, Brisotist faction in France who had been purged by the Jacobins. He insisted that for the '4 or 5 months past' he had been 'almost the sole labourer upon whom the fatigues, the danger and the exertions of the LCS (the only avowed sans culottes in the metropolis)'. He aggressively asserted his political allegiances with the Jacobins in ways which would later endanger his individual freedom: 'I tell you in plain terms I am a republican, a down right sans culottes.'

Thelwall's defence of his position as an active radical is constituted through critical engagement with both the American and French revolutions. He distances himself from the violent conduct of Jacobin factions in France, tempering his expression of allegiance with the Jacobins by noting that he was 'by no means reconciled to the dagger of the Maratists'. He also produces a keen sense of critical engagement with the political trajectories of the American revolution. Requesting that his friend send him material on 'the state of politics and society in America', Thelwall expressed his reservations about the political character of the new American polity: 'I fear you are somewhat short of the true sans culotte liberty; that you have too much veneration for property, too much religion and too much law.' Through his political activity Thelwall, then, actively negotiated these multiple trajectories of Atlantic radicalisms. This emphasizes the particular, and contested, geographies of these networks and how different kinds of democratic identities were generated in relation to them.

The forms of democratic political community generated through the LCS were constituted through connections with transnational political cultures. The links between anti-slavery networks and the campaigns for parliamentary reform headed by the LCS emphasize the shifting and contested articulations generated through these geographies of connection. The early correspondence of the LCS shaped a 'multi-ethnic' conception of liberty which contested restrictive notions of the 'Rights of Man'. This shaped the political identities constituted through the reform networks which the LCS facilitated. The reply from the Sheffield Constitutional Society to Hardy's enquiries about reform societies in Sheffield applauds Hardy's 'noble observation' that 'no man who is an advocate for Principle of the Liberty of a Black man but will strenuously promote and support the Rights of a White man and vice versa'.[51] As chapter 7 argues in detail, transnational political networks are still theorized in rather reductive ways. The social movement theorist Sidney Tarrow, for example, has argued that they are most useful as conduits for the transmission of information (Tarrow, 2005). This ignores their multiple, generative effects. The connections between Hardy and Equiano demonstrate how such connections and networks were constituted through 'more than rational' forms of affective connection. They were not just about the transmission of information, but were about the shaping of particular kinds of connection, radical identities and democratic political communities.

The multi-ethnic friendship between Hardy and Equiano shifted the geography of the antagonisms contested by the LCS, shaping a contestation not just of the lack of democracy in England, but also of slavery. This dislocated a narrow notion of English liberty, such as that shaped by its more genteel predecessors like the Society of Constitutional Information, and led to Hardy's advocacy of multi-ethnic notions of political community. Friendships like those between Hardy and Equiano, for example, shifted the antagonisms constituted through the LCS and the notions of who was included in the constructions of 'political community' shaped through the LCS. In the spring and summer of 1792, Equiano continued his association with Hardy and the LCS. On his tours to promote his book he sought out contacts for the newly formed society. From Edinburgh he sent Hardy 'My best respect to my fellow members of your society. I hope they do yet increase – I do not hear in this place that there is any such society – I think Mr . . . Matthews in Glasgow told me that there was (or is) some there.'[52]

The friendship between Hardy and Equiano, however, developed in ways that emphasize the fragmentary, contested and uneven relations between anti-slavery networks and reform networks. There is evidence of a divergence between Hardy and Equiano, which illustrates the ongoing and contested formation of solidarities, democratic political identities and political friendships. Thomas Hardy and his brother-in-law George Walne, a tailor who was also an early member of the LCS, were both subscribers to early editions of Equiano's *Interesting Narrative* published in 1789 (Carretta, 2005: 297). Hardy's ongoing friendship, association and identification with Equiano shaped his political outlook in important ways. Equiano's impact is also demonstrated through correspondence from Hardy's wife Lydia, which evokes a sense of the relationships between Equiano and subaltern anti-slavery networks. Lydia commented:

> the people are here as much against [slavery] as enny ware and there is more people I think here that drinks tea without sugar than drinks with. . . . all are very fond of Vassa's book. I suppose he is about going of[f] give my respects to him and I wish him a good journey to Scotland.[53]

Lydia Hardy's letter suggests that her friendship with Equiano shaped a broader culture of resistance to slavery. It points to her involvement in the sugar abstention campaign, promoted by abolitionists in 1791, which Drescher suggests had an impact on sugar prices at its height in 1792 (Drescher, 1987: 88–91). Her participation in the boycott suggests how subaltern agency could be constituted through contesting the constitution of everyday material practices. The sugar boycott ceased to be promoted by the Abolition Society, however, after 1792 'as part of the Society's general wariness of any extra-Parliamentary campaigning which might be viewed as subversive in the reactionary climate of the period' (Midgley, 1992: 40; see also Griggs, 1936: 71). This emphasizes how radical political activity was formed through uneasy alliances and intersections between subaltern and elite networks and repertoires of activity.

This 'reactionary climate' stemmed from the hostile reaction to the French revolution, which fostered the rise of loyalist reaction and intimidation of radicals. This exerted pressure on Equiano's relations with Hardy. While the LCS faced severe political repression through the 1790s, in 1792 Equiano faced public accusations that he was never in Africa, but 'was born and bred up in the Danish Island of Santa Cruz in the West Indies' (Carretta, 2005: 351). Equiano fought to maintain his sense of respectability and good character and dropped subscribers to his book who were known for their radical associations. The names of Hardy and Walne, and of Ottabah Cugoana, the black radical and author 'who had encouraged slave resistance, disappeared from the fifth and later editions' (Carretta, 2005: 353). Radical subscribers from 'Jacobin' Norwich were similarly excised (Carretta, 2005: 361). Nonetheless, Equiano continued his association with the LCS and Hardy. In the wake of Thomas Hardy's arrest for treason in 1794, Equiano gave 10 shillings and 6 pence to a fund to give relief to 'those families, whose husbands and fathers are now languishing in Prison, on charges of High Treason' (LCS, 2002, vol. 2, 280). That Equiano dropped Hardy from his subscriber list suggests his unwillingness to continue making a public association with Hardy.

Thomas Hardy also distanced himself from anti-slavery campaigns. Only months after writing of the LCS's commitment to a multi-ethnic concept of 'the Rights of Man', he was subordinating the campaigns against the slave trade to campaigns for reform of parliament. He wrote to his uncle in Falkirk on 4 June 1792 that 'you are all petitioning for the abolition of that accursed traffick denominated the slave trade'.[54] He argued that 'so far you are in your duty but that is not all, there are other evils existing in this country which it is equally our duty to endeavour to remedy and a principle way to remove these prevailing evils is to have a more equal representation of the people in parliament.' For key LCS figures, it seems, anti-slavery activity quickly became subordinate to the campaign for parliamentary representation (see also Barrell, 2006: 62). It appears that Hardy came to view the anti-slavery campaigns as something that would detract from the campaign for parliamentary reform, rather than intersect with it. This produced a particular construction of democratic practices, where parliamentary reform was constructed as a remedy for all other ills. The LCS did, however, continue some limited engagement with anti-slavery politics, publishing articles against slavery in its *Moral and Political*

Magazine and pamphlets by LCS supporters such as Henry Edward Illiff continued to advocate multi-ethnic forms of liberty (LCS, 2002, vol. 3: 114, 192–3; vol. 5: 175–6).

The subordination of anti-slavery demands to the campaign for parliamentary reform is related to a broader ambiguity in the relations between the London Corresponding Society and subaltern grievances. The LCS was composed primarily of artisans, but often actively defined itself against repertoires of subaltern political activity, especially those that exceeded the responsible forms of political activity they promoted. Thus an LCS pamphlet entitled 'Reformers No Rioters' argued that 'one of the fundamental principles of this society . . . is that riot, tumult and violence are not the fit means of obtaining a redress of grievances' (LCS, 2002, vol. 1: 290). The pamphlet itself, however, emphasizes the contested political identities and practices produced through the LCS (see also Preston, 1817). The original draft, written by the bookseller John Bone, was, according to the spy William Metcalfe, 'full of the most violent and seditious expressions' (Thale, 1983: 215). The LCS members Joseph Burks, a bookseller, and James Parkinson, a radical pamphleteer, produced a 'corrected' version of Bone's address that was approved and ordered to be printed as 'Reformers No Rioters' (Thale, 1983: 215). This official LCS line against riot, then, was constructed and disseminated only through excluding dissenting voices and by reiterating that parliamentary representation was to be the means of redress for all grievances.

This suspicion of forms of political activity that exceeded representation shaped the LCS leadership's attitudes to slave revolts. In the *Rights of Nature*, John Thelwall criticized Edmund Burke's 'naturalization of slavery'. The terms on which he engaged with slave revolts, however, are symptomatic of the partial solidarities and identification with slave resistance shaped through the LCS. Thelwall contests Burke for writing 'with exaggerated horrors' of the 'tribunals of Maroon and Negro slaves, covered with the blood of their masters' (Thelwall, 1995: 408). He continues:

> I deplore, as ye do, the 'robberies and murders', committed by these poor wretches – the blind instruments of instinctive vengeance. But, I cannot, like you, forget by whom those lessons of murderous rapacity were taught. I cannot forget, that slavery itself is robbery and murder; and, that the master who falls by the bondsmen's hand, is the victim of his own barbarity. . . . I am no apologist for the horrible massacres of revenge; whether perpetrated by negroes, by monarchs, or by mobs. I abhor revenge. Vengeance, Mr Burke, with me is crime.

There is a clear empathy with slaves here. Slave resistance is situated and rationalized as an inevitable product of slave relations. In a powerful image, the master felled by the 'bondsmen's' hand is seen as a victim of nothing but his own barbarity. But while contesting Burke, and asserting support for slave resistance, Thelwall distances himself from the forms of activity constituted through resistance to slavery. The agency and identity of slaves is reduced here to 'instinctive vengeance', erasing any sense that the slaves may possess political cultures. This raises questions about what kind of political practices, actors and identities were included in the transnational democratic networks that the LCS was part of. Thelwall doesn't mention the revolution in St Domingue explicitly here, but it would have been an important context to his writing on slave resistance. The revolution was widely publicized in London and debated by abolitionists (Geggus, 1982: esp. 127; see also Blackburn, 1988: 303).

Thelwall, then, excluded events like the slave revolt in St Domingue from the transnational democratic imaginary that he invoked in the letter to his American friend. This emphasizes the exclusionary practices through which transnational democratic imaginaries and practices could be constructed. It draws attention to some of the practices through which they were constituted, formatted and policed. Interrogating the practices through which such political networks were constituted, then, permits a focus on such exclusions, rather than seeing such transnational democratic networks as 'smooth spaces' produced without power relations. Bruno Latour has argued that humans and non-humans are 'seduced, manipulated or induced into' collectives through distinctive practices of enrolment which generate networks in particular ways (Latour, 1994: 46; see also Callon, 1998). Following the construction of these transnational democratic political networks emphasizes how only certain forms of political practices, and certain political actors, were enrolled into these networks. Slave resistances, through developing forms of political activity that exceeded representation, did not conform to the LCS leadership's notion of responsible political activity. Slaves were not hailed by Thelwall as potential democratic subjects. Instead, radical anti-slavery politics was excluded from Thelwall's vision of a transnational democratic political culture. This contrasts markedly with other appropriations of the Haitian revolution in London's radical politics. Thomas Clarkson defended the revolution arguing that the 'self-emancipated slaves' there were 'endeavouring to vindicate for themselves the unalterable Rights of Man' (Clarkson cited by Rediker, 2007: 331). Robert Wedderburn, the black radical preacher and Spencean, engaged explicitly with the Haitian revolution in his series of pamphlets 'The Axe Laid to the Root', written in 1817 (see Linebaugh, 1993: 199–201; Wedderburn, 1991).[55]

The fragmentary and contested relations between the LCS and anti-slavery networks suggest that the LCS's relations to transnational networks were particular and contested. They support Fischer's argument that the 'cultures of anti-slavery were no more convenient in the European metropolis than they were in the plantation zone' (Fischer, 2004: 226). These articulations between different groups of activists were not smooth, not the immanent production of a 'multitude', but were formed through the shifting and contested negotiation of trajectories of political activity. They emphasize how these transnational networks were generative and productive and shaped activists' political identities in important ways. Finally, they suggest that these transnational democratic networks were formatted, policed and constituted through the enrolment of particular kinds of activists associated with particular kinds of political practice. These transnational democratic networks were largely, though not exclusively, male and white (see Clark, 1996; Landes, 1996). They also excluded forms of subaltern political activity that exceeded the forms of democratic representation that were constructed as approved forms of political activity by the LCS. These forms of political activity suggest the dynamism of relations between political activity in the past and transnational networks. They also emphasize the ongoing and contested character of these relations.

Conclusions

During the trials of Horne Tooke and John Thelwall for treason, Chief Justice Eyre described the LCS as a political monster 'spreading itself every hour from division to division, and each division producing its sub-divisions, those sub-divisions becoming divisions, and so on ad infinitum' (cited by Barrell, 2000: 87–8). Eyre mobilized this threatening image to dramatize the movement of the LCS across the capital. The pretensions of working-class men to democratic organization were as threatening as the movement of the LCS across London. This chapter has sought to recover the diverse forms of agency and identity they made through mobilizing forms of democratic organization. I have argued that they generated democratic practices through networked sites of association across the capital. These were constituted through productive forms of democratic and spatial-temporal orderings. Finally, they were produced in dynamic relation to transnational flows of democratic ideas and practices.

Through this account I have outlined a way of understanding democratic practices as a productive and contested form of relationality. I have argued that this unsettles the account of the spaces of democracy outlined by Barnett and Low. I have stressed the importance of understanding the geographies of connection that shape democratic practices. Through interrogating these relations between democratic practices and geographies of connection I have sought to contribute to Slater's agenda for relational approaches to democracy. I have also argued that understanding the overlapping temporal *and* spatial rhythms helps foreground the diverse forms of subaltern identity and agency constituted in relation to democratic practices. This project has sought to demonstrate the potential of theorizing democratic practices in explicitly relational ways. Chapter 5 takes up the challenge of articulating a relational account of nationalisms, which have frequently been theorized in relation to bounded and given spaces.

Chapter Five

Counter-Global Networks and the Making of Subaltern Nationalisms

On 19 April 1800 John Pollard, an Irish sailor late of HMS *La Nymphe,* went in the company of another sailor to a dockside tavern in Plymouth called the Turk's Head.[56] 'After having seated himself in the public room, he 'called for a pint of beer'. Upon receiving his pint 'he took up the glass in his hand and holding it to his mouth to drink said – "success to the rebels" "success to the French" and "damn the dog that opposes them."' 'On uttering these treasonable and seditious words the Master of the House', John Barrett, reprimanded him for 'speaking against Government'. Pollard immediately replied ' "damn and bugger government I never took but one oath in my life" if that be the case says Barrett – "I hope that oath was in behalf of you're king and country" – to which Pollard immediately replied – "no that oath was at Spithead and I will live and die by it."' By this Pollard was referring to the 'great mutiny' at Spithead in 1797, where sailors had taken over the fleet, raised the red flag and shocked the nation both by mutinying in time of war and by the forms of 'order' that they demonstrated. The shock to 'the British Empire' was, as Herman Melville later noted, 'what a strike in the fire brigade would be to London threatened by general arson' (Melville, 1995: 18).

Pollard was arrested and imprisoned. The brief prepared for his trial by a Plymouth solicitor noted that Pollard 'was certainly intoxicated at the time of his uttering these words'. He was thought a 'fit object of prosecution', however, because he was 'an incorrigible offender'. The brief recounts how Pollard had been among the leaders of the mutineers on *La Nymphe* at Spithead. He had 'ran away from her to avoid punishment for his behaviour in the mutiny' and joined the *Montague*. Pollard was later recognized by his former Captain Frazer on the *Montague*. While on the *Montague* it was alleged that he had 'at various times been guilty of mutinous seditions and disorderly conduct'. He was accused of having 'twice struck his capt

(Knight) on the Quarter deck and been guilty of other acts for which (but for the humanity of Captain Knight in not bringing him to a court martial) he would by the articles of war have forfeited his life'. Within an hour of being back on *La Nymphe* the brief alleges that 'Pollard was endeavouring to excite the crew to mutiny', boasting that 'he had in the *Montague* been instrumental in sending Lord Vincent on shore at Gibraltar – and that if they [the crew of *La Nymphe*] had a dislike to any of their officers he would assist them ashore also'. For his 'treasonable and seditious words' Pollard received a six-month prison sentence.[57]

This chapter engages with some of the issues raised by Pollard's conduct and his 'treasonable and seditious words'. It explores the relations between the heterogeneous, multi-ethnic subaltern cultures of the lower deck and emerging forms of Irish 'nationalist' political activity. This foregrounds the role of subaltern agency in constituting nationalist identities and nation-building practices. The first section explores the dynamic trajectories of shipboard subaltern politics in the 1790s. I then draw out the implications of these networked forms of subaltern politics for ways of theorizing subaltern nationalisms. The second section explores the relations between the United Irishmen and what Bolster has called the 'rough egalitarianism' of shipboard cultures (Bolster, 1997: 91). The third section uses a focus on the different performances of oaths to engage with the diverse forms of identity formed through sailor's politics. It suggests oaths could be used in ways which shaped very different forms of political collectivity and explores the ways in which oaths were formed at the intersection of relations between gender, race, labour and violence. The final section of the chapter draws together the key arguments to explore the dynamic relations of subaltern nationalism to Atlantic/counter-global networks.

'To banish all tyrants':[58] The Dynamic Trajectories of Mutiny

In 1797 and 1798 in the wake of the Spithead and Nore, mutinies and conspiracies among the British navy convulsed the Atlantic. There were mutinies and 'disorders' off Cape Nicola Mole (in present-day Haiti) and off Havana in the Caribbean, at Plymouth, among the Mediterranean fleet, and at the Cape of Good Hope, as well as unrest among Irish regiments in Newfoundland (see Boucher and Penn, 1992: 187; Byrne, 1992; Gill, 1913: 252–3; Wells, 1983: 145–51). That many of these mutinous events and conspiracies occurred after 29 sailors had been hanged in the severe repression of the mutiny at the Nore is notable (Manwaring and Dobree, 2004: 277). These mutinies and conspiracies, such as the conspiracy among Irish and black sailors aboard the *Remonée* in the Caribbean, have been dismissed as 'distant echoes' of the mutinies at the Spithead and the Nore in 1797. Conrad Gill saw them as being like the 'milder recurrences that sometimes follow, at an interval, an epidemic of fever' (Gill, 1913: 252).

Irish sailors were central to many of these mutinies. In 1798, for example, there was a conspiracy led by Irish sailors aboard the *Defiance*. The conspirators were heard to take oaths pledging allegiance to the United Irishmen and to claim that they 'should have equality and freedom in Ireland'.[59] Some of these mutinous events and conspiracies were directly related to the rising associated with the United Irishmen in 1798. The account of Pollard's various mutinous actions emphasizes some of the practices through which such action travelled with and between naval vessels in the late 1790s. It gives a sense of how sailors were involved in different mutinous events, and how their different experiences of these were significant. Pollard's boasts about sending officers ashore are a testament to the dynamic unofficial geographies of knowledge sailors used to negotiate their maritime labour (see Rediker, 1988a: 134–5). These mutinies were the product of combination between sailors on different ships. Sailors produced connections between different mutinous vessels and mutinies in different places, through organizational forms such as Round Robins (Rediker, 1988a: 234–5). Seamen used the Round Robin 'to engage one another', 'while guaranteeing that it might not be known who were the beginners or Ring Leaders' (Nathaniel Uring, cited by Rediker, 1988a: 234).

Roger Wells writes of the mutinies in the Channel fleets in 1797 'that petitions for increased pay were circulating from ship to ship, and it is probable that two delegates were elected by each ship's company [who] oversaw these proceedings' (Wells, 1983: 85). A revised petition including 'new demands over the quality of food, pursers' deductions from the rations, the low standard of medical care on board, the denial of shore leave, and the absence of pensions for disabled men, were added to the initial wage demand' (Wells, 1983: 85; see Gill, 1913: 10–15; Rodger, 2004: 445). The decision to ignore these petitions by the admiralty was a key cause of the mutiny at Spithead (Gill, 1913; Wells, 1983). The Nore mutineers demanded 'more regular pay, advance wages for pressed men, a right to leave in port, a more equitable distribution of prize-money and an effective veto on the appointment of officers' (Rodger, 2004: 447). This latter demand speaks to a significant attempt to democratize these work places structured by hierarchical power relations (see Moore III, 1991). Similar demands were made by mutineers in the Caribbean, the Mediterranean and off the Cape of Good Hope.[60]

These mutinous events and conspiracies were shaped by dynamic, spatially stretched forms of subaltern knowledge. The reach of these knowledges is demonstrated by a petition from the squadron of eight ships that mutinied off the Cape of Good Hope in 1797. After demanding the 'expulsion of such officers as the several ships concerned have turned on shore, and who by their former conduct have justly rendered themselves obnoxious to their respective ships' and listing a set of grievances regarding the quality of the provisions aboard ship, the petition notes:

> The people of this squadron has heard something of the conduct of HMs fleet in England and the regulation that has taken place in consequence with regard to the extra allowance of pay and provisions, but as we do not expect that you have received any official intelligence how to act on the occasion, we do not expect those regulations to take place until that time may arrive, and we are determined to patiently wait the event.[61]

This petition, then, not only develops assertive demands such as the expulsion of particular officers who had rendered themselves 'obnoxious'. It also strategically mobilizes the sailors' knowledge of the mutinies at Spithead and the concessions made to the mutineers by the naval authorities. The petition boasts of the superior knowledge Tars had of these events and the official response to them. This is particularly notable as sailors were not outgoing from ports in England, but were returning from the 'East Indies'. That they mobilized knowledges of the events in the Channel earlier that year is a testament to the spatially stretched forms of political activity which shaped sailors' political cultures. This also powerfully demonstrates how these knowledges were mobilized in strategic and inventive ways through their political activity (see Bolster, 1997; Rediker, 1988a; Ross, 1983; Scott, 1986).

Peter Linebaugh and Marcus Rediker have argued that ships in the early modern Atlantic were 'an extraordinary forcing house of internationalism' (Linebaugh and Rediker, 2000: 151). This assessment of maritime social relations is supported by the crew lists of ships involved in the Spithead and Nore mutinies and the various mutinous events that ricocheted around the Atlantic in their aftermath. On the *Grampus*, a storeship involved in the mutiny at the Nore and in disturbances off present-day Haiti later in 1797, there were sailors from Jamaica, Barbados, Boston, Rhode Island, New York and Philadelphia, many sailors from Ireland, Wales and Scotland, and from English seaports such as Dover and Yarmouth.[62] The crew of the *Hermione*, which mutinied in 1798, was similarly diverse (see Pope, 2003: 338–40). The multi-ethnic character of such crews unsettles claims that the mutinies at Spithead and the Nore were solely the product of a 'native political tradition of shipboard organization' (Rodger, 2003: 563).

Such diversity also runs against the grain of much theorizing of transatlantic Irish identities. Examining the ship as a site of political activity challenges influential accounts of the Irish diaspora which have constructed the Irish as a sealed, ontologically discrete unit of study (Kenny, 2003: 135).

Rather than suggesting that some mutinies were the product of distinct 'labour' grievances, and some purely the work of Irish 'republicans', I seek to explore the relations between these nascent forms of nationalist political activity and the 'rough egalitarianism' that shaped the politics of the lower deck. This situates Irish subaltern political identities as part of the ongoing negotiation of Atlantic networks. It illuminates subaltern articulations of Irish nationalist politics which have been rather marginalised in the historiography of the United Irishmen (see Elliott, 1982; Wilson, 1998).

Existing work on the relations between Atlantic connections and the United Irishmen have focused on the significant number of key, often elite, United Irishmen who were exiled to the United States in the aftermath of the rebellion (see Durey, 1997; Ignatiev, 1996; Wilson, 1998; see also Binns, 1854). Irish radicalisms, however, were crafted through ongoing relations to various Atlantic trajectories and flows of political activity. The United Irish radical and weaver James Hope pointed to the impact of the American revolution on Ireland, arguing that 'the American struggle taught people, that industry had rights as well as aristocracy . . . which gave extension to the forward view of the Irish leaders' (Hope, 2001: 47). His engagement with the American revolution was critical: his poem 'Jefferson's Daughter' had a scathing indictment of slave-holding in the early republic (see Gibbons, 2003). The French revolution had a major impact on Irish politics in the 1790s and Tom Paine's *Rights of Man* became a bestseller in the 1790s (Dickson, 1993; Whelan, 1996, 2004).

Irish radicalisms were also constituted in relation to the 'black Atlantic' (see Rodgers, 2007; Whelan, 2004). Equiano toured Ireland in 1791 and had diverse contacts in Belfast, where he stayed for several months in 1791 (Equiano, 1995: 235). There he kept company among dissenters such as Samuel Neilson, the United Irishman who acted as Equiano's patron, 'so that the well dressed, middle aged African appeared with his *Interesting Narrative* not only at the local booksellers but at Neilson's drapery business at the commercial heart of the town' (Rodgers, 1997: 75). These connections and exchanges had effects. Key United Irish radicals, including Neilson and Napper Tandy, were subscribers to the Dublin edition of the *Interesting Narrative* (see Equiano, 1995: 25–6). Neilson gave 'anti-slavery' issues a prominent place in the *Northern Star*, the newspaper of the United Irishmen. The prominent United Irish agitator Thomas Russell contested Britain's relationship to the geopolitics of slavery in his pamphlet *A Letter to the People of Ireland on the Present Situation of the Country* (Russell, 1796: 22). Many United Irishmen who were exiled to the United States, however, were to become slave-holders or hold pro-slavery positions (see Binns, 1854; Ignatiev, 1996; Wilson, 2005: 155).

It is paradoxical that while relational accounts of the political have become increasingly influential in geography, the nation is often still theorized in restrictively territorial ways. Thus Penrose has argued for the importance of particular 'strategies of territoriality' in nationalist thought, but treats these strategies as bounded within particular nations rather than engaging with how these strategies negotiate spatially stretched relations (Penrose, 2002: 282). John Agnew has argued:

> The nation's territory is not a simple block of space but a complex set of relationships between local, regional, and national levels of social practice and geographical imagination. Nationalism relates to territory, therefore, in more complex ways than most students of nationalism have tended to believe. (Agnew, 2004: 228)

Agnew begins to open up a relational construction of the nation and nationalism here. This argument is framed by a restricted relationality. It is only relations *within* the nation that he treats as constitutive of nationalist political identities. Similarly, Jones and Fowler's useful exploration of the role of particular places in the formation of nationalist identities and politics only treats places within the bounds of the nation as constitutive of nationalist politics. Further, their account of the relations of Welsh nationalist identities to flows of political activity – such as the influence of the US civil rights movement – is poorly developed (Jones and Fowler, 2007: 347). Understanding the formation of identities in relational terms, however, opens up different ways of thinking about the constitution of nationalist political identities. In this context it means that Irish identities, particularly those of sailors, were being constituted in relation to the ongoing and unfinished political, cultural and material networks that traversed the Atlantic.

There is a strong sense of this in Pollard's 'seditious words'. His identity is configured through relations with the 'rebels', the United Irishmen, with the French, and through relations to a distinctive set of subaltern grievances and forms of organization. This insistence on viewing nationalist identities as produced in relation to geographies of connection situates nationalisms as always already products of various relations. This opens up more multiple accounts of the spatial and temporal relations of nationalisms than have structured dominant ways of theorizing nationalism. Benedict Anderson's influential thesis on the nation as an 'imagined community', for example, depends both on a notion of 'empty homogeneous time' and on a sense of the nation as constituted through a 'deep horizontal comradeship' (Anderson, 1991: 7). This produces a linear, homogeneous framing of the nation and forecloses the agency of the competing trajectories of different nationalist identities in constructing the nation (Chatterjee, 1993, 2004; Guha, 1997). Anderson's analysis depends on rendering space a passive fixed backdrop to the dynamism of 'empty homogeneous time'. This produces an account of the nation as a fixed, bounded territorial container of political activity, subordinated to the dynamic temporal constitution of the nation. To consider the multiple forms of identity generated in relation to nations/nation-building projects it is necessary to foreground more multiple spatial and temporal relations in constituting the 'nation' (Chatterjee, 2004; Mulligan, 2005). This is a condition of possibility for examining the diverse forms of agency and identity generated in relation to the 'nation'.

Foregrounding the plural and diverse forms of agency involved in shaping the nation unsettles the dominant roles accorded to elites in shaping nationalist identities and nation-building projects. Contrasting theoretical approaches have centred the role of elites in shaping both nationalist identities and nation-building approaches (see, for examples, Anderson, 1991; Hobsbawm and Ranger, 1983; Kornprobst, 2005; Nairn, 1977: 339–41; 1997). These approaches are structured by simplistic divisions between nationalist elites and masses and concentrate agency in particular elites (see Kornprobst, 2005: esp. 417). Linda Colley's influential thesis about the centrality of the making of a Protestant 'ruling class' in the formation of 'Britain' is a good example here (Colley, 1992: 370). This is a 'top down history' that produces a 'univocal nation of "Britons"' (Thompson, 1994b: 323, 328; see also Wilson, 2003: 43). This approach to the theorizing of the nation occludes the role of subaltern groups in appropriating, reworking, contesting and shaping narratives of the nation and nation-building practices. Interrogating the multiple spatialities generated through nationalist practices allows a focus on these different forms of agency, as well as illuminating the practices of exclusion in relation to differences such as gender, race, class and sexuality produced through nationalist forms of political activity (see Guha, 1997; Hall, 2000; Wilson, 2003).

Placing 'nationalist' political activity aboard ship dislocates dominant geographical imaginings of nationalism as territorially bounded. This helps foreground the constitution of Irish nationalisms through dynamic spatial practices. As Mulligan argues, they were formed 'on a transatlantic terrain' where nationalism functioned as 'a highly mobile construct which could be reactivated in a multitude of contexts overseas, so as to make a sense of place, the world and one's own predicament' (Mulligan, 2005: 452). These nationalist practices were also constituted through interaction with the heterogeneous subaltern cultures of the lower deck. This is not to argue that such nationalisms couldn't produce bounded, exclusionary forms of politics and identity. Rather, adopting a relational ontology of the political has resources for understanding the diverse outcomes of nationalist political activity. This included both exclusionary, bounded forms of politics and more open ways of generating nationalist identities. The rest of this chapter argues that different subaltern nationalist identities were generated through negotiating the geographies of connection formed through Atlantic networks. It argues that exploring how these geographies of connection were negotiated opens up possibilities for understanding different ways in which agency and identities were constituted through mobilizing Irish nationalisms.

Shipboard Spaces and Irish Nationalisms

In 1796 Wolf Tone, one of the key leaders of the United Irishmen, composed an address to Irish sailors in the British navy. Tone dramatically appealed to Irish sailors to mutiny and steer their ships into the ports of Ireland. He addressed the sailors thus:

> You are aboard the British navy. You will probably be called upon immediately to turn your arms against your native land, and the part which you may take on this great occasion is of the very last importance. I hope and rely that you will act as becomes brave seamen and honest Irishmen. Remember that Ireland is now an independent nation. You are no longer the subjects of the King of England; you are at the same time a great majority of those who man his fleet, in the proportion of two to one. What is there to hinder you from immediately seizing on every vessel wherein you sail, man of war, Indiamen or merchantman, hoisting the Irish flag and steering into the ports of Ireland? You have the power, if not the inclination . . . (Cited by Gill, 1913: 331–2)

The sailors were positioned in potentially useful ways in relation to the geopolitical strategies of the United Irishmen. A key strategy of the UI leadership was to develop an alliance with the French, as the prospects for a rebellion in Ireland were seen as dependent on support from the French (Elliott, 1982). Tone's address views Irish Tars primarily as a 'means' to the 'end' of the formation of an independent Irish republic. He displays little interest or feel for the ongoing grievances of sailors or for their distinctive organizing traditions. His address to the sailors displays the social distance, the 'paternalistic stance' he displayed when aboard the *Cincinnatus* towards political exile in America in 1795 (Elliott, 1989: 260).

The historiography of the United Irishmen has reproduced Tone's construction of Irish sailors as passive figures who needed to be led. Accounts of the United Irishmen figure such sailors and mutinies merely as a means to a greater end. The struggles of Irish Tars are constructed as playing out the already formed designs and demands of the UI movement and leadership (see Elliott, 1982: 140–2; Wells, 1983: 145; Whelan, 1996: 123). These interpretations marginalize the agency of the sailors in constituting the character of these mutinies and in turn shaping the character of Irish nationalisms. They ignore the distinctive contributions these events made to the constitution of subaltern Irish nationalisms and political identities. They also ignore how the social relations aboard the ships where they conspired, mutinied and revolted shaped the political identities crafted through these mutinies. To explore the relationships between the geopolitical strategies of the United Irishmen, Irish sailors and the character of these mutinies and conspiracies involves thinking about the geographies of connection and contestation that shaped the mutinies. This necessitates a more dynamic relation between Irish nationalisms and the spaces of the ship than is posed in the rather straightforward infiltration stories that underpin the arguments of Elliott, Wells and Whelan. In turn this suggests that the mutinies shaped different possibilities for the articulation of Irish subaltern nationalist identities.

The mutinies emerged at the intersection of routes of political activity shaped by the Atlantic revolutions of the late eighteenth century. The existence and precise nature of contacts between political organizations like the United Irishmen and the London Corresponding Society and the mutinies has long been a source of contention (see Elliott, 1982; Gill, 1913; Rodger, 2003; Thompson, 1968; Wells, 1983). There is some direct evidence of influence of these organizations on some of the mutinies under discussion here. In the court martial of the lead mutineers from the *Grampus* involved at the Nore, a 'Committee man', James Smart, was accused by other sailors of being a member of the LCS.[63] This was an accusation he didn't deny. Both Wells and Elliott have argued that there were particular individuals with links to the LCS/ UI (Elliott, 1982: 140–1; Wells, 1983: 95–9).[64] The LCS activist John Gale Jones had toured the Kent towns of Rochester, Chatham, Maidstone, Gillingham and Gravesend in the mid-1790s, making important contacts especially in Rochester (Gale Jones, 1796). Thompson avers that these contacts may have been 'among the threads which link the Jacobins to the naval mutineers at Spithead and the Nore' (Thompson, 1968: 162).

The practice of punishing United Irish and Defender prisoners by impressing them into the navy also influenced shipboard politics.[65] The exact numbers of such prisoners are difficult to ascertain and subject to much debate (see Kennedy, 1990; Rodger, 2003). An official attempt to quantify the number of Defenders and United Irish prisoners sent to the fleet from Dublin suggested there were 74 in 1795, 18 in 1796 and 23 in 1797.[66] Official correspondence suggests significant official confusion about how many of these political prisoners had been sent into the fleet. It notes that 'numbers of them were allowed to enter as volunteers into the service' and 'not stamp[e]d with the appellation of United Irishmen or Defenders although certainly of that class'.[67] There were attempts to stop the practice of putting prisoners in the fleet, especially for those not 'immediately bound for the West Indies', due to concerns that they 'might produce bad consequences in the navy and army by contributing to a mutinous disposition'.[68] That it was discussed in 1803 whether Irish 'rebels' who had arrived in

Scotland should be detained or sent into the navy, together with the navy's chronic shortages of labour, suggests that these attempts might not have been that significant (Mitchell, 1998: 67; see Wells, 1983).

The central significance of the LCS and the United Irishmen, however, would not appear to have been direct infiltration. Rather, their influence seems strongest in the democratic cultures that characterized the mutinies. The mutineers' attempts to democratize the space of the ship bear important similarities with the democratic spatial practices of the LCS (see also Moore, 1991). The mutineers at Spithead and the Nore elected delegates to a general committee. The sailors' use of democratic systems of representation at Spithead was applauded by the *Moral and Political Magazine* of the LCS (LCS, 2002, vol. 4: 180). Though, interestingly, there were also continuities in some of the tensions that emerged in both these experiments with democratic spatial practices. Whether or not these forms of organization can be directly attributable to the LCS/United Irishmen, they demonstrate the circulation of democratic practices and cultures.

The mutineers, however, did not passively mimic the forms of democratic political culture associated with the LCS and the United Irishmen. Through using democratic principles to attempt to regulate and transform life aboard ship, they not only intervened in maritime social relations, turning bow to stern, as Moore argues (Moore, 1991). These were inventive uses of democratic practices, extending them to regulating workplaces which were usually defined by strict and violent hierarchies. These mutinies, conspiracies and revolts, then, can't be seen as just a simple extension of the activity of the United Irishmen aboard ship. These intersections with sailors' grievances and combinations reworked, unsettled and transformed United Irishmen political practices. These unsettle the power relations which structure Tone's address where sailors are hailed as becoming part of an Irish navy, but where social and labour relations are still posed in hierarchical terms. This was also a function of the linkage/articulation of this nationalist project with subaltern grievances.

As argued in chapter 4, the LCS had ambiguous relations with subaltern struggles. The United Irishmen were similar. They sought to produce alternative forms of democratic culture, but they had limited notions of whom and what should be democratized. The United Irishmen, for example, were often hostile to labourers' combinations both in Ireland and in America. The leadership was initially extremely wary of participation of workingmen and were wary of links with weavers' combinations lest they be accused of 'corresponding with a mob' (Wells, 1983: 17). David Wilson has argued of the United Irish exiles in America that not only 'did their egalitarianism stop at the boundaries of white male society', but they 'refused to countenance class conflict within those boundaries', and he notes their hostility to labour combinations (Wilson, 1998: 134). James

Hope, the most working class of the United Irish leadership, was critical of the forms of social élitism that shaped the organization. He argued that 'none of our leaders seemed to me perfectly acquainted with the main cause of our social derangement', 'the condition of the labouring class', 'if I except Neilson, McCracken, Russell, and Emmet' (Hope, 2001: 59).

A final aspect of these maritime social relations is the way these naval vessels brought together Tars from all over Ireland. This can be demonstrated by the sailors brought to a court martial in 1798 for the conspiracy on the *Defiance* associated with the outbreak of the United Irish rebellion. The *Defiance* had a history of mutinous activity. There was a mutiny among its crew in 1795 in the Firth of Forth against five-water grog 'as thin as muslin and quite unfit to keep out the cold': five men were hanged (Rodger, 2004: 445). It was 'the most troublesome ship' at Spithead: something that has been related to the high numbers of Irish sailors on the vessel (Elliott, 1982: 143). Twenty-five men, including eighteen sailors, were court-martialled for their alleged role in the conspiracy in 1798.[69] The places of birth of the sailors underline the pan-Irish character of the conspiracy: six were from Dublin, three from Cork or County Cork, two from Wexford, and one apiece from County Down, Donegal, Carrick On Suir, Longford, Queen's County, Wicklow, Meath and Gourley.[70] This suggests that sailors were involved in producing a sense of assertive Irish political identity that transcended significant regional affiliations and tensions. This is significant, as regional identifications could be potentially conflictual and impacted on the Atlantic trajectories of Irish subaltern politics, moving, for example, with seasonal migrants to Newfoundland (see Byrne, 1992).

Irish sailors made their identities and politics in relation to the 'rough egalitarianism' that characterized Atlantic maritime cultures (see Bolster, 1997: 91). The unruly, heterogeneous spaces of the lower deck brought together multiple trajectories and routes of subaltern activity. Foregrounding the forms of political activity constituted through these shipboard spaces offers possibilities for asserting and following the dynamic trajectories of subaltern political identities. This permits a focus on the agency of Irish sailors in constituting, engaging with and negotiating the spatial relations made and remade through Atlantic networks. Irish sailors familiar with traditions of secret societies and of combinations were part of the diverse, multi-ethnic crews such as those on the *Grampus*. The meeting up of these different trajectories had multiple outcomes. They could be productive of forms of collective identity, of cooperation. They could also be productive of exclusionary negotiations of identity. The next section will demonstrate that how these negotiations and practices between Irish Tars and sailors of other ethnicities were crafted and performed had significant impacts on the formation of Irish subaltern identities. The ways in which these identities were formed produced different possibilities for the articulation of subaltern nationalisms.

Oaths: Key Repertoire of Irish Subaltern Political Activity

John Pollard's 'altercation' with the loyalist Plymouth publican rested in part on the significance of the oath. The account of their encounter dramatizes the binding legitimacy of the oath and its importance as a form of subaltern mobilization. The administering and taking of oaths was a key form of mobilization, intimidation and potential solidarity among sailors in the mutinies of the 1790s. An Act of Parliament passed during the repression that followed the mutinies made administering illegal oaths an act punishable by transportation for seven years. The act noted that mutineers had used oaths to incite 'Acts of Mutiny and Sedition, and have endeavoured to give Effect to their wicked and traiterous Proceedings by, imposing upon the Persons whom they have attempted to seduce the pretended Obligation of Oaths unlawfully administered'.[71] Oaths were a key ritual through which Tars created forms of collective identity and bonds. They shaped a set of paradoxical practices. They were used to produce and cement forms of solidarity among sailors. They also produced exclusionary identities and forms of intimidation. Oaths constituted particular relations between forms of masculinity, violence (if often threatened rather than practised) and solidarities. This section explores the different uses of oaths among these mutinies and the different collective identities produced through the use of oaths.

The practice of administering and taking oaths was a significant repertoire of Irish subaltern political activity. In the mid-to-late eighteenth century oath-bound secret societies and combinations emerged as powerful subaltern forms of organization in Ireland as well as elsewhere. These deployed the use of oaths in innovative and strategic ways. The administering of oaths was a formative spatial practice through which the Whiteboys moved across Munster in the early 1760s.[72] Donnelly argues the Whiteboys 'invested oaths with a great practical and symbolic importance in fusing local activists into the wider network of a regional movement' (Donnelly, 1978: 27). The swearing of oaths also became a key feature of the significant labourers' combinations active both in Dublin and smaller towns such as Carrick-on-Suir.[73] Oath-bound forms of organization moved with Irish labourers. As noted in chapter 3, they moved with Irish dockside labourers and weavers to London.[74] They moved with seasonal migrants to Newfoundland. In July 1800 the Governor of Newfoundland was informed 'that almost all the male population' in the outports of Newfoundland 'especially those to the southward, had taken the United Irish oath' (Byrne, 1977).

Oaths were a key form of mobilization associated with the United Irish-men and the Defenders. They were used for envisioning particular forms of solidarity and discipline, and were part of the United Irishmen's politi-cization of subaltern popular cultures (see Whelan, 1996). Their use was not uncontested. James Hope 'lamented that we should shrink from an open declaration of our views into conspiracy; that oaths would never bind rogues, that I would rather act openly' (Hope, 2001: 48). Aboard ship swearing and administering oaths became a key way through which Irish sailors negotiated multi-ethnic, rough forecastle cultures. Oaths were taken and administered in different contexts and in different spaces aboard ship. Oaths were sworn publicly on the decks of mutinous ships at Spithead and the Nore.[75] At Spithead every 'man in the fleet took an oath to support the mutiny' (Gill, 1913: 26). Oaths were also integral to conspiratorial prac-tices aboard ship. Their use suggests ways in which they could be used as part of repertoires of activity of multi-ethnic subaltern cultures.

The location of oaths as part of the 'ordinary multiculture' that shaped the lower deck can be gleaned from the court martial of four sailors from the *Renommée* (Gilroy, 2004: 105). The ship was sailing off Havana when a conspiracy was detected, reputedly bearing the influence of the mutiny on the *Hermione* (Pope, 2003: 228; Wells, 1983: 149). Gabriel Johnson, an African American from New York, Thomas Hennigan from Dublin, and J. McDonald and Patrick Hynes, who the *Renommée* pay book merely records as coming from Ireland, were court-martialled and sentenced to death for their part in the conspiracy.[76] Evidence given to the court martial by William Allen, a sailor on the *Renommée*, turns on the way oaths were administered:

> Patrick Hynes and me were drinking our grog together (he being a messmate of mine) [he] told me, he wanted to speak something sincerely to me. I asked him what is meant. He told me they were going to take the ship into the Havannah and whether I would take an Oath upon it. I told him I would take no oath on that subject then he said whoever did not, that the word was . . . Death or Liberty. I told him it was foolish to think of that, and that surely every man would be hung then he said, whoever did not make Oath upon it, it would be death for them in any part of the ship they found them in. Upon that discourse he left me, and Gabriel Johnson came to me that evening, just after six O clock and asked me if Pat Hynes had asked me any-thing. I just told him he had not; he said, if he had You may as well tell me as not.[77]

His evidence suggests the use of the oath was part of strategies of ongoing intimidation and mobilization. It situates the administering of oaths as part of rough cultures of the lower deck and as part of particular sites of asso-ciation. Allen's testimony situates the administering of oaths as a form of ongoing intimidation. His evidence notes that he was subjected to ritualistic and repeated intimidation by different fellow Tars.

The court martial evidence for the conspiracy is suggestive of how the use of oaths was located at the intersection of different sailors. The oath is not seen as restricted to one group of sailors, and it is not just 'Irish' sailors who are sworn. These attempts to administer oaths suggest how they could be used to generate multi-ethnic practices of rebellion. The revolutionary edge of the watchword 'death' or 'liberty' is also notable. In their court martial testimony even fellow sailors who gave hostile witness do not mark out Johnson as black, suggesting that his status as a fellow sailor transcended his 'difference'.[78] As Gilroy has argued in a different context, 'racial difference is not feared. Exposure to it is not ethnic jeopardy but rather . . . unremarkable' (Gilroy, 2004: 105). The use of the oath, however, suggests how particular masculinities cemented these ordinary forms of multiculture (see Bolster, 1997). The court martial records of the conspiracy on the *Renommée*, then, suggest a conspiracy that drew together Irish and other sailors in multi-ethnic cultures of resistance and that oaths were a formative part of this multiculture.

On other ships, especially in mutinies and conspiracies related to the United Irish rising in 1798, the use of oaths generated different forms of collective identity and antagonism. There is evidence that suggests the use of oaths as part of the formation of exclusionary collective identities associated with aggressive forms of territorialization. The court martial of those accused of being part of a conspiracy on the *Defiance* accuses Irish sailors of being part of a 'mutinous assembly or meeting on the starboard side of the galley'.[79] On the *Captain*, fifteen or twenty conspirators were said to meet 'under the forecastle on the larboard side of the galley'.[80] The administering of oaths was central to cementing these exclusionary identities and collectives.[81] This suggests how the conspiracies of Irish sailors were conducted through aggressive forms of territorialization of particular sites of the lower deck.

The testimonies also suggest how these forms of association of Irish sailors were defined in very hostile ways against English Tars. William Howell of the *Defiance* recalled that he had 'heard David Reed say the English buggers we'll kill them all and make Orange boys of them'.[82] On the *Caesar* it was reported that 'Englishmen hardly dare go thro' the Galley by day time without being insulted and his heels tripp'd . . . from under him' and that Irishmen 'threw bottles at Englishmen from the Galley' (Wells, 1983: 148). These exclusionary identities were also produced through particular small acts of violence aboard ship, such as the intimidation of English sailors and Irish sailors who didn't support the UI. In his testimony Lawrence Carroll of the *Defiance* noted the response of the messmates in his birth after reading a letter he had written to his brother in Dublin which concluded, 'I hope the country is quiet and the rebels defeated'. 'Cornelius Callaghan told me I ought to be knocked down for I was no Irishman for writing such a letter.'[83] This suggests how notions of Irishness became the site of contestation through these mutinous events and conspiracies. It also suggests that sailors constituted different notions of Irishness in relation to events such as the 1798 rebellion.

Jeffrey Glasco, in a discussion of the different and conflictual forms of masculinity performed through the mutinies at Spithead and the Nore, has argued that maritime masculinities were generated through different notions of skill. He usefully demonstrates how particular gendered hierarchies were developed and notions of leadership in the mutinies drew on and reproduced these hierarchies (Glasco, 2004). He also suggests that more radical sailors brought these gendered hierarchies into contestation through drawing on notions of equality and liberty (Glasco, 2004: 47). Consideration of the significance of violence to maritime notions of 'manliness' is absent from Glasco's account of these mutinies. The use of oaths as a central form of mobilization and intimidation in sailors' politics emerges from particular relations between subaltern masculinities and gendered forms of violence.

Routinized violence and the routinized threat of violence were central to maritime social relations in the eighteenth century. Violence was integral to the labour of these 'military seamen' (Glasco, 2004: 41). The forms of hierarchical discipline aboard ship were produced through flogging, and importantly through the threat of the use of such discipline (see Christopher, 2006: 98–9; Dening, 1992: 113–24; Rediker, 1988a: 207–9, 212–15). These routinized forms of violence were productive of sailors' identities. Sailors were not only constituted in relation to the violent and hierarchical social relations that characterized naval vessels. They were also constituted in relation to subaltern cultures where notions of manliness and violence were co-produced and cemented through forms of gendered violence (see Clark, 1996; Creighton and Norling, 1996; Featherstone, 2005a: 261). Young sailors were socialized aboard ship through boxing (see Bolster, 1997; Equiano, 1995: 70). As chapter 3 demonstrated, the traditions of combinations and secret societies that Irish sailors drew on were constituted through relations between violence and masculinity. The diverse cultures of violence that intersected on the lower deck, then, shaped the political responses of sailors and the conduct of mutinies. This reinforced notions of Irish nationalisms as the preserve of men, and defined by relations between manliness and violence.

Mo Hume has argued that there are mutually constitutive relations between notions of gender, violence and the nation (Hume, 2006: 75). These relations between masculinities, violence and subaltern political cultures shaped the possible articulations of subaltern nationalisms in significant ways. For the United Irishmen, republicanism was a 'manly calling' constituted through 'paramilitary homosociability' (Curtin, 1991: 135). The active male citizenship they advocated depended on a passive construction of women's roles in the struggle.[84] The rhetoric of the United Irishmen was also based on a gendering of the nation, where the nation became a woman that needed to be defended. Such a passive construction of the role of women was not uncontested or inevitable. Mary Ann McCracken, for example, contested the limits of republicanism and the exclusionary forms of masculinity associated with violence and drinking through which republicanism was constituted (Curtin, 1991: 139). These exclusionary associations, however, were reinforced by the kind of relations between gender, violence and nationalist political identities constructed through the mutinous events and conspiracies aboard ship.

Subaltern Nationalisms and Geographies of Connection

The preceding discussion has suggested that in the 1790s nationalist identities were ongoing, contested, in formation. What it was to be 'nationalist', here, was not finished or complete. Further, nationalist practices were being produced in relation to Atlantic circulations of radical and republican ideas. Different practices were formed in relation to these geographies of connection, whether this was through the geopolitical alliances of the United Irish leadership with the French, or through Irish Tars defining their identities with or against the sailors with whom they laboured. Foregrounding these geographies of connection allows different ways of constructing 'nationalist' identities to emerge. It also permits a sense of how different 'nationalist identities' were produced through relations such as those between Irish subaltern nationalisms and the grievances of sailors and notions of equality and freedom.

This is not to argue that these nationalisms weren't formed through practices of inclusion/exclusion (see Hall, 2000: 110). It does suggest, however, that there were different ways of generating these demarcations. The contacts between Equiano and the United Irishmen in Belfast, the motley forms of politics that characterized the conspiracy on the *Renommée*, the arguments of Thomas Russell against the geopolitics of slavery, all suggest there were different ways of generating Irish nationalisms than the association of Irishness and exclusionary notions of whiteness which emerged in the US in the nineteenth century (see Ignatiev, 1996). These different nationalist practices suggest that what it was to be 'nationalist' could be formed through positive relations with others and forms of connection, rather than through an inevitable hardening of identities. If Atlantic networks and spatial relations were in process in the 1790s and up for negotiation, then the forms that territorialization and nations might take were also up for negotiation.

Sibeylle Fischer has discussed the relations between transnational proc-esses and the formation of nationalisms in imaginative ways in her accounts of the early Haitian constitution. She argues that the 'vagueness on citizen-ship in the early constitutions' is 'a trace of the transnational nature of radical antislavery'. She continues:

> That the early constitutions do not give criteria for citizenship should not be seen as an omission or oversight that is later amended. Rather, it is evidence that the revolutionaries did not think of the new state along the lines of a new nation finally liberated from the fetters of colonialism. Indeed, we may go so far as to argue that the later specifications of citizenship are a measure of how far subsequent politicians had been pushed away from the original transnationalism of antislavery. (Fischer, 2004: 241)

This account positions the formation of Haiti through dynamic relations with the geographies of connection and contestation shaped through the transnational cultures of anti-slavery. She positions emergent notions of Haitian statehood and nationalism as exceeding narrow and exclusionary forms of citizenship. This emphasizes that the dynamic relations between transnational forms of political culture, such as anti-slavery, and emergent nationalisms in the Atlantic world shaped different possibilities for what nationalisms and statehood could be about. That the formation of the Haitian state was 'pushed away' from the transnational political cultures of anti-slavery is further testament to the relational construction of nation-alism. Fischer goes on to argue that 'both internal and external pressures forced' Haiti's politicians 'to build a polity on the model of the modern Western nation-state' (Fischer, 2004: 240).

My point here is not to suggest a direct comparison between Haiti and Ireland. They were positioned in very different relation to Atlantic geogra-phies of connection and exchange. Fischer raises an important set of questions, however, about the relations of emergent nations in the Atlantic world to geographies of connection and transnational political cultures. Interrogating the relations of dynamic geographies of connection to subaltern nationalisms in Haiti or Ireland allows a focus on the multiple, contested forms of nationalism. Such connections and geographies were not somehow just marginal to the constitution of nationalist identities, nor were they just strategically useful. These connections were generative and shaped emergent nationalist identities in significant ways. Positioning such transnational articulations, and the heterogeneous forms of social relations constituted through the site of the ship, as productive, emphasizes why thinking about the nation in relational terms can be significant.

Homi Bhabha has pointed to the potentially generative character of such relations through affirming the role of 'culture's transnational dissemination' in generating new kinds of 'solidarity' (Bhabha, 1994: 170). His focus on the different temporalities of the nation, however, edges out a serious engagement with the spatialities through which such essentialist forms of identity are threatened and disrupted. This is limited to a rather celebratory and uncritical focus on the role of 'margins' and 'borders' (see Bhabha, 1994: esp. 148–9). I think it is useful to position the kinds of geographies of connection foregrounded in this chapter, of multi-ethnic solidarities, as part of the practices through which such 'essentialist identities' are challenged and disrupted. They can 'disturb those ideological manoeuvres through which "imagined communities" are given essentialist identities' (Bhabha, 1994: 149).

This suggests the potentialities of different political cartographies of nationalisms to those often demarcated by theorists on the left. Edward Said reflects a much broader common sense of left theorizing of the nation when he argues:

> The history of modern and indeed pre-modern nationalism suggests that the telos of nationalism is the fundamental reinforcement of a kind of native identity which becomes tyrannical in the end and of course dissolves or occludes important questions as well as issues of class, race, gender, and property. (Said, 2004: 340)

This contention is symptomatic of some of the costs involved in theorizing nationalism in a predominantly temporal way. The hardened antagonisms between Irish and English sailors aboard naval vessels discussed in the last section might be seen to support such claims about the inevitable reinforcement of closed forms of 'native' identity. This chapter, however, has also asserted that there were other ways in which nationalism was articulated. To interrogate these different ways of articulating nationalisms it has been necessary to assert the coexistence of difference in the formation of nationalist identities (see Massey, 2005). It has been necessary to situate nationalisms as a terrain of contestation and production of different identities. Thinking about the dynamic geographies through which these subaltern nationalisms were constituted can foreground how class, race, gender and property generate different nationalist identities that the temporal focus of Said ignores.

Positioning these contested, multiple geographies of connection as impacting on the constitution of nationalisms unsettles the linear development of nationalism towards a horizon of closure figured through Said's argument. This allows a sense of the constitution of the ongoing and contested character of nationalism through various ways of engaging with spatially stretched relations of power. This is to argue that nationalism is inevitably plural and unfinished. This opens up possibilities for engaging with subaltern articulations of nationalism. Interrogating how geographies of connection are negotiated through nationalist political activity, then, becomes central to understanding the forms of political identities generated through such activity. Laclau has argued that there is no positive core of meaning to 'nationalism', but rather that its 'meaning will vary depending on the chain of equivalences associated with it' (Laclau, 2005a: 227). Following the practices through which geographies of connection are constructed, mobilized and negotiated through nationalist political practices can be integral to understanding how 'nationalism' becomes articulated in different ways.

Conclusions

This chapter has interrogated the relations between shipboard political activity and emergent Irish nationalisms in the late 1790s. I have suggested that these shipboard spaces of politics dislocated dominant ways of generating Irish nationalisms. This permits a focus on the constitution of subaltern nationalisms in relation to various geographies of connection. I have demonstrated that different kinds of nationalist identities were generated in relation to the rough egalitarianism of the lower deck. I have noted the different forms of collective identities generated through uses of the oath, for example. These could generate different kinds of relations between labour, gender, masculinities and violence. These forms of subaltern nationalist activity could generate both multi-ethnic articulations and exclusionary spaces of politics aboard ship.

Interrogating the relations between nationalist political practices and geographies of connection has been productive. It opens up accounts of diverse forms of subaltern identity and agency constituted in relation to nationalist political activity that have been closed down by bounded and temporal constructions of the nation. This emphasizes that there are histories and geographies of the formation of nationalist identities in relation to transnational flows and networks. Further, it emphasizes the markedly different strategies and political identities mobilized in relation to such flows and networks. This generation of different kinds of identities, both through nationalist and other political practices, is developed through the discussion of the contemporary counter-global political networks in Part III.

Part Three

Political Geographies of the Counter-Globalization Movement

Chapter Six

Geographies of Power and the Counter-Globalization Movement

Part II examined the diverse geographies of connection and contestation formed through subaltern political activity in the eighteenth-century Atlantic world. I have challenged assumptions that subaltern movements of the past were bounded. I have demonstrated that there are histories and geographies of subaltern political activity that have contested globalizing practices through deploying 'cosmopolitan', multiple forms of identity and solidarities. The final two chapters of this book develop these themes through exploring the geographies of the powerful forms of contemporary opposition to neo-liberal globalization.

These inspiring movements have contested the neo-liberal forms of discipline that constitute globalization. They have shaped powerful, unusual alliances and developed novel forms of political activity, identity and forms of organizing. These have had significant impacts on global politics through such events as the protests against the World Trade Organization in Seattle and the planetary opposition to the Second Gulf War on 15 February 2003. The forms of networked political activity they generate have also unsettled and challenged existing ways of understanding and theorizing the geographies of social and political movements. These burgeoning movements against neo-liberal globalization, in particular, pose important challenges to ways of theorizing the relations between space, power and political activity. This chapter focuses in depth on these challenges.

Firstly, these movements are defined by an explicit transnationalism. They have generated alternative geographies of connection through their opposition to neo-liberal globalization. Secondly, these movements have been defined through the ways in which they contest the spatially stretched power relations of neo-liberal globalization. Making these power relations part of the terrain of contestation and political debate has been one of these movements' most significant achievements. This raises key questions about how resistances negotiate spatially stretched relations of power. Thirdly, these movements have contested the terms on which political discourses such as environmentalism are defined. These alliances have articulated subaltern political ecologies, for example, which contest assumptions that environmentalisms are a middle-class privilege (Featherstone, 2007; Martinez-Alier, 2002).

This chapter uses an engagement with the geographies of these diverse movements to interrogate the relations between space, power and political identities. These concerns are then developed through a detailed discussion of one particular set of political alliances, the Inter-Continental Caravan (chapter 7). The first section of this chapter interrogates one of the most iconoclastic interventions in thinking about the resistance to neo-liberal globalization and which has in turn impacted on these forms of resistance: the work of Hardt and Negri. I argue that the inspiring, visionary account of the multitude as a new form of radical political collectivity rests on problematic ways of understanding the relations between space, politics and identity. The second section of the chapter engages with the practices through which 'these movements' have brought neo-liberal relations of power into contestation. I argue that this has been one of the key achievements of these movements and that it has been productive, for example, of different geographies of connection. The third section of the chapter examines the very different forms of political identity constituted in relation to opposition to neo-liberal globalization. It uses a focus on the distinctive maps of grievance produced through the activity of different movements to analyse the constitution of different political identities through these forms of resistance. Finally, the chapter explores some of the populist logics at work in the construction of the political identities mobilized through the counter-globalization movement. It uses a discussion of these populist logics to develop an alternative account of the relations between power, space and identity.

Counter-Global Networks and the Spatial Politics of the 'Multitude'

Of all the multifarious engagements with the emergent political identities, alliances and experiments of the counter-globalization movements, Hardt and Negri's *Empire* and *Multitude* have been the most iconoclastic and influential. Their work has even been hailed as a new Communist Manifesto for the 'anti-globalization movement' (see Fotopoulos and Gezerlis, 2002). For Hardt and Negri, contemporary neo-liberalism is characterized by diffuse relations of power. Neo-liberalism functions neither through dominance, nor even through eliciting consent in the Gramscian sense of hegemony, but through the very production of bodies and subjectivities. They suggest that Empire, the political form which they associate with contemporary neo-liberalism, is a diffused form of political control and production. As Allen argues, 'their Empire is a decentred, deterritorialized apparatus of rule that admits no transcendental centre of power' (Allen, 2003: 87).[85] Others have interrogated in depth the (problematic) geographies of power that are developed through their discussion of Empire (see Allen, 2004; Gibson-Graham, 2002; Sparke, 2005). This section engages with Hardt and Negri's arguments about the 'multitude'. In particular, I interrogate the forms of spatial politics this version of radical collective subjectivity depends on.

Hardt and Negri argue that the diffused character of the production of power through neo-liberalism has undermined the existence of an 'outside' from which oppositional politics can organize. They insist that oppositional politics cannot be constructed from such an 'outside', but rather constitute a 'field of pure immanence' (Hardt and Negri, 2001: 354). The implications of this are that 'Empire cannot be resisted by a project aimed at a limited, local autonomy' (Hardt and Negri, 2001: 206). This unsettles a particular style of left critique that stands outside the activity of knowing and engaging with the world. It also undermines metaphors of 'autonomy', which seek to produce pure, uncorrupted spaces outside of such relations (see Sale, 1993: 275). Rather, their arguments suggest that radical politics is always already enmeshed in cross-cutting relations of power and is itself productive. Their focus on politics as immanence, the dynamic forms of constitution, becoming through political activity, gives their account of social relations an effervescent vitality.

This emphasis on the productiveness of political activity frames their insistence on the transformative power of the 'multitude' (Hardt and Negri, 2001, 2004). Hardt and Negri define the multitude as a new form of radical political collectivity. They conceive of the multitude as 'an open and expansive network in which all differences can be expressed freely and equally, a network that provides the means of encounter so that we can live and work in common' (Hardt and Negri, 2001: xiv). These ongoing experimentations with forms of radical political collectivity draw inspiration in both political and theoretical terms from Negri's experiences as part of the 'autonomist' movement in Italy in the 1970s (on Negri's political trajectory, imprisonment and exile, see Negri, 2005). A concern with the productiveness of political struggle and a sustained critique of the institutions of the organized left are just two of the key threads that link *Multitude* and *Empire* with his earlier political writings (Negri, 2005: xxxix). As Negri has suggested, his political and theoretical engagements in the 1970s sought to 'reweave the web of insurrection against a new organization of capitalist domination' (Negri, 2005: xlix; see also Guattari and

Negri, 1990: 75–102). Central to this was a critique of the 'traditional organization of the Official Labour Movement' and an engagement with the 'new experiences of organization and centralization of the struggles on the part of the movement of the seventies' (Negri, 2005: xxxix; see also Lumley, 1990: 309–10). Hardt and Negri conceive of the multitude as an immanent expression of a globalized opposition to Empire. This brings together diverse forms of resistance and marginalized groups through shared subjectivities such as an 'enormous desire for global democracy' (Hardt and Negri, 2004: 290).

This account of the multitude depends on a particular version of spatiality. For Hardt and Negri, the multitude is constituted through 'smooth' space in contrast to the more bounded, national spatialities of 'traditional social organizations' such as labour unions (Hardt and Negri, 2004: 136–7). Hardt and Negri draw on Deleuze and Guattari's notion of 'smooth space', which they define against forms of striated space. This is 'a fluid space of continuous variation, characterized by a plurality of local directions' (Patton, 2000: 112; see also Deleuze and Guattari, 1987). Hardt and Negri's account of the production of the multitude depends on a particular relationship between immanence, smooth space and the formation of political identities. Situating the multitude as 'an open and expansive network in which all differences can be expressed freely and equally' produces a singular account of the network which is experienced in the same way by different movements and groups. This privileges the temporal as the decisive, generative element in the constitution of political identities and renders the spatial as a mere backdrop for the constitution of revolutionary temporal subjects.[86] In their account, the multitude springs fully formed as an already constituted radical subject unified by common revolutionary desires. This makes it hard to see the different political identities being generated through resistance to neo-liberal globalization, let alone begin to account for the contested relations and solidarities being produced between them.

Their attempts to 'ground' the notion of the multitude through discussions of particular struggles demonstrate these tensions. In *Empire*, the one example of the multitude they develop is the Industrial Workers of the World (IWW) active in the US and beyond in the early twentieth century. They celebrate 'the perpetual movement of the Wobblies' and argue that they constituted 'an immanent pilgrimage, creating a new society in the shell of the old, without establishing fixed and stable structures of rule' (Hardt and Negri, 2001: 207). The IWW was inventive. It produced forms of multi-ethnic organizing in opposition to the exclusionary or segregationist official labour movement in the US. Its experiments with multi-ethnic organizing, however, were situated, limited and partial. Its most successful multi-ethnic organizing was on the Philadelphia docks through Local 8 of the IWW Maritime Transport Workers Union (Bird et al., 1987; Cole,

2003). There, approximately 'half of the peak membership of four thousand was black, with the remainder composed mainly of Poles, Lithuanians, and Latin Americans from various nations. The major organizer was Ben Fletcher, the most important black leader to emerge in the IWW, and the local chairmanship was rotated monthly between blacks and non-blacks' (Bird et al., 1987: 177–8). Multi-ethnic organizing was made central to the activity of the Local. This multi-ethnic character, however, was achieved at the expense of a more craft-based unionism which the IWW contested elsewhere. The Local exercised significant autonomy from the IWW nationally, and levied much higher dues from its members than was stipulated by the IWW constitution (McGirr, 1995: 388).

The IWW's experiments with multi-ethnic organizing, though productive and significant, were also situated and localized. They were produced through particular contested relations and spatial practices. This undermines a sense of the multitude as merely immanent. It emphasizes how radical, collective political identities have to be made and constructed through particular forms of association and spatial practices, and how this is always a partial process done in and between particular sites. The problems that flow from Hardt and Negri's problematic construction of collective political identities are further apparent in their discussion of the protests against the WTO in Seattle in 1999. They suggest that the 'magic of Seattle'

> was to show that these many grievances were not just a random, haphazard collection, a cacophony of different voices, but a chorus that spoke in common against the global system. This model is already suggested by the organizing techniques of the protesters: the various affinity groups come together or converge not to unite into one large centralized group; they remain different and independent but link together in a network structure. The network defines both their singularity and their commonality (Hardt and Negri, 2004: 288).

The concept of the multitude usefully foregrounds the dynamism and vitality of counter-globalization movements and their multiplicity. Their account indicates how these struggles are constitutive of new forms of identity and power relations. Hardt and Negri's use of the network metaphor to examine the formation of the multitude in Seattle, however, collapses diverse movements with radically different trajectories into the same structure of 'commonality'.

Their account allows no space for the discussion of the terms on which, and the practices through which, different collective political identities come together. Arguing that the network defines both 'singularity' and 'commonality' is to evade a focus on the practices of articulation through which solidarities and alliances are constituted. Hardt and Negri, as Massey has argued, 'have no serious way' of engaging 'with the heterogeneity within the multitude' (Massey, 2005: 175). This singular account of *the* network erases the constitutive differences, fissures, antagonisms and striations that cross-cut the solidarities and collective identities formed through counter-global networks (see Routledge et al., 2006; Routledge, 2008). This lack of attention to the constitutive differences in collective political identities, alliances and solidarities has important effects politically as well as theoretically. Hardt and Negri's a-spatial account evades some of the key tensions that have emerged through the conduct and activity of the movements against neo-liberal globalization.[87]

In the wake of the euphoria over the Seattle protest, a number of thoughtful critiques questioned the marginalization of activists from the South and North American activists of colour and the organizing practices that preceded it (DN, 2001; Martinez, 2000; Rajah, 2001; Wong, 2001). They have foregrounded the unequal geographies of power produced through these emerging networks of opposition to neo-liberal globalization. Commentators from the global South have pointed to the pressures that lack of internet access, incomes and visa privileges exert on the involvement of activists from the South in these networks (DN, 2001). The movements that are brought together through these globalized networks of opposition also negotiate and contest practices of globalization through mobilizing markedly different imaginative geographies. They are not a uniform mass of revolutionary fervour, unified by an 'enormous desire for global democracy' (Hardt and Negri, 2004: 290). Rather, the solidarities constructed through these networks can be undermined by or can coexist with exclusionary, 'nationalist' constructions of grievance (see Featherstone, 2003; Greenfield, 2005; Vanaik, 2004). Thus, Rupal Oza, in an insightful discussion of the resistance to the Miss World pageant in Bangalore in 1996, has argued that both left and right shared an understanding of globalization as a threat to the 'nation' where the construction of the 'nation in opposition to globalization rested on deeply problematic constructions of gender and sexuality' (Oza, 2001: 1069). Such exclusionary nationalist articulations of struggles against globalization can limit and exert pressure on the possibility of transnational alliances constituted through shared opposition to neo-liberal practices and institutions.

Hardt and Negri's account of the immanent resistance of the multitude to Empire evades these tensions. The rest of this chapter seeks to foreground these contested relationalities through situating these movements as part of multiple, overlapping networks and trajectories. I draw on Routledge et al. here in viewing resistances to neo-liberal globalization not as a 'movement of movements' or as a fully-fledged global civil society, but as a 'series of overlapping, interacting and differentially placed and resourced networks' (Routledge et al., 2006: 838). This makes it possible to interrogate the effects of activists' different locations in relation to global networks and flows. In contrast to Hardt and Negri's approach, this seeks to produce a partial, situated account of the relations between space, power and the formation of collective identities. Through this account I engage with five key issues which are occluded in Hardt and Negri's work to foreground the diverse forms of identity and agency constituted through these counter-global networks.

Firstly, this account seeks to follow the spatial practices through which neo-liberal power relations are brought into contestation. I argue that these practices are productive and generative. Rather than suggesting that the opposition of the multitude to Empire is uniform, spontaneous and immanent, I argue it is necessary to follow the situated practices through which neo-liberalism is brought into contestation. This allows different geographies of power constituted through counter-global networks to emerge. It also allows different movements some agency in shaping the terms of the antagonisms which they produce, in contrast to Hardt and Negri's account which assumes that resistance to neo-liberalism is almost natural rather than being constructed (see Laclau, 2005a: 240; Munck, 2007: 132).

Secondly, this account focuses on the different power relations and identities that are being constituted through counter-globalization movements. It seeks to foreground rather than evade the different tensions and unequal relations of power being produced both within and between movements.

Thirdly, it seeks to examine the ways in which past traditions of political cultures exert pressure, set limits and open up possibilities for the formation of political identities. The political practices of the counter-globalization movement in Western Europe and particularly in the US, for example, have been constituted in relation to shifting definitions of whiteness that have structured the histories and geographies of alternative political movements (see Martinez, 2000; Ross, 2003). The political forms of the counter-globalization movement, while inventive, are not a decisive break from past struggles as Hardt and Negri's theorization of the multitude often assumes (Hardt and Negri, 2004: 136). In particular, I seek to interrogate the significance of different forms of nationalism in shaping resistance to globalization, and to explore the impacts of such nationalisms on the formation of identities and solidarities through counter-global networks (see also Munck, 2007: 133–4; Wainwright and Oritz, 2006).

Fourthly, a focus on the constitution of collective political identities through political activity can allow a sense of how such political activity is constitutive and productive. If these networks are seen as partial, situated articulations between different unlike actors, then this permits a focus on the different forms of agency produced through their activity. It also allows a focus on the productiveness of the meeting up of different trajectories of political activity, which is occluded by collapsing them into an overarching 'multitude'.

Fifthly, this account, drawing on the argument developed in chapter 2, situates the solidarities these movements create as dynamic and situated interventions in the geographies of transnational networks. Situating these solidarities as particular interventions in the formation of transnational networks unsettles the disembodied 'global' demands which Hardt and Negri suggest the multitude should adopt: the rights to global citizenship, a minimal income and the reappropriation of the new means of production (i.e. access to and control over education and information and communication) (Hardt and Negri, 2001). Following the solidarities and identities produced through counter-global networks suggests much more generative and recursive relationships between networks of resistance to neo-liberalism and place-based struggles than does Hardt and Negri's insistence on a 'total' opposition to Empire (Hardt and Negri, 2000: 206–7). As I argued in chapter 1, 'universal demands' don't float as global demands apart from struggles in particular sites, but rather are constituted through articulations and practices between different place-based struggles.

The next section takes up the first of these issues and follows some of the spatial practices through which counter-globalization movements have brought neo-liberal globalization into contestation.

Contesting Neo-Liberal Geographies

On 7 February 2006 a motion was presented at the McDonel Hall Government, a student association at Michigan State University, calling attention to major disputes about Coca-Cola in both Colombia and India. The motions read as follows:

> WHEREAS a fact-finding delegation of labor, educator, and student representatives led by New York City Council member Hiram Monserrate concluded, based on a 10-day trip to Colombia, that "there have been a total of 179 major human rights violations of Coca-Cola's workers, including nine murders," more troubling were the "persistent allegations that paramilitary violence against workers was done with the knowledge of and likely under the direction of company managers," and that Coca-Cola Company's "inaction and its ongoing refusal to take any responsibility for the human rights crisis faced by its workforce in Colombia demonstrates, at best, disregard for the lives of its workers," and its "complicity is deepened by its repeated pattern of bringing criminal charges against union activists who have spoken out about the company's collusion with paramilitaries," and

WHEREAS there has been a growing outcry by Indians against Coca-Cola Company's business practices in India due to its overusing and polluting of the common groundwater, giving toxic sludge to farmers as fertilizer, and selling contaminated soda to the citizenry, leaving Indians at risk of dehydration, starvation, and poisoning . . . (McDonel Hall Government, 2006)

The motion goes on to argue that since 'the Coca-Cola Company has repeatedly refused to contribute to any independent investigation of the aforementioned allegations', Michigan State University should 'desist from renewing their contract with the Coca-Cola Company'. The motion was passed. A similar motion passed at the University of Michigan lost Coca-Cola the lucrative contract for supplying soft drinks to the University of Michigan campus, which was estimated to be worth $1.27 million (Hardikar, 2006). Students have now 'thrown Coke products out of [at least] thirteen colleges and universities' in the US (Higginbottom, 2007: 283). Student associations in Ireland, Italy and the UK have taken similar action.

The McDonel Hall motion demonstrates the way that these campaigns have brought together different grievances against Coca-Cola. Through transnational organizing practices the boycott links different places where Coca-Cola has been contested. The boycott of Coke introduces some of the key aspects of the relations of counter-global networks to neo-liberal forms of globalization. These movements have brought the unequal power relations and 'hidden' forms of violence that generate globalized commodities into contestation. They have attempted to make the forms of unequal power relations, human rights abuses and environmental degradation associated with Coca-Cola visible and contestable. It also suggests that these practices are productive. These campaigns have brought together different movements struggling against Coca-Cola. It also emphasizes that these are ongoing works of articulation and connection, rather than merely immanent, and that these transnational resistance networks are not ungrounded, but work through connecting particular sites of political activity.

Coke has been contested on various grounds. As the MSU motion notes, Coca-Cola has been the subject of mobilization around the rights of trade unionists because of its links to the assassination of trade unionists in Colombia. As with the record of other multinationals in Colombia, such as BP, there is strong evidence of both complicity and collusion by multinationals with attacks by paramilitaries on trade unionists (see also Novelli, 2004). SINALTRAINAL, the local branch of the food and drink workers union, has been active in bottling plants and initiated calls for a boycott in 2003. There have been nine assassinations of unionized workers from Coca-Cola plants (Higginbottom, 2007: 279). These include the assassination of Isidro Segundo Gil, 'who was murdered by paramilitary forces inside the Carepa plant of . . . Bebidas y Alimentos' bottlers/franchise for Coca-Cola (United Steel Workers Union and the International Labor Rights Fund, 2001; Higginbottom, 2007; War on Want, 2006: 8).

This violence against unionized Coca-Cola workers has had effects. In 1993 SINALTRAINAL 'had 1,440 members in Coke plants, by 2004 this had fallen to just 389' (Higginbottom, 2007: 280). Despite 'the loss of nearly half of its membership to violence, fear, and corporate restructuring over the last ten years, SINALTRAINAL continues to challenge multinational corporations, especially the Coca-Cola Company' (Gill, 2006: 9). On 22 July 2006, the International Day of Protest Against Coca-Cola, it staged demonstrations in several Colombian cities to condemn the degradation of work that has accompanied the global shift to neo-liberal capitalism, and to denounce corporate complicity in paramilitary murders of Coca-Cola workers. Coca-Cola's anti-trade union practices have also been contested in Guatemala, Nicaragua, Peru, Russia and Turkey (War on Want, 2006: 8–9). The boycott is also part of longstanding transnational mobilisation against Coca Cola. There was concerted international organising in support of workers in the Coca Cola bottling plant in Guatemala City in 1979 and 1980 (Levenson-Estrada, 1994: 190–2, 203).

There has been significant international trade-union mobilization in support of trade unionists in Colombia and against Coca-Cola. These campaigns are significant as they have been defined by forms of labour internationalism based primarily around human/trade union rights rather than around developing common economic interests. In 2004 the conference of the UK public sector union UNISON voted to support the boycott of Coca-Cola (UNISON, 2007). On 20 July 2001 the United Steel Workers Union and the International Labor Rights Fund filed a lawsuit in US District Court for the Southern District of Florida (Miami) against Coke and Panamerican Beverages, Inc., the primary bottler of Coke products in Latin America. Additional defendants include owners of a bottling plant in Colombia where trade union leaders have been murdered. The suit alleged that 'With respect to their business operations in Colombia, the Defendants hired, contracted with or otherwise directed paramilitary security forces that utilized extreme violence and murdered, tortured, unlawfully detained or otherwise silenced trade union leaders of the Union representing workers at Defendants' facilities' (United Steel Workers Union and the International Labor Rights Fund, 2001). The international trade union response hasn't been uniform, however. The UK Trade Union Congress's campaign Justice for Colombia, for example, doesn't currently support the boycott of Coca-Cola, arguing that other unions than SINALTRAINAL in Colombia don't support a boycott (Justice for Colombia, 2004: 21–2; see the refutation of this position in Higginbottom, 2007). This gives a sense of the specific and contested practices through which articulations are made between different sites, struggles and movements.

Coca-Cola has also been contested due to its poor environmental record. There have been major campaigns against Coca-Cola in India due to the role of Coca-Cola plants in 'exacerbating water shortages' (War on Want, 2006). The most high profile of these has been the ongoing campaign in Plachimada, a tiny hamlet in the state of Kerala. Here a diverse coalition has campaigned against the effect of the company's plants on water supplies. The multinational has been accused of 'creating severe water shortage, of polluting its groundwater and soil, and also of distributing toxic waste as fertilizer to farmers in the area' (Raman, 2005: 2481; see also Bijoy, 2006). The company has been subject to mounting pressure from local communities, particularly among adivasis and dalits. On 16 December 2003, in a landmark verdict, the single bench of the Kerala High Court upheld the position of the panchayat and directed the company to seek alternative sources of water for its bottling plant in Plachimada. The single bench maintained that groundwater belonged to the people and that the government did not possess the right to allow a private party to extract it in such huge quantities, it being 'a property held by it in trust'. It also ruled that the company should be allowed to use only that quantity of groundwater equal to the amount normally used for irrigating crops in a 34-acre plot, the actual area occupied by the company (Raman, 2005: 2481). Coca-Cola were forced to stop production in March 2004, but legal battles over their attempts to resume production in Plachimada continue (Bijoy, 2006; Raman, 2005).

As the McDonel Hall motion demonstrates, this opposition to Coca-Cola's environmental record has in turn been networked globally as well as across India. The National Alliance of People's Movements has been influential in this regard, mobilizing through sites such as the World Social Forum (Drew and Levien, 2006; see also Raman, 2005: 2484). These protests have led to further contestations of Coca-Cola in India. Prompted partly by the protests in Plachimada, the Centre for Science and Environment in Delhi conducted studies in 2003 which found that 12 brands of soft drink manufactured by PepsiCo and Coca-Cola contained toxic pesticide residues, a situation which was unchanged in 2006 (Centre for Science and Environment, 2006). The study 'revealed that the soft drinks produced by Coca-Cola and PepsiCo contained toxic pesticide residues; a Joint Parliamentary Committee led by Sharad Pawar was constituted to verify the findings of the CSE which in fact were found to be true' (Raman, 2005: 2483). This suggests how bringing companies into contestation can be productive. As Brian Wynne suggests, 'expert dissent is often only encouraged and sustained by the existence of a public backcloth of scepticism or alienation' (Wynne, 1996: 48–9).

The diverse practices through which Coca-Cola has been contested suggest a set of significant issues around the conduct of the political activity of counter-globalization movements. Firstly, there is the way that these movements are active in bringing the geographies of power that shape neo-liberal globalization into contestation. Making the geographies of power shaping neo-liberalism part of the terrain of contestation has been a significant achievement of these movements. Secondly, there is the generation of connections and solidarities between different movements, partly mediated through particular campaigns such as those on different university campuses. These bring together movements which have contested Coca-Cola on different grounds and hence can be productive, for example of struggles which link campaigns over environmental inequalities with struggles for the human rights of trade unionists. Thirdly, there is a sense of the productive character of bringing power relations into contestation. For, contrary to Hardt and Negri, these forms of resistance are generated through practices which bring power relations into contestation and through specific, situated articulations between different struggles. Fourthly, these practices speak to a set of questions about the spatialities of democratic practices, particularly those involved in holding powerful actors to account. The conduct of these forms of democratic politics exceeds the container of the nation-state. This necessitates an understanding of the diverse geographies of power constituted in relation to democratic practices, which (as I argued in chapter 4) were closed down by Barnett's nation-centred account of the spaces of democracy.

These diverse and innovative political movements problematize the claims of theorists and politicians associated with the radical centre that antagonisms are no longer a constitutive part of the political. Anthony Giddens, for example, has claimed that the political is a domain which can now be characterized by harmonious negotiation rather than the definition of adversaries or enemies. Giddens's consensual construction of the political, however, is constituted through isolating citizens from engagements with spatially constructed power relations. He argues that 'the overall aim of third way politics should be to help citizens pilot their way through "the major revolutions of our time"' (Giddens, 1998: 64). He eradicates antagonism from the political through setting up 'globalization, changes in family structure and the transformations of our relationship to nature' as transformations that citizens should be 'piloted through'. This language is instructive. For Giddens outlines a passive construction of citizenship and political agency. He refuses to hail citizens as part of the changing space-time configurations of 'globalization' with some agency to negotiate, shape and engage with such transformations. Engaging with the multiple ways that the changing space-time configurations of 'globalization' are being negotiated allows very different conceptions of political activity and agency to emerge.

The consensual politics associated with the 'third way' has been subjected to rigorous critiques by a number of authors who have characterized the current 'era' as being 'post-political' (Mouffe, 2005; Swyngedouw, 2007; Žižek, 1999). Thus Žižek argues that 'in the post-political universe of pluralist negotiation and consensual regulation' 'the foreclosed political returns' in the guise of fundamentalisms (Žižek, 1999: 35). As noted in chapter 2, Chantal Mouffe, one of the most significant and vociferous of these critics, has persistently argued for a reassertion of the importance of antagonism for contemporary politics (see Mouffe, 2000, 2005). While I share the frustrations of these theorists with the depoliticizing moves that characterize the current conjuncture, their epochal delineation of the contemporary period as 'post-political' is problematic. It rests on a limited notion of what constitutes the political and of the spatialities of the political. This is based around a construction of national politics as the only site where political antagonisms are to be constructed and practised and tends to miss the significance of the diverse, heterogeneous alliances shaped through counter-global networks.

Mouffe has insisted that democratic politics depend not on the exclusion of power relations from the political, as theorists associated with deliberative democracy have argued. She argues that instead of 'trying to erase the traces of power and exclusion', democratic politics requires 'us to bring them to the fore, to make them visible so that they can enter the terrain of contestation' (Mouffe, 2000: 33–4). This is a significant and useful argument. But as I argued in chapter 2, Mouffe is not attentive to the practices through which this is achieved. Take the example of the Coca-Cola boycott as a practice through which traces of power and exclusion have been brought into contestation. The unequal geographies of power produced by Coca-Cola have had to be actively dragged into the terrain of contestation through concerted transnational mobilization. They haven't just rendered themselves visible. The practices through which this has been achieved have also been markedly disruptive of the nation-centred ways of imagining the political that have framed the arguments of proponents of the post-political thesis. This has been achieved through articulations between different groups struggling against Coca-Cola in different parts of the world.

Following the political practices through which movements have brought powerful multinational companies into contestation produces more productive and generative geographies of contestation. These spatial practices of resistance exceed the fixed containers of the nation-state, which function as rather idealized spaces where Mouffe envisions agonistic politics are practised. Bringing these relations of power into contestation involves following and contesting relations of power that stretch beyond the nation-state. As the contestation of Coca-Cola demonstrates, this is a productive process. It brings together different movements contesting these multinationals on different terms and in different places. This demonstrates how solidarities are actively produced through contesting the generation of transnational networks and the heterogeneous relations between 'commodities', labourers, water-tables, trade unionists, that they produce. In this sense the politics of the Coke boycott is both spatially and materially heterogeneous.

The forms of political activity deployed through counter-global networks, then, disrupt the theoretical and political positions of both 'third way' politics and theorists like Mouffe, Swyngedouw and Žižek who define the contemporary epoch as post-political. These networked forms of politics show that globalization is something to be shaped, contra Giddens. The transnational articulations of antagonisms generated through the opposition to Coca-Cola emphasize how contested forms of the political are still being generated. But they suggest how they are not neatly confined within the arenas of nation-state politics which Mouffe associates with agonistic pluralism. In this sense they have dragged into the terrain of contestation aspects of the neo-liberal constitution of globalization that are placed outside the limits of the political consensus of political life, especially in Britain and the US.

This helps articulate more generous assessments of counter-globalization politics than the rather dismissive responses of some left academics. Graeme Thompson, for example, has referred to the 'global social justice movement' as 'an unstable amalgam of anarchists, environmentalists, international protectionists, disillusioned reformers, well-meaning third worldists, well-intentioned debt forgivers, and rabid US haters' (Thompson, 2003: n.p.). John Allen's discussion of the spatial practices of resistance to the World Trade Organization argues that the violence that characterized the protests was antithetical to the formation of productive power relations (Allen, 2003: 184–5; see also Cameron and Palan, 2004: 21). He contends that the protests were characterized by a 'politics of rejectionism' that 'does not amount to the kind of collaborative engagement where political solutions are negotiated and differences accepted' (Allen, 2003: 185). One of the key achievements of the protests, however, was to make visible and contestable the role of the WTO in generating, shaping and formatting globalization in a neo-liberal fashion. The protests took a relatively obscure, uninteresting financial institution and made its role in fashioning globalization in a neo-liberal way absolutely central.

The practices through which geographies of neo-liberalism have been brought into contestation have been productive. They have opened up political spaces for the possibility of generating globalization in other ways. These movements have brought the cartographies of power of neo-liberalism into contestation. Unlike Hardt and Negri, they have demonstrated that it is necessary to target particular sites, particular companies, particular institutions, particular events, to bring neo-liberal globalization into contestation. Through this focus on particular sites, however, the strategies of counter-globalisation movements have largely ignored neo-liberalisms' 'pervasiveness as a system of diffused power' (Peck and Tickell, 2002: 400). Through targeting particular key sites counter-globalisation movements have perhaps neglected an engagement with the subjectivities being produced and shaped through neo-liberal practices (Wainwright and Oritz, 2006). In doing so they have tended not to engage with the practices through which neo-liberalisms elicit consent and legitimacy. This gives rise to important questions about what maps of grievance that did contest the terms on which neo-liberal subjectivities are produced might look like. The terms on which these neo-liberal geographies of power have been brought into contestation have varied. The next section examines the different forms of political identities constituted through these political practices.

Contested Networks

In 2001 José Bové, the charismatic leader of Confédération Paysanne, was deported from Brazil for his part in the 'tearing up of an experimental plot of transgenic crops' at a farm located in 'Nao me Toque, 300 km from Porto Alegre, capital of Rio Grande do Sul state', which belonged to 'the US-based transnational Monsanto' (Osava, 2001). These actions against transgenic crops were the product of alliances between Bové and activists from the Brazilian land rights campaign Movimento Sem Terra (MST). Confédération Paysanne and MST both have a formidable reputation for assertive non-violent direct action and both are engaged in collective experiments involving the reconstitution of agricultural practices (see Bové and Dufour, 2001; Movimento Sem Terra, 2001; Fernandes, 2005; Wolford, 2004, 2005). These organizations have been powerful actors in the making of counter-global networks such as the international peasant/small farmers organization Via Campesina (Desmarais, 2002). These alliances illustrate how the political identities produced through counter-globalization networks have been formed through ongoing negotiation and contestation of the practices through which non-humans are enrolled into globalized networks.

The action emphasizes how solidarities/articulations are not just about bringing together activists from discretely bounded struggles, but rather can intervene in shaping and contesting the geographies of transnational networks. These solidarities also emerge at the intersections of different experimentations with ways of generating relations between humans and non-humans. Both MST and Confédération Paysanne have developed a commitment to alternative social and ecological farming practices. After initially mimicking intensive agriculture on the land gained through their occupations, MST has begun to experiment with alternative forms of agriculture and has produced the first organic seeds in Latin America (Branford and Rocha, 2002: 211–39; MST, 2005). Confédération Paysanne has backed alternative proposals for rural development based around 'solidaristic agriculture' related to radical non-agricultural actors in rural communities (Herman and Kuper, 2003: 106–7).[88]

The articulations crafted between these movements, however, suggest that the kinds of engagements with associations/collectives did not produce smooth, consensual alliances. There were important geographies to these transnational networks of resistance. These solidarities brought together actors and non-humans such as seeds, formed in different relation to such entities as the Common Agricultural Policy of the European Union. Bové and Joao Pedro Stedile of the MST offered markedly different ways of negotiating these geographies of power. Stedile disagreed with Bové's position of 'fighting the European Union's farm subsidies on the grounds of their "distorting international trade to the detriment of developing countries"' (Osava, 2001). He argued that 'the problem is not the subsidies in Europe . . . but the lack of subsidies in Brazil and elsewhere' and he condemned 'the transformation of food products into a simple tool for business and profits' (Osava, 2001; see also Stedile, 2004: 34).

These tensions suggest some of the conflictual maps of grievance that are constructed through the politics of counter-globalization movements. The tensions between Bové and Stedile over subsidies and world trade signal some of the key ways in which opposition to neo-liberal globalization constructs resistance on different terms. Thus Bové and Stedile mobilize different maps of grievance in relation to neo-liberal globalization. For Stedile, it is important to protect the nation through the generation of subsidies (though the MST hasn't necessarily constructed exclusionary versions of the nation in relation to globalization as some other movements have; see chapter 7). The terms through which these antagonisms are constructed, and the geographies of these antagonisms, then, are multiple and contested. Rather than there being a spontaneous 'resistance' to 'Empire' which automatically links different struggles, the terms on which neo-liberal globalization is brought into contestation can themselves be the source of contestation and also different forms of agency can be constituted through these different practices. This section explores the relations between the way geographies of power are brought into contestation and the political identities produced through the activity of these movements. It then engages with the contested power relations within these movements, especially relating to tensions over race, gender and ethnicity. It argues that there are strong connections between the terms on which neo-liberal globalization is contested and these tensions.

Confédération Paysanne has been active in articulating the grievances of French peasants/small farmers in inventive ways. It has been active in the opposition to intensive farming and to the existing form of the Common Agricultural Policy. It has also unsettled a tendency to present opposition to junk food in terms of an exclusionary French nationalism. A particularly significant issue here is the ways in which Bové differentiates his politics from 'chauvinist' opposition to globalization. He argues against chauvinist opposition to globalization, arguing that 'their idea of sovereignty relates to the nation-state, and theirs is a selfish, frightened and irrational response'. As an alternative to such a bounded, exclusionary opposition to globalization, he argues for a 'concept of sovereignty' which 'enables people to think for themselves, without any imposed model for agriculture or society, and to live in solidarity with each other'. Further, he argues against a fetishization of the national or local. 'The globalization of trade must be counteracted on the same level – that is to say, on a world scale rather than on a narrow-minded nation-state basis. Nationalists worry about the mixing of races, whereas we welcome fair trade, cultural exchange and solidarity: we stand for a dignified and free life under real democracy' (Bové and Dufour, 2001: 159; see also Massey, 2005: 169–72).

Bové's account here gives a rather neat sense of there being two different kinds of opposition to neo-liberal globalization: exclusionary versions of 'nationalist' opposition to globalization and a more progressive, multifaceted opposition which rejects alternatives based around a narrow articulation of the nation-state. Bové's distinction is important and necessary in political terms, and highlights the ongoing contestation over the different terms on which neo-liberal globalization is opposed. There is also a tension here. That is that the overlapping networks through which counter-globalization movements are constituted bring together different groups/identities which shape very different politics in opposition to globalization. In line with the argument of chapter 5, different movements also articulate very different versions of the nation in relation to globalization. Morris-Suzuki notes that 'while some movements try to forge new identities and to win recognition for suppressed forms of knowledge, others seek to buttress existing national or ethnic barriers and to reassert established certainties' (Morris-Suzuki, 2000: 82). What is significant about the counter-globalization movements is that often these different forms of identities coexist within these overlapping networks. Thus Vandana Shiva's appeals to a bounded, exclusionary version of the Indian past can coexist with the

EZLN or Bové's appeals for a rejection of chauvinistic, nationalist opposition to globalization (on Shiva, see Mawdsley, 2006). The 'process geographies' of these overlapping networks will be explored in depth in the next chapter (Routledge, 2003).

Such exclusionary forms of resistance to globalization have structured different forms of political activity. It hasn't only been movements in the global South that have opposed globalization through exclusionary forms of nationalisms and localism, as sometimes is implied. One of the contexts for Bové's arguments is the mobilization of grievances against globalization in racist, chauvinistic ways by the Front National in France. The rightist forms of opposition to the North American Free Trade Agreement (NAFTA) in the US have likewise mobilized racist, exclusionary nationalist arguments (see Sparke, 2005: 177). Geographies of exclusion have shaped the political activity of these movements in more subtle and mundane ways. This raises significant questions about how the geographies of power produced through the activity of these movements/networks are negotiated and generated.

The networked opposition to globalization associated with counter-globalization movements has deployed and generated innovative forms of political activity and organization. These forms of organization are integral to the political alternatives being generated through these movements. As David Graeber has argued, 'this is a movement about reinventing democracy':

> It is not opposed to organization. It is about creating new forms of organization. It is about creating and enacting horizontal networks instead of top-down structures like states, parties or corporations; networks based on principles of decentralized, non-hierarchical consensus democracy. (Graeber, 2004: 212)

Autonomous forms of organization such as the affinity group, a key form of movement organizing, however, have often been fetishized as free of contaminating power relations (see also Pickerill and Chatterton, 2006). These concerns are central to debates over the ways in which the political practices of counter-globalization movements negotiate geographies of power through their organizing practices.

One of the tensions that has arisen in relation to these forms of organizing has been their fragmentary ways of dealing with and negotiating unequal relations of power within these movements through their activity. Stephanie Ross has been particularly incisive around some of the tensions produced by the anarchist insistence on the 'autonomy to make local decisions' (Ross, 2003: 290). Ross usefully illustrates how constructions of autonomy can allow leadership practices, such as key spatial practices like decisions over locations of actions, to be denied. In this she highlights a significant dilemma. It is not leadership practices themselves that are necessarily problematic, but the denial of their existence, since this 'results in leadership unbound by structures of accountability, and/or the castigation of those who take on necessary leadership functions' (Ross, 2003: 294). This also has significant implications for the formation of a transnational opposition to neo-liberal globalization, based on alliances between different place-based struggles. As Ross argues, an insistence 'on absolute freedom from higher levels of legitimate authority and decision-making can have serious negative consequences, both for effectiveness and for the democratic capacities of others' (Ross, 2003: 290).

The organizing practices of these movements have been brought into contestation in various ways, particularly in the US, in relation to issues of race and gender. In the wake of the Seattle protests, for example, Elizabeth Martinez published an article entitled 'Where was the color in Seattle?' Martinez's article, while engaging positively with the protests, suggested that activist subcultures were constituted through exclusionary forms of whiteness and failed to make connections between local and transnational issues. She argued that these tensions were exacerbated through use of the internet to mobilize for the protests, as this failed to broaden the constituency involved, given the unequal access to the internet, particularly among poor black and Hispanic communities in the US (Martinez, 2000). Martinez's critique of the Seattle protests has in turn been the subject of critique. Amory Starr, for example, has contested many of the key points in Martinez's article. Starr claims, for instance, that she 'cannot find a single piece of data from the anti-globalization movement that suggests anybody is not interested in making connections between international injustices and domestic ones' (Starr, 2003: 272). She also implies that the 'race' issue has become mobilized, not as part of a project to contest inequalities within the movement, but as a form of sectarianism (Starr, 2003: 273). In her prescriptions for action she suggests the importance of dealing with 'specific incidents', but isolates these questions from the broader ways in which these activist subcultures are constituted.

Martinez's article moved the discussion on, however, from considering not only the presence/absence of activists of colour, or specific incidents, through discussing the potentially exclusionary organizing practices and activist subcultures. These tensions have also been raised in relation to how they impact on ways in which grievances are constructed. In a discussion of the relationship between the Coke boycott and activism of color, for example, Ashwini Hardikar argues of the coalition she was involved in at the University of Michigan:

> Although the coalition looks very 'representative' – that is, students of color and womyn are at the center of the coalition – the process through which the coalition was built over the period of a year has been a point of contention

among some. I do believe that this campaign was initiated with the intention of synthesizing anti-racism and anti-globalization struggles, yet to some the outreach and coalition-building process seemed to put the racist aspects of Coke's violations as more of an afterthought rather than at the center of the movement. (Hardikar, 2006: n.p.)

Hardikar's analysis of the process of coalition building against Coke usefully indicates that even when coalitions look 'representative', practices of marginalization can still exert pressure on the ways through which maps of grievance are shaped and defined. Thus she argues that the coalition didn't make anti-racism central to the contestation of Coca-Cola, and that there was a disjuncture between the anti-racist and anti-globalization aspects of the coalition. In similar terms, Mohanty (2003) has argued that these movements have tended not to make the unequal gender relations that are produced and reproduced through neo-liberalism central to their analysis.

These movements are positioned in relation to shifting definitions of whiteness which structure the identities of alternative political movements in the US. As Fletcher and Gapasin argue in an incisive account of the politics of labour and race in the US, 'race has been the trip-wire of progressive and radical movements in the USA' (Fletcher and Gapasin, 2003: 246). They problematize 'US labour's historical tendency to define its constituency in exclusively "white" terms', which they argue 'has been one of the greatest limitations on US trade unionism' (Fletcher and Gapasin, 2003: 246; see also Du Bois, 1972; Ignatiev, 1996). The significance and legacy of these exclusionary geographies of labour organizing have been underplayed in the emerging 'new labour geography' (see Herod, 2001; though see also Jepson, 2005). It is precisely the continuing importance of such histories and geographies of political activity and their generative impact on the forms of organizing and political identity that are closed down by Hardt and Negri's amorphous construction of the 'multitude'. To engage with the diverse forms of opposition to neo-liberal globalization that are being constituted it is necessary to follow and interrogate the histories and geographies of these trajectories of political activity. It is also necessary to explore the generative, multiple and contested effects when political trajectories shaped through different political cultures coalesce.

One of the key contributions of the counter-globalization movement has to form spaces through which different movements come together, on at least potentially equal terms. This involves the negotiation of the unequal geographies of power that structure emerging transnational spaces of politics, riven as they are by exclusionary visa regulations and unequal access to mobilities. There have, however, been attempts to challenge rather than reproduce these uneven geographies of power within the organizing practices of the counter-globalization movements. Thus there was early contestation of the limited geographical range of participants in the first and second World Social Forums. At the second World Social Forum, for example, only 15,000 out of 80,000 participants were from outside Latin America, and there was poor representation of Asian/African organizations (Waterman, 2003; see also Sparke et al., 2005). Thus it was decided to make the 2006 World Social Forum 'polycentric' and to hold it in Bamako (Mali), Caracas and Karachi. As Mustafa argues, dispersing the meetings 'has made the forum more accessible, as has its unstructured format that is not hierarchical' (Mustafa, 2006: n.p.).

These attempts to disperse the meetings were also attempts to deal with some of the tensions that emerged through the rapid growth of the WSF. Peter Waterman argued of the 2003 Forum that it 'is too big; it is lacking in openness, transparency and accountability' and 'thus, it reproduces the traditional politics of party and "bingo" (big international non-governmental organizations) alike' (Waterman, 2003: n.p.; see also Klein, 2003). Despite these tensions in the organizing of the WSF, Waterman argues that the mushrooming of the WSF is also producing creative possibilities. He suggests the 'centre (its initiators) can no longer control the process they themselves invented and developed, now that the idea of social forums is out of the bottle and subject to numerous and varied, local or specific . . . claims, forms and inflections' (Waterman, 2003: n.p.). As the WSF process moves with the emerging regional versions it is also producing some interesting political subjectivities and possibilities. These possibilities were celebrated by a feminist and ex-member of the Indian Communist Party (ML) who attended the 2003 Asian Social Forum in Mumbai, who affirmed the importance of moving beyond the rigidities of 'formal ideologies'. She argued that such ideologies 'had been suffocating, as it quelled difference of opinion, debate and transformation' and affirmed the way it 'gave the space to form new alliances, shape new formulations, design new approaches, and maybe even new theories to underpin all the alternatives' (cited by Jain, 2003: 100).

This emphasizes the productiveness of the articulations and solidarities generated through these movements. The coming together of different movements, alliances and articulations can generate new forms of political identities, and practices and solidarities are generated. As well as some of the tensions and inequalities that I have foregrounded in this section, this can be productive. In an account of the transnational alliances formed in opposition to NAFTA, which brought together Canadian, Mexican and US activists, Cavanagh et al. quote a Mexican activist who commented that before the 'trinational work on NAFTA, he saw Canadians as simply gringos in overcoats' (Cavanagh et al., 2001: 156). They also note how the transnational networks of opposition to NAFTA unsettled a discourse around 'national' sovereignty, which raised serious questions about whether

US activists 'would be willing to accept a supranational body that may at times rule against the United States' (Cavanagh et al., 2001: 155). In this way these alliances brought into contestation the unequal geographies of power that shape opposition to neo-liberalisms. These solidarities thus reshaped the maps of grievance constituted through opposition to NAFTA, challenging opposition based around narrow defences of US sovereignty (see also Danaher, 2001: 198–204).

This section has developed a concern with the multiple and contested political identities produced through opposition to neo-liberal globalization. It has dislocated Hardt and Negri's work in two major respects. Firstly, it has demonstrated the necessity of thinking about the dynamic trajectories of political activity out of which counter-globalization networks are constituted. It has argued that it is partly through interrogating the generative effects of the coming together of these trajectories that the productive character of these forms of politics can be foregrounded. Secondly, it has foregrounded the multiple and contested identities which are produced through these practices, which are again closed down by the forms of radical immanence favoured by Hardt and Negri.

The final section of the chapter develops the theoretical implications of these concerns with the relations between space, politics and the formation of collective political identities through turning to Ernesto Laclau's work on populism.

Populist Logics and the Construction of Maps of Grievance

The preceding section examined the different political identities constituted through counter-global networks of opposition to neo-liberal globalization. I have argued that these movements construct particular maps of grievance and also generate contested geographies of power through their organizing practices. This section explores the practices through which these identifications are made and the effects they have on the formation of political identities. It does this through examining how maps of grievance are mobilized through constructing particular 'populist logics'. Ernesto Laclau has used a focus on the constitution of populist logics to address precisely the kinds of questions about the constitution of collective political identities that Hardt and Negri evade (see also Laclau, 2005a: 239–44). Laclau, however, like most political theorists who have addressed populism as a serious political set of practices, theorizes populism within a restrictively nation-centred account of the political. I argue that following the different populist logics at work in the politics of the counter-globalization movement permits a different geography of populist logics to emerge. I use this to offer a distinctive account of the relations between space, the political and the formation of collective political identities. The section concludes by arguing for an engagement with the terms on which such populist logics are constructed, rather than a dismissal of populist articulations of grievances *per se*.

In *On Populist Reason* Laclau develops an analysis of the constitution of what he terms 'populist logics' to understand the formation of collective political identities. In contrast to Hardt and Negri, who he argues dissolve the question of the formation of collective political identities into the 'multitude', he argues for the necessity of understanding the formation of collective political identities (Laclau, 2005a: 239–44). This emerges from Laclau's concern to theorize the logics through which populist political articulations are made, rather than merely engage with the actual forms of politics that get labelled populist (Laclau, 1977, 2005a, 2005b). This leads Laclau to adopt a definition of populism as the practices through which politicized notions of the 'people' are constituted. He argues that populism 'means putting into question the institutional order by constructing an underdog as an historical agent – i.e. an agent which is an other in relation to the way things stand' (Laclau, 2005b: 47). Laclau contends that populism is not an irrational set of practices that somehow undermines more rational, coherent forms of political conduct (see also Arditi, 2005; Canovan, 1999; Panizza, 2005). Rather, he insists that all politics contains a populist dimension. 'No political movement will be entirely exempt from populism', Laclau avers, because 'none will fail to interpellate to some extent the "people" against an enemy through the construction of a social frontier' (Laclau, 2005b: 47). The necessary analytical question in Laclau's terms becomes not 'are movements populist?' but 'to what extent is a political movement populist?' 'The degree of populism' in Laclau's terms depends on the 'depth of the chasm separating political alternatives' (Laclau, 2005b: 47).

Laclau proposes an analysis of populism based around the following three elements. He argues that populism needs to be understood as an ensemble of relations of 'equivalences, popular subjectivity, dichotomic construction of the social around an internal frontier' (Laclau, 2005b: 38). For Laclau, notions of popular subjectivity, politicized constructions of the people, are constituted through drawing an internal frontier through the construction of 'equivalential logics'. Here the relational constitution of political identities is decisive. As I noted in chapter 5, Laclau argues that the 'meaning' of any given political practice such as populism or nationalism will 'vary depending on the chain of equivalences associated with it' (Laclau, 2005a: 227). Further, he argues for an understanding of populism as an 'empty and floating signifier' (see Laclau, 2005b: 38–43). For Laclau, populism is not a politics with a positive content, such as claims for particular rights. Rather, it is a set of practices, ways of doing politics, that can be taken up by different political movements (see also Kazin, 1995).

These concerns about the formation of populist logics speak to some of the key tensions that have arisen in the movements against neo-liberal globalization. There are the constitution of various 'underdogs' and oppressed groups against common enemies. There is the interpellation of various groups as part of this common set of resistances. There is the mobilization of these grievances by particular charismatic figures/leaders. Despite the significance of non-hierarchical forms of mobilization to the political identities and practices of those involved in these movements, certain charismatic leadership figures such as José Bové, George Monbiot, Vandana Shiva, and Professor Nanjundaswamy of the KRRS have been significant. Chapter 7 develops an engagement with some of the implications of their leadership practices. As the preceding discussion has emphasized, there are key differences in the ways in which these friend/enemy distinctions are mobilized. One of the key differences here has been around the often conflicting maps of grievance constructed through their political activity. Thus Bové has argued for the significance of a transnational resistance to globalization eschewing 'chauvinistic nationalism', a project also signalled by the slogan 'our resistance is as transnational as capital'. Others have argued for a much more nationalist construction of political opposition to neo-liberal projects like NAFTA (see also Greenfield, 2005). Vandana Shiva has mobilized around a rather atavistic, and potentially very exclusionary, celebration of past social/ecological relations (see Mawdsley, 2006; Shiva et al., 1997). To make sense of the relations between these maps of grievance and the formation of distinctive populist logics it is necessary to interrogate the spatial practices through which populist logics are constituted.

Political theorists have tended to theorize populism as being constituted 'within the bounds of national traditions' (Kazin, 1995: 289). Laclau's accounts of the formation of populist logics in *On Populist Reason*, for example, are all constituted within the framework of the nation-state (Laclau, 2005a; see also Laclau, 1977, 2005b). Arditi's thoughtful account of populism as a 'shadow of democracy' shares this nation-centred framework. He argues for an account of 'the populist experience as an *internal periphery* of liberal-democratic politics' (Arditi, 2005: 77, emphasis in original). For Arditi, however, such an internal periphery exists within the bounds of already constituted nation-states. This obscures the ways in which populist logics and particular spatial practices are co-produced. This widespread assumption that populist political practices are mobilized through the bounded geographies of national politics has effects. It obscures both the role of populist practices in reinforcing the nation as central to political activity and forms of populist political practice that stretch beyond the confines of the nation-state. A more plural sense of the populist articulations of grievances emerges if the relation between populist articulations and nation-centred accounts of politics is dislocated.

If political theorists have been uninterested in the geographies of populism, political geographers have displayed a profound lack of interest in populism. Sparke's account of the 'rise of Perot's populist anti-free trade movement in the US' is instructive here (Sparke, 2005: 166). Sparke's use of the term 'populist' is limited to a reproach for the politics of those like Ross Perot or Pat Buchanan who produced a starkly exclusionary US nationalist opposition to NAFTA. He uses the term merely as a dismissive label rather than a term with analytical power. Further, Sparke doesn't explicitly theorize the geographies through which these populist articulations of grievance are constituted. These tensions are also present in Erik Swyngedouw's discussion of Laclau, Žižek and Mouffe's various theoretical interventions around populism (Swyngedouw, 2007). Swyngedouw usefully signals the importance of these interventions for debates on the relations between space and politics, but reproduces the nation-centred account of the political that frames these interventions. He also follows Žižek's problematic critique of Laclau for adopting a focus on the construction of populist logics as a deviation from engaging with the 'proper' politics of class struggle (Swyngedouw, 2007; see Žižek, 2005).

What then are the geographies through which populist logics are constructed? Further, what difference does it make to think explicitly about the relations between spatialities and populist articulations of grievances? As the preceding sections of this chapter have demonstrated, different movements construct political identities through bringing into question the power relations shaping neo-liberal globalization. These movements have constructed populist logics in Laclau's sense. They have radically put into question the institutional order of neo-liberal globalization and constructed the ways in which globalization is generated and produced in antagonistic terms. Further, these movements have interpellated diverse political subjects as part of a common opposition to neo-liberal globalization. To examine the political geographies through which these populist logics are constructed, however, dislocates some of the key terms of Laclau's account of the constitution of populist logics. Here I am not attempting to say that these are populist movements, but rather I think it is useful to explore the populist logics constructed through their political activity. Exploring the spatial practices through which populist logics are formed can help interrogate the different collective political identities and articulations constituted in relation to neo-liberal globalization. This has the following key elements.

Firstly, following the ways in which opposition to globalization is mobilized emphasizes that the articulation of grievances through 'national' terms through populist discourses is not inevitable. The articulation of such grievances within the 'bounds of particular national traditions' is actively produced through distinctive spatial practices. The practices through which national spaces, and imaginations of national political traditions, such as E. P. Thompson's invocation of English democracy in his account of the London Corresponding Society, are productive (see also Schwarz, 1982: 88–9).[89] Through such articulations populism, nationalism and spatial relations become recursively constituted. Arguably, the extent to which the national is taken for granted in the theorizing of populism is a testament to how powerful populist practices have been at equating their forms of political practice with the nation.

The exclusionary construction of the nation through populist logics in relation to globalization can be demonstrated through Ross Perot's rhetoric against NAFTA. During his campaigns against NAFTA he subsumed fears of 'threatened American employment . . . into the larger fearful discourse about a looming loss of American jobs south of the border' through dubbing this 'the giant sucking sound' (Sparke, 2005: 133). This metaphor dramatizes the significance and precariousness of the US border, making it both a site of political contestation and a site of anxiety and tension. It also constructs enemies, in this case Mexican immigrant workers who are 'taking US jobs' aided and abetted by NAFTA. If such 'national' geographies of populism are not analysed but are seen as 'natural', the work that populist articulations of grievances do in constructing exclusionary spaces of the nation through opposition to 'globalization' can be missed. Further, this can close down the extent to which different, more politically plural and progressive versions of the nation can be mobilized through populist logics/practices and how this can become contested through different forms of opposition to globalization. It can also close down engagement with the frequently regressive gender and race politics co-constituted with such bounded articulations of the nation.

Secondly, Laclau's analysis moves towards a practice-based account of the formation of populist logics. This is a significant break with the work of theorists like Canovan who have advocated a more structuralist approach to understanding populist politics (Canovan, 1999). Following the spatial practices through which populist political logics are constituted, however, can be very disruptive of nation-state centred accounts of the political. The discussion in this chapter of opposition to genetically modified seeds and the Coke boycott has demonstrated how political activity spills out of, refuses and exceeds the confining spaces of, the nation-state. Following the resistance to neo-liberal globalization, then, produces radically different spatialities of contestation than Laclau's nation-centred account. As I argued in chapter 2, thinking the construction of antagonisms spatially means attending to the multiple, differentiated geographies of contestation through which political identities are constructed.

Thirdly, as the discussion of the solidarities between Bové and MST demonstrates, these populist logics are made through political practices that mobilize heterogeneous associations of humans and non-humans. This is disruptive of the notion of practice that informs Laclau's account of populist logics. It demonstrates, paradoxically, that politicized notions of 'the people' are rarely produced in purified ways, but rather are often constituted through mobilizing particular relations between humans and non-humans. This can work in different ways. During the BSE crisis in the spring and summer of 1996, as Bill Schwarz has evocatively noted, 'the imagined frontiers of the English nation were marked out in the traffic of gelatin, tallow and bull semen' (Schwarz, 1997: 25). Indian opposition to genetically modified seeds, as I will argue in the next chapter, has often mobilized an exclusionary nationalist opposition to such seeds, constructing them as a threat to 'the nation'. The alliances between Bové and MST signal more productive possibilities for the constitution of populist logics through particular articulations of heterogeneous associations. They demonstrate how producing heterogeneous associations on different terms to those envisioned by neo-liberal conventions and principles can be at stake through opposition to globalization. Further, these different articulations of associations between humans and non-humans can be the grounds on which friend-enemy relations are constituted.

Fourthly, following these practices through which maps of grievance are constructed foregrounds the dynamic, ongoing construction of populist logics. This permits a focus on constructions of 'the people', of collective identities, that aren't tied restrictively to notions of 'the nation'. This has resources for disrupting the tendency for 'the nation' to become 'the only way to imagine community' (Hardt and Negri, 2001: 107). Where Bové and activists involved in opposing NAFTA shift the terms of debate from 'national sovereignty' to 'popular sovereignty' they are producing very different populist logics through very different maps of grievance. These maps of grievance construct 'the people' through mobilizing opposition to common enemies that stretch beyond the nation-state, such as neo-liberal institutions and particular multinational companies. This opens up possibilities for experimenting with forms of collective political identity which reject nation-centred opposition to globalization, but which are also situated, partial and collective, in contra-distinction to Hardt and Negri's account of the multitude.

For critics on the 'left', populism is frequently a 'reproach' (see Brass, 2000; Sparke, 2005; Swyngedouw, 2007). Thus Žižek argues that the 'main task of today's emancipatory politics, its life-and-death problem, is to find a form of political mobilization that, while (like populism) critical of institutionalized politics, will *avoid* the populist temptation' (Žižek, 2005: n.p.; emphasis in original). Surely a politics that seeks to purify itself of any populist forms of articulation, however, represents a retreat into élitism or vanguardism (see also Laclau, 1977: 196–7). I contend that rather than simply dismissing these movements as 'populist', a useful intervention can be made through following the ways in which these populist logics are articulated. For it is through transnational articulations of popu-list alternatives that some of the exclusionary nationalisms that structure the opposition to neo-liberalisms are being challenged. By engaging with the innovative spatial practices through which these movements have refused exclusionary oppositions to globalization, left theorizing can con-tribute to the shaping of these alternatives in plural and productive ways.

Conclusions

This chapter has interrogated the relations between counter-global net-works and neo-liberal geographies of power. I have traced some of the practices through which these movements have brought neo-liberalization into contestation. I have argued that this has had effects. Counter-globalization movements have made the relations between neo-liberalism and globalization part of the terrain of contestation. Through this process they have also generated multi-facetted, transnational forms of organizing that have delineated alternative ways of generating globalized practices. I have argued, however, that these relations to neo-liberal geographies of power are not uncontested. I have sought to make differences in the way these geographies of power are contested, and the multiple geographies of power generated through these forms of organizing, central to the account of these movements.

I have argued that Hardt and Negri's account of the multitude, while giving a useful sense of the generative character of these movements, is ultimately problematic. It evades many of the key tensions being generated through these movements, and also makes it hard to see the agency of these movements, such as the shaping of distinctive maps of grievance. To engage with these tensions I have drawn on Laclau's arguments about the constitution of populist logics. The chapter has emphasized that if a defini-tion of populism as the articulation of different political identities in relation to common enemies is adopted, then the formation of populist logics, is central to the activity of the counter-globalization movement. It is these practices through which different political identities are brought together which will be crucial in shaping what kinds of collective political identities and alternatives are shaped through the interventions of different counter-globalization movements. Through linking the constitution of populist logics with the formation of distinctive maps of grievance, I have sought to intervene in these relations between space, power and political identity. The next chapter develops these concerns through a detailed account of one set of transnational alliances, the Inter-Continental Caravan.

Chapter Seven

Constructing Transnational Political Networks

In late May 1999 the Nuffield Council on Bioethics released a report which concluded that there was a 'moral imperative' for research and development of genetically modified crops because of their potential 'to conquer world hunger' (*Guardian* 28/5/99; see Nuffield Foundation, 1999). The report mobilized a very particular story about the global South to justify its support for genetically modified crops. It argued that these crops had the potential to be a technical fix for 'world hunger'. Though the report mobilized a strong argument in favour of the benefits of genetically modified crops for the South, it made no attempt to consult with Southern actors in reaching this decision. Perspectives from the global South had also been absent from the expert process and panel that had formulated the report's recommendations (see also Levidow, 2001).

It would be usual for the mobilization of the 'South' in such an official report to remain uncontested. On the day the report was released a number of Indian farmers associated with the BKU, together with UK anti-GM activists, gathered outside the Nuffield Foundation's headquarters in Bedford Square, London. They watched and chanted as some of the Indian delegation and a small number of UK activists jostled past bemused security guards into the building. Between fifty and a hundred activists waited outside for the delegation to emerge. Musicians from 'Seize the Day!' performed their anti-Monsanto anthem 'Food "n" Health "n" Hope'. The Indian activists contested the uncritical version of relations with the 'South' that had been mobilized in the report to support the development of biotechnology (Ainger, 2003). They also criticized the way that although the 'South' had been powerfully mobilized in the report, 'Third World' perspectives had been absent from the expert process and panel that had formulated the report's line. The delegation told the Nuffield Foundation:

> We will not let your corporations justify genetic engineering with the lie that it will alleviate the suffering, dispossession and poverty that these same corporations are responsible for. (Cited by *Do or Die*, 1999: 98)

The activists asked for a consultancy fee for their advice. They emerged and joined London-based activists in chanting anti-WTO slogans on the steps of the Nuffield Foundation, connecting the action to a wider critique of neo-liberal globalization.

This action against the Nuffield Foundation took place as part of the Inter-Continental Caravan (ICC), an ambitious project which united activists from the Indian New Farmers Movements with West European green activists in contesting neo-liberal institutions and biotechnology. The event was not part of the planned activity of the Caravan, but rather the Nuffield Foundation became a site of grievance during the Caravan's stay in London. In terms of media coverage this action had a low profile, but it brought vehement opposition to the report to the Foundation's headquarters. It dragged this organization, which through its report had deftly constructed itself as a 'neutral and objective body', into a terrain of active political contestation. It produced a challenge to the stories about the South being mobilized through the report. Further, rather than articulating genetic modification as a threat to an imagined purity of intrinsic natures, it contested the power relations through which genetically modified crops were produced. The character of this contestation was distinctively located at the intersections of routes of political activity and alliances between Indian farmers and anti-GM activists in Western Europe. In this way these inter-relations were productive. They changed the terms on which the Nuffield Foundation's report was being challenged, and articulated a transnational opposition to genetically modified agriculture.

This event introduces the key themes of this chapter. The chapter focuses in-depth on the Inter-Continental Caravan to explore the productive geographies through which transnational alliances are made. It also explores how the practices through which geographies of power are made sense of have effects on the making of political identities and the conduct of solidarities. The chapter begins by outlining the Caravan project and relating it to the shifting maps of grievance of the different movements involved in the project. It then argues that the productive alliances produced through the Caravan unsettle the way transnational forms of political activity have been theorized. It then explores aspects of the conduct of the Caravan. Firstly, I engage with the 'process geographies' through which the Caravan was constituted (Routledge, 2003). I then explore the contested and productive outcomes of the Caravan project.

The Inter-Continental Caravan

The Caravan project brought to Western Europe '450 representatives of grassroots movements from the South and East of the world', including 400 drawn from the Indian New Farmers Movements (People's Global Action, 1999a). There were also a small number of activists from outside India, including from MST and the Nepali human rights organization INHURED. The project, initiated by the Gandhian influenced Karnataka State Farmers Union (KRRS), sought to foster solidarities between different counter-globalization movements. The Caravan shaped alliances that were defined by collective mobilization and joint actions against transnational capital and agribusiness. It was structured by a desire to 'link North and South not by the usual calls for solidarity with the South, but by a campaign against common enemies (with the South helping the North more than the reverse!)' (ICC, 1999b: n.p.). These vibrant solidarities produced through the ICC were constituted through antagonistic relations with the emerging spatialities of neo-liberal globalization. The project emerged from transnational networks of resistance to neo-liberal globalization, which have been strongly influenced by the Zapatistas. The stories activists themselves told about the ICC's formation focused on the catalysing role of the Zapatistas and their support networks.[90] The transnational support networks of the Zapatistas produced People's Global Action Against Free Trade (PGA), the network of counter-globalization movements that convened the Caravan.

The PGA network is defined by 'a rejection of reformist, NGO-style "top down" approaches to resistance' (Townes, 1999; see also Routledge, 2003). It draws on the involvement of major grassroots movements of the South such as the KRRS and the Brazilian land rights campaign Movimento Sem Terra, as well as movements from the North such as Reclaim the Streets and the French peasant organization Confédération Paysanne. The Caravan project was decisively shaped by the KRRS, which has led an anti-neo-liberal articulation of Indian farmers' grievances (Assadi, 1995b: 218–19; 1997). These alliances have begun a collective experiment with the kinds of organizational forms and practices and activities that might generate an internationalist opposition to globalization. They have experimented with forms of solidarity that might produce and generate joint actions between movements from different political traditions.

That the project was defined by spatially stretched and multiple trajectories of resistance posed challenges for the research. I was concerned to engage with the activity of these networks rather than to conduct interviews or focus groups outside the context of such activity (see della Porta and Mosca, 2007; della Porta, 2005). It was not possible or desirable to seek a position outside of these multiple networks. Rather, taking on Latour's argument that even long networks remain local at all points, it was necessary to become part of the ongoing activity of these networks (Latour, 1993: 117–19). Thus the research was initially based around attending meetings of the London Welcoming Committee (LWC), one hub of the ICC networks. This chapter also draws on participation in ICC events in London and Cologne. This specific site in the activity of the formation of the Caravan was constituted through interrelations with London-based activist networks. Being part of the committee's often-chaotic and vitriolic meetings enabled engagement with how this particular site of action negotiated and generated differences and tensions. Attending these meetings and taking notes on how key issues were negotiated enabled a stress on how these practices are constitutive of political identities. It also allowed a distinctive engagement with how these transnational networks were constituted.

These transnational networks and identifications emerged from common involvement in campaigns against genetically modified agriculture and globalization that utilized tactics of non-violent direct action. The KRRS was seen by many London activists as an organization with its 'credentials intact' (Townes, 1999: n.p.). The KRRS thus was recognized by activists in London and elsewhere as involved in similar and inspiring struggles against neo-liberal globalization. The organization's high-profile opposition to the Dunkel Draft of the Uruguay round of GATT in 1993 had attracted international acclaim among activists outside India (Assadi, 1995a: 194; Escobar, 2001; Townes, 1999). This strategy represented a significant shift in the way that the movement constructed maps of grievances, from targeting rural-urban division in India to contesting transnational power relations. Similar acclaim followed for assaults on the Cargill Seed Factories and Kentucky Fried Chicken outlets. Their 1998 Cremate Monsanto! Action, when activists burned a crop of genetically modified cotton, was widely publicized through email networks. The KRRS's longstanding leader Professor Nanjundaswamy articulated these actions as a legitimate form of 'Gandhian violence'. These acts explicitly linked opposition to neo-liberal globalization with opposition to genetic modification and bio-technological innovations (Nanjundaswamy, 1998, 2003). Through their opposition to neo-liberal globalization, the KRRS have become progressively linked to other counter-globalization struggles (see Desmarais, 2002: 112; Starr, 2000: 71).

The activity of the KRRS in contesting neo-liberal institutions and forms of globalization was an intervention in the political identities and imaginations of power of the Indian New Farmers Movements. The New Farmers Movements came to prominence in the 1970s and 1980s. The KRRS was founded in 1980. These movements attempted to redraw the lines of political antagonism in rural India through mobilizing a distinction between the countryside and a corrupt and exploitative urban India (Brass, 1995; Bentall and Corbridge, 1996). They have constructed this antagonism through denoting the countryside as '*Bharat*', or India, and in doing so have produced an exclusionary elision between the nation and the countryside. As Omvedt argues, 'rather than organizing wage-earners against property owning employers they have organized entire village communities against the state' (Omvedt, 1995: 126). These movements have drawn on the practices and idioms of Gandhian mass action and on powerful symbolic narratives which celebrate an authentic Gandhian Indian countryside where the village is the appropriate unit of political organization. Nanjundaswamy has referred to the movement both as a 'village movement' and as 'a movement for independence' (Krishnarajulu, 1986: 31).

These movements are uneven and differentiated. The support of some movements, such as the Bharatia Kisan Union in Uttar Pradesh, is drawn predominantly from particular caste constituencies (Bentall and Corbridge, 1996: 34; Gupta, 1997: 60–1). Their forms of mobilization have tended to ignore differences within the village. Thus Assadi argues that although 'there was a strong influence of socialist ideology' on the leaders of the KRRS, they believed that the interests of the rural poor could 'be best served in organizing the peasantry and not by splitting it into its various sections' (Assadi, 1997: 41). This position, however, has been contested. Further, the New Farmers Movements have tended to ignore the grievances of landless labourers and those from lower castes, and in particular contexts to be actively hostile towards them (see Assadi, 1995b; Brass, 1995; Gupta, 1997; Lerche, 1999). Thus Gupta states it is easier for Tikait, leader of the BKU, 'to stand shoulder-to-shoulder with the Muslims of West UP than with the Scheduled Castes of the village, such as the Harijans and the Valmikis'. Further, he argues that the BKU has not said anything 'about uplifting the ex-untouchables or even the landless labourers' (Gupta, 1997: 60).

Through the 1990s there was a key shift in the maps of grievance of the KRRS. The KRRS targeted key neo-liberal political projects, particularly the Dunkel Draft of GATT. This emphasizes how the articulation of friend-enemy relations can be continually formed through activity. The KRRS led vociferous opposition to the Dunkel Draft, forming alliances with Mahendra Singh Tikait of the BKU Uttar Pradesh and the BKU Punjab (Assadi, 1995a: 194). This articulation of Indian farmers' politics against neo-liberal globalization was neither inevitable nor uncontested. Sharad Joshi, the leader of the Maharashtra-based Shetkari Sanghatana, supported the Dunkel Draft, arguing that 'the interests of the Multi-National Corporations and the farmers coincide' (Joshi, interview with Bentall, 1996: 298). The opposition of the KRRS to neo-liberal projects like the Dunkel Draft was articulated through opposing the way they envision the control and regulation of seeds.

The KRRS organized mass mobilizations such as the 'seed satyagraha'[91] in Bangalore on 2 October 1993, attended by a *lakh* (a hundred thousand) of farmers. Speakers at the rally argued that the proposals of the Dunkel Draft to allow private companies to patent seeds 'would have devastating effects on their livelihoods in general and on their control of seeds in particular' (Rane, 1993). A declaration read out at the rally argued:

> We do not recognize intellectual property rights on biological materials being granted to companies for their private profits. The knowledge on which crops to plant and on which seeds to use was evolved by generations of farmers and not by the corporations. Therefore we do not accept that they have a right to profit from our knowledge and our experience. Instead, we adhere to the concept of common property rights, where the right to seeds cannot be owned by private companies. Seeds should be allowed to be exchanged freely among farmers in the country and the world, as has been the practice till now. (Cited by Rane, 1993)

The opposition to proposals for patenting seeds in the Dunkel Draft was articulated through a defence and mobilization of unofficial practices of exchange. The declaration emphasizes that the seeds are more than just fixed, material goods. It articulates the importance and histories of the right to craft and intervene in practices which produce seeds as part of unofficial exchanges between farmers. It also suggests that farmers produce distinctive identities in relation to these practices and that pride is produced through the skill and knowledges crafted in relation to seeds. This pride and independence is articulated by the KRRS as being threatened by attempts to patent seeds (Assadi, 1995a: 197).

Through these campaigns against the Dunkel Draft the KRRS became involved in transnational resistance networks. The KRRS was involved in the formation of People's Global Action and also became a prominent movement within Via Campesina (Desmarais, 2002). The shifting maps of grievance of the KRRS opened up possibilities for the articulation and formation of alliances with different groups campaigning against similar enemies, institutions and processes. They also brought the KRRS into contact with NGOs, campaigning groups and environmental activists such as Suman Sahai and Vandana Shiva (Assadi, 1995a; Rane, 1993). This anti-neo-liberal line of Indian Farmers Movements like the KRRS and the BKU, the national farmer's union with a strong base in Uttar Pradesh, is a particular intervention in the articulation of farmers' grievances. Other farmers' movements, notably the Maharahstra based Shetkari Sanghatana, have persistently argued that neo-liberal practices reflect the 'true interests' of farmers (Omvedt, 1991). Shetakri Sanghatana was involved in a counter-tour of ten Indian pro-biotech farmers organized by the industry lobby group EuropaBio and PR company Burson-Marsteller (*Corporate Europe Observer*, 1999). These antagonisms over the articulation of farmers' grievances thus moved the Caravan to Europe. The terms on which these antagonisms were constructed also moved.

Activists involved in the Caravan in Western Europe were similarly shaped by dynamic trajectories of political activity. Many activists were involved in various struggles against neo-liberalism. Conway has argued these had significant impacts on the emerging 'anti-globalization' movement (Conway, 2004: 995). These movements also shaped changing maps of grievance. This can be illustrated through The Land is Ours, a land rights campaign which some of the London-based activists involved in the Caravan had also been involved in. The Land is Ours shaped a politicization of land in Britain in the 1990s, trying to forge a positive political agenda for the anti-roads movement (Featherstone, 1997). The campaign's political activity had always had an internationalist edge. The high-profile occupation of a derelict site in Wandsworth, London, for example, resulted partly from the influence of MST. The MST's commitment to a strategy of 'pedagogy by example', demonstrating what can be achieved through practical alternatives, was a significant influence on The Land is Ours (Monbiot, 1998: 180; Stedile, 1999). The Caravan project, however, was productive of a shift towards more intense relationships with activists from the South defined by joint actions; these emerged particularly through opposition to transgenic seeds.

The Caravan project produced solidarities through tracing some of the key common 'enemies' of movements like the KRRS and European green and social justice activists. These enemies were contested through joint 'non-violent actions against the most important centres of power of the [European] continent' (PGA, 1999a: n.p.). The Caravan followed and intensified two key strands of resistance articulated together by organizations like the KRRS: opposition to neo-liberal globalization and to the genetic modification of plants. During the three-week project there were demonstrations and actions at key financial centres and concerted actions against genetic modification of seeds (see figure 7.1).[92]

The political activity of the Caravan thus moved as it followed different spatially constituted relations of power, making them localizable and contestable. Its political agency and identity were constructed through dragging into contestation those relations of power that are not confined within the neat boundaries of nation-states. The emergence of these transnational institutions and companies as common enemies of diverse resistance movements was a condition of possibility for the alliances that emerged through the Caravan project. These grievances were significant in that they emerged through the political activity of these diverse movements and became

Site(s) of Grievance	Date
Cargill, Amsterdam	26 May, 1999
Monsanto, Technical European Center, Louvain La Neuve, Belgium	28 May, 1999
City of London	29 May, 1999
Nuffield Foundation, London	29 May, 1999
GM Test Site, Bishop Stortford, Hertfordshire	30 May, 1999
Transgenic Colza Field near Toulouse with Confédération Paysanne	3 June, 1999
European Union Summit, Cologne	3–4 June, 1999
World Trade Organisation, Geneva	9 June, 1999
European Patent Office, Munich	16 June, 1999
Bayer Plant, Leverkusen	18 June, 1999
G8 Summit, Cologne	18-19 June, 1999

Figure 7.1   Key sites of grievance of the Inter-Continental Caravan.

established as key commonalities around which solidarities could be formed. I will discuss below in more detail the dynamics and conduct of some of these particular protests and the organizing practices of the ICC. Here, I want to explore in more depth the spatial practices through which transnational alliances are constituted. I argue that both work on resistance politics and social movements has failed to attend to the generative, contested and multiple spatial practices through which transnational solidarities are made. Interrogating these spatial practices opens up important theoretical resources for engaging with the political identities and practices constituted through these movements.

The Productive Spatialities of Counter-Global Networks

The Inter-Continental Caravan was a significant, contested and innovative project. It provides a useful case of the practices through which transnational political activity is constituted. Detailed accounts of these spatial practices have in the main been absent from recent work on the geographies of resistance and in relation to social movement theorizing (see della Porta, 2005; Miller, 2004; Tarrow, 2005; for exceptions, see Davies, forthcoming; Routledge et al., 2006; Sundberg, 2007). Here I use the Caravan to unsettle some of the key assumptions about the making of political networks and alliances and how these themes figure in recent work on transnational social movements. In this I dissent from Walter Nicholls's argument that it is adequate merely to add geographical concerns onto understandings of existing processes identified by social movement theory (Nicholls, 2007: 607, 619; see also Miller, 2000). This section explores some key tensions in recent literature on the construction of transnational activist networks. It sets up the core themes which will be worked through the engagement with the ICC. In particular it argues that the dynamic spatialities and trajectories of transnational resistances demand examination of the networks that constitute, and are constituted through, political activity. It argues for accounts of the generative, productive and contested practices through which solidarities are made and constituted. Further, it emphasizes that political activity is formed both through intervening in geographies of power and through the active negotiation of interrelations.

Chapter 2 outlined a networked account of the understanding of the formation of solidarities to move beyond the rigidities of scalar accounts of political activity. I also argued for the importance of transcending accounts of solidarities as merely the coming together of fixed or common interests. This way of setting up solidarities makes it hard to see the generative character of solidarities. It also obscures a focus on the construction of solidarities between radically unlike actors. The Caravan brought together different dynamic political trajectories. Following the solidarities crafted through the Caravan unsettles assumptions that solidarities necessarily flow from the coming together of actors with common interests or understandings. These assumptions have structured emerging literatures on transnational social movements in significant ways.

Thus Thomas Olesen, in his fine study of the transnational support networks associated with the Zapatistas, argues that 'a certain common understanding must be present between the variety of actors involved before it is plausible to speak of a network' (Olesen, 2005: 20). His account of the Zapatistas' solidarity networks gives an important sense of their dynamic and productive character, but this is closed down by arguing that for a network to exist it is necessary to have a set of common understandings. This is predicated on a very singular notion of *the* network which is common across social movement theorizing (see also della Porta and Mosca, 2007; Tarrow, 2005). What I would argue, however, in relation to the ICC is that to associate a network with common understandings obscures not just the multiplicity of networked political practices, but also their productiveness. If these networks are thought in more explicitly spatial terms it is possible to see the formation of transnational political networks as the ongoing products of the coming together of diverse trajectories of political activity. The movements brought together through the ICC were already part of various routed, connective forms of political activity. The ICC was an attempt to formalize and develop these connections. Through situating these different movements as coming together through various networks, rather than closing them into one singular network, it is possible to emphasize more explicitly the productive and contested processes of making transnational solidarities. As I will argue below, the coming together of different movements can have significant effects, such as changing the terms on which grievances are contested.

Other recent interventions in social movement theorizing have also emphasized the identification of commonality in the construction of transnational organizing networks. Thus McAdam, Tarrow and Tilly have used the term 'scale shift' to make sense of how social movement action moves between different 'levels' (McAdam et al., 2001; see also Tarrow and McAdam, 2005; Tarrow, 2005). They argue:

> Scale shift is a moderately complex process within which the relative salience of diffusion and brokerage varies, but passage through attribution of similarity and emulation regularly produces a transition from localization to large-scale coordination of action. Like actor constitution and polarization, scale shift operates across the whole range of contentious politics in similar ways, yet in conjunction with other mechanisms and processes produces anything from strike waves to mass murder. (McAdam et al., 2001: 339)

The stress on practices of emulation and similarity in their account of scale shift serves a similar function as the singular notion of the network in Olesen's work. This closes down a sense of the generative relations between different place-based movements. Further, their writings on scale shift do not give a sense of these geographies as constitutive of the political identities of these movements. They ignore, for example, the productive relations between space and political activity, through bringing into contestation different geographies of power, the formation of alliances between unlike actors and the constitution of solidarities that have effects beyond merely producing a movement which works at bigger 'levels'.

How, then, is it possible to move beyond such reductive accounts of the geographies of transnational political networks? Firstly, it is necessary to assert that such alliances are not the products of a singular network, but are rather the coming together of different dynamic trajectories of political activity. This is significant. It unsettles the tendency to counterpose place and space in accounts of such movements (see Miller, 2004). It allows a focus on the relations between different place-based political movements, which are always already constituted through various interrelations. The discussion of the Caravan, below, uses this to emphasize the continued significance of place-based politics in the constitution of transnational networks. Movements like the KRRS have significant histories and geographies, which shape the way they construct grievances. This problematizes Hardt and Negri's spaceless and presentist account of the multitude. Further, these transnational activist networks are also constituted through particular key sites, both in terms of their organizing practices, and also in terms of the particular 'cuts' they make into transnational geographies of power.

Secondly, these networked forms of political activity are interventions in the relations between places in various different ways. The geographies of connection envisioned through the Caravan were multiple. One of the key ways they were produced was around particular bio-politics through interventions in the productions of transgenic seeds, both in Britain/Western Europe and in India. Making sense of such alliances demands an attention to the materially heterogeneous politics crafted through these solidarities. Social movement theory, including work on environmental politics, and much work on the geographies of resistance, remains firmly within a restrictively human-centred account of the political (see Doherty, 2002; Miller, 2000; Panelli, 2007; Tarrow, 2005). To make sense of the solidarities constituted through the Caravan, however, it is necessary to consider how political activity is constructed through interventions in the relations between humans and non-humans. It is impossible to account for the transnational solidarities that shaped the Caravan without understanding the transnational contestation of particular ways of generating seeds. Adding this concern with the non-human to accounts of solidarities shifts understandings of what solidarities are about. Rather than solidarities just being about links between fixed human actors in different places, they become interventions in how relations between humans and non-humans are constituted. These materially heterogeneous interventions can be reworked through their mobilization through transnational networks.

These solidarities have been formed through shared contestation of the practices through which seeds have been enrolled into particular collectives. Sarah Whatmore has argued that the 'enrolment' of GM-seeds into social relations has involved a set of 'volatile' practices (Whatmore, 2002: 126). She demonstrates how in their 'Roundup ReadyTM incarnation soybeans are hybrid agents of corporate science in which the entanglement of technical and business practices is incorporated in the seed' (Whatmore, 2002: 132). Her account of the various agricultural practices and techniques through which the soya bean has been enrolled, however, gives little sense of the ways in which enrolment can become a deeply contested process (Whatmore, 2002: 125–33). Though she writes of the 'volatile' practices of enrolment, she describes the ways in which practices of 'saving seed' have merely become 'redundant' through the use of patents. This ignores the multi-faceted transnational resistances that have coalesced in opposition to these particular practices of enrolment. These struggles are not constituted against capital as a myth or abstract transcendental force. Rather, they contest what Braun has argued are the 'heterogeneous associations that constitute its [capitalism's] ground' (Braun, 2005: 839).

Thirdly, situating transnational political networks as the coming together of dynamic political trajectories emphasizes the multiple and contested character of their activity. Too much emphasis on emulation, similarity and common understandings closes down a focus on the radical plurality of political identities brought together through opposition to neo-liberal globalization. The constitution of transnational political networks can be much more fissiparous, contested and productive than this focus on common understandings suggests. In particular, I want to develop the concerns of chapter 6 on the effects of the different ways in which geographies of power are brought into contestation through exploring the effects the differing maps of grievance that different activists had in the Caravan. I argue that these both opened up and exerted pressure on the formation of transnational solidarities.

Fourthly, these alliances and solidarities can have multiple effects. This disrupts the very limited 'goal'-oriented notions of political 'calculation' that have often structured accounts of transnational political alliances. Tarrow, for example, draws on a definition of coalitions as 'collaborative, means-oriented arrangements that permit distinctive organizational entities to pool resources in order to effect change' (Levi and Murphy, cited by Tarrow, 2005: 164). In similar vein, Miller has argued that despite 'the success of anti-globalization protests in calling attention to the deprivations of global neo-liberalism, very little has actually changed in either the behaviour of transnational corporations or the institutional structures of global governance' (Miller, 2004: 224). The problems with such narrow ways of evaluating the effects of alliances/solidarities is that they close down a focus on the more open-ended effects of such political activity. Miller might be right in narrow terms about the effects of the 'anti-globalization' movement. As I argued and demonstrated in chapter 6, however, these movements have brought the terms on which neo-liberal globalization is constructed into contestation in societies where consensual accounts of politics have placed these concerns off the political agenda.

It is necessary to follow the activity of such solidarities and alliances to evaluate their effects, rather than to judge them in narrow goal-oriented terms. A key outcome of the Caravan, for example, was the dislocation of the terms of contestation of transgenic seeds away from the discourses of 'purity' which had dominated the discourses of European green movements. As Jacques Rancière has argued, the guarantee of 'permanent democracy is not the filling up of all the dead times and empty spaces by the forms of participation or of counterpower; it is the continual renewal of the actors and of the forms of their actions' (Rancière, 2007: 61). Thus, the emergence of new political subjects, such as the alliances produced through the Caravan, must be seen as doing more than either meeting or failing to meet fixed political goals. It is also necessary to engage with the effects of transnational alliances on how political practices are shaped and constructed.

Process Geographies of the Inter-Continental Caravan[93]

Professor Nanjundaswamy wrote in a communiqué publicizing the KRRS's campaign to cremate Monsanto's field trials of genetically modified cotton in India:

> We know that stopping biotechnology in India will not be of much help to us if it continues in other countries, since the threats that it poses do not stop at her borders. We also think that the kind of actions that will be going on in India have the potential not only to kick those corporate killers out of our country; if we play our cards right at global level and co-ordinate our work, these actions can also pose a major challenge to the survival of these corporations in the stock markets. (Nanjundaswamy, 1998; circulated widely on email networks)

Nanjundaswamy's communiqué envisions the solidarities between different activists struggling against biotechnology as productive. It defines these solidarities as emerging through shared action against capitalist biotechnology and the key institutions shaping and producing neo-liberal forms of globalization, especially the WTO (Nanjundaswamy, 1998). The account, through its references to the role of 'corporate killers', intertwines contestation of unequal power relations with a denunciation of particular techniques for modifying living things. These solidarities are also defined through positive relations with other struggles against biotechnology and through practices which generate seeds as part of unofficial networks of exchange, rather than as patented commodities (see also Sahai, 1993, 2000).

Nanjundaswamy's communiqué and images of the Cremate Monsanto! action were circulated widely among activist networks throughout Europe. These were the kinds of inspirational action that fed into the formation of the Caravan project. The way Nanjundaswamy hailed other activists as part of a common contestation of biotechnology and neo-liberal globalization was part of the ongoing process of forming transnational alliances that came together in the Caravan. The KRRS's high-profile actions against Monsanto appealed directly to the practices used to contest biotechnology by activists in the UK and other parts of Western Europe. The forms of solidarity that were produced through the ICC were generated through shared involvement in particular practices of confrontational, non-violent direct action (PGA, 1999a). The KRRS has been part of the translation of Gandhian practices of disobedience to contemporary struggles in the Indian countryside. Through invoking Gandhian action the KRRS has drawn not only on one of the most legitimate repertoires of Indian political activity, but also on one of the internationally renowned forms of non-violent direct action.[94] Its use of 'direct action' has been central to its involvement in networked resistance to neo-liberal globalization.

The solidarities constituted through the Caravan, then, emerged not so much from common understandings or common ideological positions, as through a politics of identification on the basis of shared *practices* of resistance against common enemies. This politics of identification was produced through shared involvement in non-violent direct action and confrontational political activity. For many activists, this shared involvement in particular styles of politics was much more important than a shared 'ideological' agenda or the identification of 'common' interests. This opens up the significance of the 'more than rational' aspects of political identification which are closed down by the rationalist constructions of political activity that structure dominant forms of social movement theorizing (see McAdam et al., 2001; Tarrow, 2005). For the geographies of connection that hold together forms of transnational political activity can be constituted through 'more than rational' forms of political activity. These are missed if political actors are constructed as being involved in political activity only for narrow resource-based reasons. One of the key forms of affective geographies of connection that impacted on the Caravan was Nanjundaswamy's attempt to reproduce a transnationally networked form of political charisma.

John Allen, drawing on Weber, has argued for an understanding of charisma not as an innate characteristic of particular individuals, but as something which is a precarious and relational achievement (Allen, 2003: 120). This is a useful intervention, as the processes through which charisma is constituted are rarely interrogated in work on social movements and the geographies of resistance (see Assadi, 1997; Bentall and Corbridge, 1996; Olesen, 2005). Charisma, as Weber suggested, depends for its reproduction on the recognition of authority (Weber, 1968: 242). The recognition demanded by charismatic leadership is relationally constituted and continually formed rather than simply flowing from the innate qualities of leaders. As Allen emphasizes, 'trust may be established at a distance but only for as long as the charismatic effect is maintained. Once recognition is called into doubt . . . the relationship dissolves and any authority along with it' (Allen, 2003: 149n5). Allen's remarks are suggestive of some of the geographies through which such practices of charismatic authority and recognition are constituted. To analyse Nanjundaswamy's attempt to reproduce charismatic authority through transnational networks it is necessary to develop a more explicitly networked account of the constitution of charismatic authority.

The construction of charismatic leaders within the New Farmers Movements is a powerful legacy of Gandhian political action. The leadership styles of Nanjundaswamy of the KRRS and Mahendra Singh Tikait of the BKU are constituted in relation to histories of male, charismatic 'non-leaders' within the Gandhian mould (Bentall and Corbridge, 1996: 42). Their conduct has affinities with the way that Gandhi defined political utopia as 'a patriarchy in which the ruler, by his moral quality and habitual adherence to truth, always expresses the collective will', rather than through advocating 'participation by every member of the polity' (Chatterjee, 1984: 165). Nanjundaswamy and Tikait, however, have only been partially successful in reproducing their legitimacy and the legitimacy of their movements.

The KRRS's strategy of 'Gandhian violence' has lost them support and there was active opposition by some Karnataka farmers to the Cremate Monsanto! action (Assadi, 1996: 1186; Herring, 2006; Nagaraj, 1996; Panini, 1999: 2169; see also Omvedt's critique of the action, in Omvedt, 1998). (Nanjundaswamy's poor showing in the 1999 parliamentary election in his Karnataka constituency is also suggestive of this crisis of support.) Indeed, Visvanathan and Parmar have argued that Nanjundaswamy represented 'the failed charismatic response to biotechnology' (Visvanathan and Parmar, 2002: 2718). It is a paradox that the Cremate Monsanto! campaign constructed farmers as 'passive victims' rather than 'active agents' (Herring, 2006: 473; see also Stone, 2007). Some of the claims the KRRS made were also proven to be wrong. Monsanto didn't attempt to use 'terminator' genes, and the links that the KRRS made between GM seeds and farmer suicides were also rather spurious (Madsen, 2005; Herring, 2006). Herring also argues that farmers have embraced transgenic seeds, but have dispersed them through unofficial networks of piracy and plant breeding experiments which he describes as 'rural anarcho capitalism' (Herring, 2006: 473). Madsen suggests that the 'problem for the KRRS' in relation to its warnings on the potential dangers of transgenic seeds 'is not that it has been proved wrong, but that many potential followers have had the guile to ignore or accept the risks associated with genetic engineering' (Madsen, 2005: 482).

The flirtation of farmers' movements with electoral strategies, including the BKU's brief alliance with the Hindu nationalist BJP, has also led to a loss of legitimacy (Bentall and Corbridge, 1996: 44; see also Mukherji, 1998). This strategy has made it more difficult for these movements to clearly differentiate themselves from established political processes (see also Routledge, 1993). The KRRS has since distanced itself from electoral strategies, recognizing these effects.[95] The *Hindustan Times* of 24 May 1999 argued that the farmers were taking the struggle to Europe through the Inter-Continental Caravan, having failed to halt economic liberalization at home. This interpretation of the Caravan suggests that the increasing international strategy of the Nanjundaswamy-Tikait grouping can be read as one of reinvention as well as a tracing and contestation of the power relations of neo-liberalism.

This strategy depended on recognition of their legitimacy, and the legitimacy of their movements, by the diverse Western European green and social justice activists involved in the Caravan. Despite the existence of substantial identification with, and support for, the KRRS, forming alliances and joint actions with them was a contested process. This emphasizes both the fraught and contested practices of making transnational solidarities, but also Nanjundaswamy's failure to reproduce his charismatic authority through such networks. Tensions around the style of Nanjundaswamy's leadership emerged through the ongoing, organizational work of the London Welcoming Committee. The hierarchical style of his leadership was disliked by many activists in the London group, who almost all came out of a politics which was deeply hostile to and suspicious of formal, organized hierarchies. It was Nanjundaswamy's conduct, as much as his formal position as leader of KRRS, which was contested.

Nanjundaswamy's conduct also became progressively contested in Karnataka (Madsen, 2001, 2005). This has been directly related to his lack of democratic conduct. Thus Kadidal Shamanna, another prominent figure in the KRRS, argued after Nanjundaswamy's death in 2004:

> In my view, to a very great extent, it was the refusal of the late Prof. Nanjundaswamy to act in a democratic manner which led to dissatisfaction. There is no doubt at all that he was the most charismatic and intellectually gifted leader that the farmers' movement in India has seen. I still remember with great thrill and excitement the way we were drawn to this great leader who for the first time convinced us of farmers' rights. But as the movement grew and became a pressure group he seemed averse to taking suggestions from the others. In fact, most of the so called differences were about trivial things regarding organizational matters. Such being the case, I do not foresee too many obstacles in the KRRS unifying itself. (Kadidal Shamanna, cited in *Deccan Herald*, 10 February 2004)

The split in the KRRS that Shamanna obliquely refers to here happened in November 1999. It was primarily related to tensions over Nanjundaswamy's conduct, especially in relation to the Caravan. He excluded the State Committee of the KRRS from involvement in planning the Caravan.

Through 'appropriating these global links, he laid himself open to charges of violating democratic principles' (Madsen, 2000: 3).

Nanjundaswamy acted as the only mediating point between Indian movements and the different European Welcoming Committees. As one of the very few KRRS members with access to the internet in his own home, he was absolutely central to the flow of information between India and Europe (Madsen, 2000). It was Nanjundaswamy who accessed KRRS's email and discussed aspects of the organization of the Caravan by phone with European activists. It was Nanjundaswamy who put pressure on calls from the Dutch Welcoming Committee to downsize the project so as to make it more manageable (*Do or Die*, 1999: 29). The contestations over how shared political action should be made with the KRRS were often carried out in a fractious and bitter manner. They produced, and intersected with, uneasy tensions in the meetings, tensions which were often exacerbated by poor organization.[96] One of the most forceful personalities within the group attempted to close down discussion of the questions over the nature of the KRRS and the conduct of Swamy[97] and difficulties over procuring visas. He felt that people coming to the meetings questioning the political credentials of the KRRS and asking about the Indians' politics were obstructive. He argued there was more important and pressing organizational work to be done. It wasn't our role to evaluate the actions of the Indians and it was almost racist to contest what the Indians were doing. In later meetings, when the Caravan was about to leave for Europe, he played on a particular image of Swamy as 'this poor, overworked old man' getting up early to travel round India, gathering up people for the Caravan.[98] Some of this rhetoric and imagery suggests the influence of the orientalism of much 'hippy' culture on how these alliances were imagined.

The contestation of Nanjundaswamy's role intersected with the two main lines of contestation that emerged through the organizational process. Firstly, the unequal gender division that was proposed for the Indian delegation of the Caravan: women were making up less than a quarter of the 400-strong delegation. Secondly, there was Nanjundaswamy's insistence that the Caravan had to have at least 400 participants drawn from Indian movements. Many activists involved in the project raised concern about the unequal gender composition of the caravan. These included an activist who had recently returned from making a video in India about actions against transgenic seeds. She had taken out a list of questions to ask Swamy, to help clarify organizational issues about the movements that would make up the Indian contingent of the Caravan and about the Caravan's gender composition. Rather than gaining accurate and complete answers, she was frustrated with what she saw as the unpleasant evasiveness of Swamy. She argued he had been 'refusing to answer' questions about the composition of the Caravan.[99] Again, concern about the selection procedure was also present in Karnataka. Two organic farmers who were prominent KRRS activists, Juli and Vivek Cariappa, 'were expelled from the KRRS for questioning the authoritarian selection procedure used by Nanjundaswamy' (Madsen, 2001: 3739).

Not only was Nanjundaswamy's charismatic authority not fully recognized by West European activists involved in the Caravan, it was also challenged by the prominent Indian environmentalist Vandana Shiva. Shiva wrote a vehement critique of the project, which was circulated widely on email networks. This revered and internationally renowned figure dissociated herself from the ICC in the harshest possible terms. She argued that most of the 'so called 500 farmers who will be travelling to Europe as part of the "Caravan" are basically Bank officials, pesticides and seed agents and commission agents' (Shiva, 1999).[100] The impact of Shiva's comments was on a much broader constituency than the small circle of people involved in organizing the Caravan. The circulation of the email had a major effect in discrediting the ICC in the activist networks which it was necessary to mobilize if the project was going to work. Her critique was considered seriously within the meetings. Partly responding to Shiva's criticisms, one activist commented that it was obvious it was not 'going to be the perfect Caravan', but it was still an exciting project. Others were harsher in their criticism of Shiva, seeing her as 'out of order' for circulating such a vehement critique. Discussions in the meetings situated Shiva's critique as part of longstanding 'personality' and 'ego' clashes between Shiva and Swamy. This clash coalesced around a power struggle for the leadership and control of the Indian 'anti-globalization' movement that was being constituted in relation to transnational activist networks. It suggests that there was a struggle for 'whose' charismatic authority would be produced and reproduced through these networks (see also Madsen, 2001; 2005: 483).

These struggles for charismatic authority, and to reproduce charismatic authority, demonstrate the ongoing spatially stretched power relations that were negotiated through the Caravan. The Caravan also had to negotiate unequal geographies of power between activists in the North and South, which became a contested issue through the organizing process, particularly in relation to visas. In chapter 6 I argued that it is necessary to interrogate the geographies of power that structure the counter-global networks being generated through opposition to neo-liberal globalization. As a correspondent of the Indian *Economic and Political Weekly* argues, the counter-globalization movement is riven by inequalities, with Euro-American participants shored up by 'their incomes and visa privileges' with 'at best token representation from the rest of the world' (DN, 2001). How these unequal geographies of power between diverse movements are negotiated has emerged as a key challenge to the counter-globalization movement.

The Caravan was an attempt to disrupt this tendency towards tokenistic representation. Nonetheless, the specific trajectories of these movements and their very different locations in transnational power geometries had effects on the kinds of solidarities and equivalences that were crafted through the Caravan. Uneven relations of power within and between the movements that were brought together through the project exerted pressures on the solidarities formed through the ICC. The joint actions of the ICC negotiated the differentiated geographies of power and uneven operation of visa regulations across Europe; controls that exert significant pressure on the formation of what Held has described as 'cosmopolitan citizenship' (Held, 1995: 233, 267–86). Despite having letters of welcome from MPs, only 37 out of 80 Indians on the UK delegation of the Caravan were allowed into the UK. Those belonging to the KRRS were refused entry, arguably for political reasons because of their high-profile involvement in direct action. KRRS activists complained of being treated 'like untouchables' by the British High Commission in Madras, where 19 activists were arrested while protesting against being refused visas (*Guardian*, 27 May 1999; *Economic Times*, 24 May 1999).

Rather than contesting or trying to circumvent the unequal operation of visa controls, some UK activists saw the very process of negotiating and engaging with these geographies of power as compromising the political integrity of the project. These concerns were intensified by the Foreign Office's insistence on vetting the Caravan's itinerary. An internal critic of the project argued that 'large-scale brown-nosing of politicians and non-governmental organizations (NGOs) was needed to get the applications through. Apart from being utterly odious, this affected the political nature of the project' (*Do or Die*, 1999: 28). The geographies of power Indian activists faced in participating in the project were thus dismissed as unimportant. These London-based activists, who had little experience of these oppressive visa regulations, articulated them as compromising the integrity of the project rather than challenging them. These unequal geographies of power were seen as something that should be avoided rather than something that could be imaginatively brought into the terrain of contestation through the conduct of the ICC demonstrating the limits exerted on transnational political activity. This emphasizes the partial negotiations with these inequalities that structured the process geographies of the ICC. The next section develops this concern with the relations between the Caravan and geographies of power through interrogating the maps of grievance formed through its activity.

The Maps of Grievance of the Inter-Continental Caravan

The maps of grievance crafted and produced through political activity are part of the work of making unequal geographies of power contestable. Following different spatially constituted power relations can be productive. Though the solidarities constituted through the ICC were formed in relation to common enemies, the terms on which maps of grievance were constructed were not necessarily the same. The specific trajectories of these movements and their very different locations in transnational geographies of power had effects on the kinds of solidarities and equivalences that were crafted through the project. The 'sites of grievance' that were to be targeted through the Caravan, for example, became the subject of intense debate within the meetings of the London Welcoming Committee. Tensions emerged in these meetings when some of the Indian participants of the Caravan expressed an interest in holding a demonstration outside parliament. These proposals spoke to the deep symbolic significance the British parliament had for their histories of political activity. They also made issues of how and where relations of power could be made contestable, central to the political identities being shaped through the project.

The idea of holding a protest outside parliament met with considerable hostility from activists in the London Welcoming Committee. One activist argued that to protest at parliament was to miss the point, because it was no longer government that controlled things but multinationals.[101] She also argued that because we were doing the work of organizing the Caravan in the UK they would have to fit into our analysis of politics. This point raised severe criticism for refusing to incorporate the ideas of Indian activists into the planning of the project. But the hostility to making a protest at parliament was widespread. Strongly held arguments were put forward that any action at parliament was contrary to the spirit of the Caravan and that attendance would confer on parliament a 'false legitimacy'. This position rubbed up against other stances in the group. A genetics activist argued that it was an opportunity that could be creatively exploited rather than simply a problem. He argued against a simple dismissal of parliament, pointing out that it still had a role in legislation over genetic engineering.

But there was to be no ICC presence in or outside parliament. 'The City' emerged as the key site of grievance, targeted in a demonstration of the ICC and some London-based activists on 29 May 1999. A position emerged that it would be much more desirable to march and construct actions in the City, London's financial district, as this was where the 'real power' was located. The City was seen as the part of London that was intertwined with the Indian activists' lives through processes of globalization. At later meetings, a British Asian activist argued that this march through London to the key sites of power of the City would invoke the Gandhian non-violent practices such as the salt marches.[102] These contestations illustrate some of the effects that the construction of maps of grievance have on the ways different routes of political activity are brought together.

The political identities of the action were negotiated through contesting how power geometries should be related to and engaged with. There was no simple consensus about which sites of grievance should be contested. Rather, these sites of grievance emerged as the focus of disputes. This related at least in part to different understandings and knowledges about the geographies of power being reshaped through neo-liberal globalization. Further, the way that this was negotiated had effects. The orientation of action towards contesting the financial power of the City and away from the centres of 'political' power produced a politics that accepted key claims of proponents of contemporary neo-liberal globalization. A result was that the maps of grievance of the ICC, in London at least, were produced through accepting the logic that the nation-state was no longer relevant, either as a political actor or as a site of grievance. These 'practical-moral knowledges' about globalization were co-produced through the identification of particular sites of grievance. In this case there was detailed and lengthy deliberation about the ways in which maps of grievance were constructed. But there were other instances when adversaries were quickly defined, located and contested through the political activity of the Caravan. In these instances the explicitly transnational constitution of the Caravan had significant effects on the conduct and identities of place-based political activities.

The action at the Nuffield Foundation with which I started this chapter is a good example here. This was a productive practice enabling militant political identities to come together at this site of grievance. The political agency of the ICC was constituted through spatial practices that attempted to make visible and contestable key relations of power. This agency was produced from the circulation and formation of 'practical-moral knowledges' about the Nuffield Foundation and its report. This adversary was defined quickly and activist networks mobilized to contest it through localizing and making contestable wider power relations at this key site. Crucially, the transnational networks that constituted this place-based activity changed the terms on which the Nuffield Foundation could be contested. Locating the opposition to genetically modified agriculture at the intersection of movements from the North and South illustrates that these are not just questions that can be dismissed as the concerns of a 'wealthy few' in the North. It also changed some of the terms on which the debate was constructed. In this instance it wasn't just about transgressions of 'pure' natures, but was broadened out to contest the terms on which stories about the South are deployed to legitimate the development of genetically modified crops.

The Nuffield Foundation emerged as a site of grievance around which the different political trajectories of the Caravan project could cohere. But tensions between the different constituencies mobilized through the Caravan emerged in relation to other sites. A proposal to join a vigil against nuclear testing outside the Indian Embassy in London was angrily denounced by one Caravan participant as 'anti-Indian'. This signalled that the opposition to globalization that was produced through the Caravan was partly constituted through overtly Indian nationalist stories. This raises questions about some of the tensions that were produced by the meeting up of different trajectories and traditions of political activity. The ways in which these tensions were based around different ways of contesting the geographies of power being shaped by neo-liberal globalization raise some key questions for the political futures being articulated by counter-globalization movements.

The opposition of the KRRS and BKU to neo-liberal globalization and the Dunkel Draft has been structured by an 'unambiguously nationalist discourse' which draws on the idioms of Gandhian nationalism (Brass, 1995: 56n41; see also Assadi, 1995b: 221; Gupta, 1998: 292, 313). Nanjundaswamy has argued that the Indian government's acceptance of liberalization has rendered India 'impotent' and that 'our genetic resources are our national property' (*Economic Times*, 24 May 1999; Gupta, 1998: 292). These nationalist maps of grievance exerted contradictory pressures and possibilities on the solidarities conducted through the ICC. Nanjundaswamy's insistence that a minimum of 400 Indian activists would form the core of the project meant that a very particular Indian-nationalist story was the focus of the Caravan's activity. This tone and style of action made other activists uncomfortable, leading to accusations that it felt at times like an 'Indian Nationalist Caravan' (see also Madsen, 2001: 3741).[103] Thus, although the Caravan was conceived of as a process that would institute solidarities between different struggles against globalization, some of the particularistic ways that resistance to globalization was envisioned closed down the potential productiveness of these solidarities. This also had effects on the conduct of the Caravan. Some of the activists from the Indian Farmers Movements, for example, were uncomfortable about speaking alongside activists from Nepal. Some of the Indian delegation became angry when it became apparent that both members of the two-strong Nepali delegation would speak at a public hearing organized in London. They argued that it was an 'Indian not a Nepali Caravan', suggesting a questionable commitment to allowing the stories of non-Indian activists to be told at the hearing.[104]

Here the maps of grievance became refigured in ways which articulated opposition to globalization through a defence of the Indian nation. As Oza has argued in her insightful account of the opposition to the Miss World Pageant in Bangalore in 1996, 'local opposition was spatially manifested as preserving the nation against the larger forces of globalization' (Oza, 2001: 1068). It is crucial that the local and global are not simply counterposed through counter-globalization politics and networks. For this can lead to a position where exclusionary nationalisms or localisms are supported, which can exert considerable pressure on the possibilities of forming equivalences between different place-based struggles. The ICC juxtaposed movements and participants who articulate grievances against neo-liberal globalization in both chauvinistic and plural, expansive ways.

The practices of Western activists, some of whom sought funding (unsuccessfully) from the right-wing Eurosceptic Goldsmith Foundation and talked of the possibility of making alliances with the political right, are implicated here, as well as the participation of Indian activists influenced by exclusionary nationalisms. These are tensions that can be related in part to the imaginations and performance of spatial relations that emerge through political activity. Bounded and particularistic forms of political identity proved to have impacts on the durability of the solidarities that were constructed through the activity of the Caravan. The way spaces of politics are imagined and performed has important effects on political identities. For how relations of power are imagined and made contestable has effects on whether political activity produces new identities or buttresses fixed, existing interests.

When Nanjundaswamy complained of India's 'impotence', when BKU activists bullied the two-member Nepali contingent of the Caravan in London, the activity of the Caravan refigured fixed, particularist and nationalist political identities. This reproduced a fixed spatial imagination of protest that articulated maps of grievances as existing only between rural India and transnational power geometries. These articulations of power relations didn't allow positive identifications to be constructed with others struggling against similar power geometries. These political identities were even defined negatively against other participants within the Caravan. At its most problematic this produced a kind of internationalism with guarantees that structured the Caravan so that it would tell only a particular Indian story about the effects of globalization. But the way these militant particularisms moved and were reconfigured also allowed more productive engagements to emerge, as the next section will argue. This suggests that political identities might be unsettled and positive identifications might be formed through the process precisely because it located opposition to neo-liberal globalization at the intersection of diverse routes of political activity.

Productive and Contested Outcomes of Transnational Organizing

Donna Haraway has argued that she 'cannot help but hear in the biotechnology debates the unintended tones of fear of the alien and suspicion of the mixed' (Haraway, 1997: 61). She notes that the mobilization of 'intrinsic natures' in these debates gives 'short shrift' to the 'mixed up history of living beings' (Haraway, 1997: 61). One of the significant achievements of the ICC project was that it located the opposition to genetically modified organisms at the intersection of different routes of activity and experience. These interactions opened up the possibility of the coming together of potentially unsettling routes of activity. The ICC was not mobilized around a consensual version of what constituted 'the environment'. The process brought together activists who constructed their identities through diverse and contested relations and practices with non-humans. These different practices cut across the groups who were brought together through the ICC.

The maps of grievance formed by the KRRS in opposition to the Dunkel Draft mobilized unofficial ethical practices through contesting the power relations and networks through which seeds are generated. The KRRS has been active in denouncing the way the Dunkel Draft envisions plant varieties as being enrolled into collectives as patented life forms (see Sahai, 1993, 2000). The KRRS mobilized a defence of the unofficial networks of seed distribution and production in opposition to attempts to establish seed varieties as the sole property of certain transnational companies, such as Cargill. Through these practices they constructed techniques for generating seeds through patents and formalized property relations as antagonisms. Here the maps of grievance were formed through the construction of practical ethical positions contesting the power relations and networks through which seeds are generated.

These practical ethical positions moved through the Caravan in ways which were both unsettling and productive. For the Caravan process brought together activists whose identities were formed through very different practices through which non-humans should be socialized. These differences emerged through activities such as a visit to a site near Bishop Stortford where GM activists had squatted and destroyed the genetically modified maize crop that had been cordoned off for testing. The Caravan was greeted with fine Irish tunes as we crossed fields to the protest camp. Activists from the Punjab BKU with whom we walked across the fields talked in very different terms about their resistance to GM crops than UK activists. They argued that the wheat that was growing in the fields around us was far thinner and less productive than the wheat they grew on their small 10–20 acre holdings. Though they were adamantly opposed to GM varieties of crops they talked about using pesticides on their crops and were strongly in support of them. They talked about how pesticides were necessary to produce successful yields.[105]

This 'productivist' tone of some of the farmers' stories had quite unsettling effects. Some UK activists, informed by orientalist notions of purity, assumed the Indians would practise only traditional farming techniques.[106] This was also based on an ignorance of the farmers' movements, which have emerged through a post-Green Revolution agrarian politics where their politics has often mobilized around the price of chemical inputs such as fertilisers.[107] This is an aspect of movements like the KRRS that has been consistently played down by Nanjundaswamy (Madsen, 2001: 3740). At one level, this dialogue confirms Haraway's concerns about the racialization of the GM debate. Here 'Indian farmers' figure only to be collapsed into nature, without dynamic social-natural practices. But this kind of interaction also brought these different attitudes to agricultural practices into question. It led to UK activists questioning, in a non-hostile way, the status of 'organic' forms of agriculture in India. This opened up the possibility of creatively unsettling how resistance towards genetic modification was conducted. As the discussion of the demonstration outside the Nuffield Foundation noted, the slogans and terms of debate used by Indian activists differed from those that frequently characterize the terms of debate in the UK. Their slogans, such as 'No patents on life', spoke far more to a contestation of the patent systems that genetically modified plants were part of than to a concern at the threat of 'mixing' and of a disruption of the imagined 'purity' of the plants they used. They brought into question some of the dynamic techniques and power relations through which seeds are generated and enrolled into collectives.

Some of the alliances and engagements formed through the conduct of the Caravan, however, were explicitly constituted in direct opposition to the pro-agricultural development politics of organizations like the biggest Indian farmers' union, the BKU.[108] Discussions between Nepali activists from INHURED (International Institute for Human Rights, Environment and Development) and the members of the Brighton-based cooking collective, the Anarchist Teapot, were constituted through common adherence to an explicitly anti-development politics. Their discussions centred on the political practices being used and developed in the mass mobilizations against big development projects, particularly dams (*Do or Die*, 1999: 209–15). But it was also significant that some activists I spoke to found their adherence to an anti-development politics unsettled by discussions with Indian activists. An Australian activist I spoke to argued that meeting up and talking with the Indian farmers had challenged her views about the outright rejection of processes of 'development'.[109] These solidarities and alliances were practices through which previous understandings of terms such as 'environmentalisms' and 'development' could be unsettled and reconfigured.

The forms of commonality mobilized by the ICC, then, were more diverse, multiple and productive than is suggested by a fixed notion of a common good or understandings, pre-existing the formation of transnational political networks. Some critical geographers have bemoaned this diverse character of the counter-globalization movement. Neil Smith has argued that the 'strength of the Seattle protest – its internationalism, resoluteness and breadth' – also harbours 'its central weakness insofar as the convergence of such an eclectic political grouping is not dependable without a sharpened political focus and enhanced organizational power' (Smith, 2000: 4). I think a more creative approach is to engage in the practices through which the terms of an internationalist opposition to neo-liberal globalization are being constructed. For, despite all its many flaws, one of the achievements of the ICC was to foreground a set of very difficult questions about what the terms of an explicitly transnational opposition to globalization might be. It demonstrates how the plural and contested populist logics formed through mobilizing different maps of grievance in opposition to neo liberalization were up for negotiation.

Rather than the formation of a common interest, the Caravan enabled the rubbing up together of many different activist identities and traditions. This process was contested but productive, not least because some of the tensions that emerged through the conduct of the Caravan became openly negotiated. Evaluations of the project highlighted the need for these political networks to engage with the implications of the unequal gender balance of the Caravan and of the reproduction of particularistic nationalist identities through the project. These concerns led to the adoption of the following political statement at the Second Gathering of People's Global Action in Bangalore:

> We reject all forms and systems of domination and discrimination including, but not limited to, patriarchy, racism and religious fundamentalism of all creeds. We embrace the full dignity of all human beings. (PGA, 1999b)

The bringing together of different activist cultures was a process that was generative of debate, negotiation and contestation rather than a simple coming together of homogeneous action or pre-existing political wills. It was part of an ongoing experimentation with what the terms and basis of an explicitly transnational resistance to globalization might be. In the Indian context this statement has been hailed as particularly important in articulating opposition to globalization on progressive 'internationalist' terms, rather than on the terms deployed by the Hindu right (Singh, 2001: 49; see also Vanaik, 2001, 2004).

These ongoing debates meant that there were some strategic moments in the research process where it was possible to engage explicitly with these kinds of experimentation with practices of solidarity. One of these moments was an evaluation meeting of the ICC, held at Kingsley Hall in London in October 1999. The meeting was held shortly after a vehement internal critique of the Caravan had been published in *Earth First!* journal and circulated widely on email networks (*Do or Die*, 1999: 28–9). This had generated considerable anger among those present. This anger was not expressed because activists were uncritically engaged in the ICC. They conceded there were problems with the project, but were angry that the critique lacked any 'positive assessment' of the ICC.[110] The discussion at the evaluation became very much defined against this position of absolute rejection of the Caravan. This opened up possibilities for asking some different kinds of questions about the conduct of the Caravan and discussing how these tensions might be negotiated.

Importantly, it opened up questions about what was 'meant by solidarity' and how practices of solidarity had been negotiated through the conduct of the ICC. I used the way these themes were emerging as an opportunity to discuss my concerns about how some of the political identities mobilized through the project adopted a quite closed nationalism. I argued that this had had negative effects on the kinds of solidarities formed through the project. This concern with the kinds of solidarities that were produced through the ICC was taken in different directions. Different activists stated very different positions on what grounds alliances should be formed. Some argued that the only key criterion should be non-violence. Others argued that alliances with right-wing groups might be a possible strategic move. This was a position that many were uncomfortable with, arguing that alliances should only be formed with groups that were broadly 'left'.

This intervention brought to the fore some of the contested practices through which solidarities were generated through the ICC. Following these practices of experimentation allowed an engagement with issues around how opposition to neo-liberal globalization is constructed, which have not been given prominence in many discussions of the counter-globalization protest (see Brecher et al., 2000; Cockburn and St. Clair, 2000; Starr, 2000). In movement debates these tensions seem to have been eclipsed by arguments over violent or non-violent strategies. But tensions over the terms on which resistance to globalization is constructed are arguably as important as these discussions. There are engagements to be made here with the kinds of maps of grievance generated through these interventions. The status of alliances here is not merely a 'means' towards the creation of small, harmonious communities (see Starr, 2000). Rather, intersections and alliances can be integral to the kinds of political identities and alternative political imaginaries they articulate. These connections, rather than just generating a larger movement, can also produce the unsettling and transformation of identities. To this extent counter-globalization movements can usefully be thought of as engaging in forms of 'collective experimentation' that are antagonistic to the collective experiments orchestrated by neo-liberalism (see Latour, 1999b).

Conclusions

The formation of the Caravan was an arduous process riven by fissures and differences. To engage with these tensions involves taking seriously the practices through which transnational resistances construct, negotiate and contest spatially stretched relations of power. Following the diverse and contested maps of grievance produced and reconfigured through the conduct of the ICC has highlighted the dynamism of these spatialities of resistance. This permits a focus on how contestations of power relations move, how they are negotiated, how they are actively constructed and how they have effects on the constitution of political identities. The ICC also demonstrates that transnational organizing is no panacea for political movements. That it contributed to the split in the KRRS demonstrates how such organizing practices can throw up tensions as well as possibilities.

Through interrogating the different 'process geographies' of the ICC I have sought to transcend the focus in the social movement literature on the role of common understandings, emulation and similarity in the functioning of transnational political networks. I have demonstrated that this is necessary to develop a focus on the contested and productive activity of such networks. Interrogating the constitution of the ICC has generated many different issues about the terms on which solidarities are constructed. It also raises important and often difficult questions about the political identities of the movements being constituted in relation to neo-liberal globalization. These movements might be spatially stretched and bring different place-based political cultures together. This doesn't mean that they necessarily generate open, solidaristic forms of identity. As Akhil Gupta has argued, the 'nationalist rhetoric' of Tikait and Nanjundaswamy might appear to be 'anachronistic'. But it is 'mixed with a shrewd recognition of the current global historical conjuncture and of the importance of forging coalitions with similar groups in other parts of the world' (Gupta, 1998: 323). The concluding chapter engages with some of the political and theoretical implications of these tensions.

Conclusion

Towards Politicized Geographies of Connection

Woody Guthrie wrote that he hated 'a song that makes you think that you are . . . bound to lose'. He was, he said, out to 'fight those kind of songs to my very last breath of air'. Instead, he sought 'to sing songs that will prove to you that this is your world', 'no matter how hard it has run you down'.[111] In the spirit of Guthrie's thoughts on song-writing this book has told stories alive to the generative and productive effects of subaltern political activity. I have sought to chart the impact of such activity on world-making processes. This has involved recovering and engaging with networked subaltern agency and identity. Through so doing I have demonstrated the significance of diverse forms of subaltern agency and identity constructed through geographies of connection.

Centring these forms of political activity in both the past and present can allow stories to be told that have significant relevance for 'global times'. I have contested dominant accounts of 'globalization' which have constructed it as heralding the end of subaltern agency and which concentrate political agency in neo-liberal networks, institutions and multinationals. In opposition to such accounts I have explored the multiple histories and geographies of counter-global networks. I have engaged with the forms of multi-ethnic solidarity and connection which subaltern struggles have articulated in opposition to dominant globalizing practices. This situates contemporary political struggles in relation to histories and geographies of productive engagements with spatially stretched and unequally constituted power relations.

This is a productive exercise in both political and theoretical terms. In political terms it can counter the marginalization and dispossession of subaltern agency in shaping globalizing practices. Such a dispossession structures much contemporary political debate and imaginaries. It has pernicious consequences especially in foreclosing political possibilities. In theoretical terms this allows a sense of the continuities in the formation of dynamic subaltern spaces of politics. These have been closed down by pervasive tendencies to counterpose a dynamic networked present to a more settled past, and which to define the dynamism of neo-liberal globalization against settled and bounded forms of subaltern political activity. This opens up important possibilities for constructing and engaging with cartographies of subaltern agency.

The first part of this conclusion develops the arguments about the making of usable pasts that have structured the logic and argument of this book. Revisiting the work of David Scott I argue that theorizing usable pasts in explicitly geographical ways offers slightly more optimistic, if perhaps more modest, ways of conceiving the relations between past, present and future globalizing practices than his arguments about tragedy allow. I then draw out the implications of the argument of this book for debates around the geographies of resistance. I do this through engaging with their implications for ways of theorizing the relations between spatialities, neo-liberalism and contestation. The final part of the conclusion draws out the key political implications of the arguments and material presented in this book. It considers their significance for attempts to reject chauvinistic, narrow forms of opposition to globalization. In particular I contend that crafting connections between different place-located struggles is crucial to opposing exclusionary nationalist oppositions to globalization and to constructing open, transnational political networks defined by solidaristic identities.

Geographies of Connection and the Making of Usable Pasts

David Scott has characterized our times as 'times that in fundamental ways are distressingly off kilter'. This, he notes, is in the 'specific sense that the critical languages in which we wagered our moral vision and our political hope (including importantly, the languages of black emancipation and postcolonial critique) are no longer commensurate with the world they were meant to understand, engage, and overcome' (Scott, 2004: 210). The implication for Scott is that:

> A tragic sensibility is a particularly apt and timely one because, not driven by the hubris of teleologies that extract the future seamlessly from the past, and more attuned at the same time to the intricacies, ambiguities, and paradoxes of the relation between actions and their consequences, and intentions and the chance contingencies that sometimes undo them, it recasts our historical temporalities in significant ways. (Scott, 2004: 210)

Scott's arguments provide a necessary injunction to take seriously 'intricacies, ambiguities and paradoxes' that have too often been elided by radical theorizing and politics. They are a significant response to the contemporary conjuncture. There are tensions, however, with this turn to a 'tragic' mode of narrating usable pasts.

This book has sought to engage with the implications of thinking about usable pasts in explicitly geographical ways. I have sought through the logic and argument of the book to produce alternative ways of rendering the relations between past, present and future than the tragic modes of narrative offered by Scott. This project has been animated by a contention that taking the geography of subaltern political activity seriously has implications for how these relations are constructed. I have argued that thinking about the geographies of subaltern political activity in networked ways allows a focus on the continuities in the dynamic and generative ways through which forms of subaltern agency and identity have been constructed. In this regard the neglected geographies of connection that structure the argument of James's *Black Jacobins* matter. Interrogating the geographies of connection that have made up subaltern struggles can foreground the following key aspects of the relations between pasts, presents and futures.

Firstly, it permits a focus on the practices through which subaltern struggles have brought unequal ways of constituting practices of globalization into contestation. This allows a focus on the processes of articulation through which connections and solidarities have been constituted through struggles in different spatial and temporal contexts. These are ways of thinking about the political that are made central to the argument and structure of *Black Jacobins*. For James, the insurgent imaginative geographies of the book were strategically necessary to 'place West-Indians in history'. They have a theoretical and political resonance far beyond this particular project. Telling stories about the multiple forms of agency and identity constructed through geographies of connection allows accounts of the relations between past, present and future to emerge which refuse simple categorization into modes of 'tragedy' or 'romance'. Unsettling teleological constructions of 'usable pasts', then, does not necessarily imply the construction of tragic modes of narrative (see also Phillips, 2007).

Secondly, these geographies of connection permit a focus on the practices through which different subaltern struggles in different contexts have sought to remake social and material relations through particular spatial practices. This focus on the 'making' of social and material practices allows a more situated engagement with the practices of subaltern political activity than Scott's concern with narrative emplotment and construction allows. This more situated account of the formation of subaltern agency and identities can be alive to the 'intricacies, ambiguities and paradoxes' demanded by Scott, but they can exceed Scott's desire to overcode these intricacies, ambiguities and paradoxes through a tragic narrative. This opens up different ways of thinking about the construction of political identities and agency. It allows, for example, stories to be told about the situated practices through which unequal practices of globalization are contested and different geographies of connection produced and reproduced. This asserts the presence of subaltern agency in shaping the makings of globalization in pasts, presents and futures.

Thirdly, following from this point one of the key aspects of the making of counter-global networks and politics that I have tried to foreground here is the different organizational practices, modes and subjectivities that have been produced through bringing globalized practices into contestation. Scott's argument is directly concerned with the (mis)fortunes of the anti-colonial state and the dissolution of the hopes associated with it. I have sought here, however, to demonstrate the diverse forms of organization, identities and solidarities generated through bringing globalized practices into contestation. I have followed different forms of subaltern political activity as they brought globalized relations of power into contestation.

What these different subaltern struggles demonstrate is something of the radical openness of political activity. They suggest that the spatial configurations of politics are in process and in becoming. Different ways of generating alternatives, different organizational forms, different subjectivities and different ways of ordering and constructing solidarities are made through the conduct of political activity. The experiments of the LCS with democracy, the mobile secret societies of Irish peasants, the transnational solidarities of the ICC, all indicate this. This openness of radical political activity dislocates Scott's positioning of radical hopes so closely with the anti-colonial/post-colonial state. Dislocating nation-centred framings of usable pasts is also helpful in this regard. It suggests that hope and possibility can be affirmed by locating situated contemporary political struggles as part of ongoing engagements with spatially stretched and unequally constituted power relations, albeit with differentiated, contested and uneven outcomes.

There is much in the conduct of the past struggles discussed here that is unpalatable to contemporary oppositional political identities: ritualistic forms of violence, exclusionary spaces of politics, male-bound forms of organization. Though significantly there are continuities with some of these tensions, such as the persistence of exclusionary forms of gender relations. These struggles, however, engaged with unequal mercantile networks through shaping their own heterogeneous alliances, solidarities and political constituencies. They produced notions of political community that were multi-ethnic. These struggles contested the formation of transnational power geometries through celebrating more than the 'parochial' and the 'local' in opposition to these relations. Their political activity was also often defined by the formation of equivalences and solidarities between unlike actors.

These forms of resistance have resources for engaging with claims that contemporary neo-liberal globalization is politically debilitating. They usefully counter the dispossession of subaltern agency done by accounts which make neo-liberal globalization seem all-powerful and which trap subaltern forms of resistance within bounded places. Thus I have engaged with the place-based experiments with democracy that connected the artisans of the LCS to Atlantic networks and flows of democratic practice. I have told stories about the political identities formed by mobile, 'motley' groups of labourers in the eighteenth century. I have recovered different forms of Irish nationalist identity generated in relation to Atlantic flows of political ideas and the rough egalitarianism of the lower deck. The project has sought to recover the vibrancy of traditions of organization which have opposed unequal geographies of power through mobilizing multi-ethnic cooperation, solidarities and through different forms of geographies of connection.

This alternative way of constructing the relations between past, present and futures has implications for ways of thinking about political agency. One of the key challenges I outlined in the introduction was how to theorize the political identities and agency constructed through counter-global networks. I have done this through constructing accounts of situated, partial and contested cartographies of subaltern agency. In contrast to accounts that have theorized subaltern agency as either existing in defined autonomous spaces or else being everywhere, I have insisted that accounts of subaltern agency can emerge through following particular interventions and engagements with networked social and material relations. I have argued that this opens up possibilities for engagements with subaltern political activity. This account of agency shifts understandings from questions about who controls how spaces and networks are produced to a concern with the different practices through which they are shaped. This allows a more plural sense of the practices through which networks are generated and produced, whether they are mercantile trading networks, or the networks that constitute neo-liberal globalization.

This is a condition for possibility for developing accounts of the forms of agency generated through networked subaltern political activity. It is through understanding situated interventions in the generating and shaping of networked social and material relations that diverse forms of agency can be foregrounded. This can bear on the different ways in which seeds or coal are enrolled into trade networks, or the different kinds of solidarities and geographies of connection shaped between places. It also permits a focus on the ambiguous effects of subaltern agency. As I have demonstrated here through different examples, the practices through which dominant globalizing practices have been contested can generate their own exclusions, whether this be the male-bound forms of democracy constituted through the LCS, or the exclusionary organizing spaces which structured the ICC. It is not enough, then, merely to foreground such forms of agency, but it is also necessary to engage with the different geographies of power and different identities produced through such agency.

This account of agency is one key element of the theoretical vocabulary developed here for engaging with networked resistances. This theoretical vocabulary seeks to allow more generous assessments of subaltern agency and identity than those generally adopted by critical geographers and left theorizing. In particular these concerns have shaped the account of place-based politics here, which has often been dealt with dismissively. Positioning place-based political activity as always already the product of negotiation of connections has allowed the telling of stories whereby localized political activity is productive. In particular I have argued that even 'militant particularisms' can be constituted through bringing together different routes of political activity. This permits a focus on the ways in which place-based political activity can be part of the shaping of political imaginaries, rather than being settled and bounded particularist struggles that require networking by 'outside' intellectuals.

To do this it has been necessary to foreground the generative geographies of connection and contestation. Through tracing the maps of grievance produced through political activity I have positioned the geographies of antagonism generated through political activity as productive. I have argued, though, that thinking the political in explicitly spatial terms can help foreground the radical openness of political activity. Thus while asserting the significance of conflict to the political, I have engaged with the diverse outcomes of political activity such as friendship and solidarity as well as conflict. I have also interrogated the interactions between geographies of solidarities and antagonisms, noting for example how the formation of solidarities can dislocate the terms on which antagonisms are constituted. The next two sections draw out the implications of these arguments for debates and political strategies in relation to neo-liberalism.

Space, Neo-Liberalism and Contestation

The success of neo-liberalism in making itself the 'common sense of the age' has been much vaunted. This assessment of the neo-liberals' achievement has become a key part of the terrain of debates on the geographies of neo-liberalism and in left theorizing more generally. Thus Peck and Tickell have charted the spaces through which neo-liberalism has constituted itself as a 'common sense of the times' (Peck and Tickell, 2002: 381; see also Larner et al., 2007). While it would perhaps be foolish to dissent too much from this broad assessment, there are tensions and risks associated with this framing of neo-liberalism that I want to engage with here. As Leitner et al. argue, 'a focus on neoliberalization as a top-down process can inadvertently reinforce its hegemonic status' (Leitner et al., 2007: 2).

This characterization of neo-liberalism as a common sense of the age too often constructs this achievement as an end-point of a particular set of political and economic processes. What remains incisive about Gramsci's writings on the relations between philosophy, politics and common sense is the extent to which 'common sense' is viewed not as a stable end-point or consensus, but as something which is characterized by instability and is part of an ongoing terrain of contestation (see Gramsci, 1971: 323–5; Hall, 1988: esp. 161–73). It locates common sense as plural, the site of conflict and the locus of different views about the world. As Partha Chatterjee argues, for Gramsci, the point of politics 'is to undertake a criticism of "common sense" on the basis of "common sense"; not to inject into popular life a "scientific" form of thought springing from somewhere else, but to develop and make critical an activity which already exists in popular life' (Chatterjee, 1989: 209).

To challenge the establishment of neo-liberalism as a 'common sense' it is necessary to assert the fragmentary, unfinished and precarious character of this achievement. It is also necessary to engage with those social and political movements that have brought neo-liberalism into contestation. There are risks in reifying neo-liberalisms and accepting too readily the extent to which they have constituted themselves as a new form of common sense (see Gibson-Graham, 2002; Massey, 2007a; Leitner et al., 2007). Such an approach is particularly damaging to alternative political imaginaries. One of the achievements of the movements against neo-liberal globalization has been to make the forms of violence and inequalities associated with neo-liberalism part of the terrain of contestation. They have also brought into contestation the unequal geographies of connection between different places produced by neo-liberal globalization. It is significant in this regard the extent to which neo-liberalism does not function as a common sense in Gramscian terms. It is perhaps remarkable given the pervasiveness of neo-liberalization the extent to which neo-liberal values and conventions are *not* the spontaneous way of thinking in many different parts of the world. Political cultures remain where there is still much more residual scepticism, even downright hostility, towards neo-liberal values, projects and identities than is often acknowledged. This does not just happen. The counter-globalization movements, as well as other social and political movements, have been integral to the reproduction of such political identities and dispositions.

The significance of such contestation, however, remains marginalized within the accounts of neo-liberalism offered by much critical geography and left theorizing. There is a marked tendency to construct resistance and contestation merely as reactions to particular processes of neo-liberalization, rather than as having their own dynamic trajectories. Thus interventions by Noel Castree on the 'neo-liberalization of nature' theorize neo-liberalism as 'one contingent way in which the enduring imperatives and contradictions of capital accumulation can be managed' (Castree, 2007b: 10; see also Castree, 2007a). He argues that 'nature's neo-liberalization' is a 'project driven by political economic elites that marginalizes the poor and calls forth resistance', conceding that such resistance 'can reconfigure the project in its specific geographical manifestation' (Castree, 2007b: 11). In Castree's account, however, resistance and the political become theorized as secondary to the logics of capital accumulation. Peck and Tickell make a similar move. They concede that there is 'a space for politics' in accounts of neo-liberalism, even 'if these are tendentially neo-liberalized politics, or limited forms of resistance to this dis(order)' (Peck and Tickell, 2002: 49). Like Castree, however, politics and resistance for Peck and Tickell become resolutely secondary to a spatial terrain already shaped by powerful and dominant political-economic processes.

The problem with these approaches is that resistances, and the political in more general terms, become added on to these stories about neo-liberalization (see also Dikeç, 2007: 6; North, 2007). They are not made integral to theorizing about practices of neo-liberalization. Instead, they are treated as secondary aspects of these phenomena, as effects or reactions, rather than as things that matter in constructing accounts of the relations between spatialities, neo-liberalization and the political. This occludes the importance of the diverse forms of agency and identity being constituted through such struggles. Further, it ignores the multiple disruptions and contestations formed through the generation of the 'heterogeneous associations that constitute' neo-liberalism (Braun, 2005: 839). Drawing attention to the many productive spatial practices through which these neo-liberal geographies of power have brought into contestation is crucial here.

In this regard one of the important achievements of the counter-globalization movement has been to make neo-liberal power relations part of a terrain of contestation. I have argued that these processes have been at once disruptive of, and more productive, than many existing critiques of the radical centre and its capitulation to neo-liberalism allow. The critiques of the radical centre by Mouffe, Žižek and Swyngedouw and others are necessary and significant. But they are limited by their search for antagonisms within already constituted national political contexts and spaces. One of the arguments of Part III of this book has been that it is necessary to attend to the dynamism and generative character of the antagonisms constituted through the counter-globalization movement. These movements have generated both antagonisms and solidarities that can't be reduced to, or effectively theorized in relation to, nation-state spaces of politics.

This is a testament to the productiveness of these political interventions. Dislocating accounts of these movements as merely defensive forms of reaction and as secondary to the logics of capital accumulation is a condition of possibility for engaging with their dynamic trajectories. Their forms of collective experimentation with new forms of organization have opened up possibilities for new ways of ordering globalization. A key achievement of these movements is the extent to which they articulate different ways of generating the geographies of globalization (see Wainwright and Oritz, 2006). The geographies of connection generated through these movements generate actually existing alternative ways of making globalized practices. They have also shifted antagonisms from being about a contestation of globalization *per se* to a contestation of the terms on which globalization is generated. Attending to these generative effects throws up particular theoretical challenges which I have attempted to engage with here. They also raise important political questions. The next section seeks to draw out the significance of such identities, solidarities and articulations for the directions of contemporary counter-global politics.

'Common Sense' Beyond Neo-Liberalism

This book has demonstrated that very different kinds of identities are generated through opposition to dominant globalizing practices. I have noted the production of different exclusionary political identities and spaces of politics in both the past and present, whether these are the nationalist articulations of resistance to neo-liberal globalization associated at times with the Caravan, or some of the violent masculinities that shaped the mutinies associated with the United Irishmen. I have argued that there are also histories and geographies of different ways of opposing unequal globalizing practices. These have constructed plural articulations of identities and 'unruly alliances and flows' through the activity of bringing unequal geographies of power into contestation. That there were different more exclusionary identities generated in relation to these geographies of power makes these multi-ethnic solidarities and egalitarian conceptions of connection and politics more rather than less significant. It is here I would suggest that some of the 'real grounds of hope' lie (Williams, 1983: 196).

One of the key concerns of the book has been to intervene in these different practices through which solidarities and identities are generated through resistance to neo-liberal globalization. I argued in chapter 6 that the tensions among these movements have tended to be reduced to divisions around the use of violence and non-violence, and to whether key institutions like the World Trade Organization should be reformed or abolished (see Brecher, Costello and Smith, 2000; Cockburn and St. Clair,

2000; Starr, 2000). In contrast I argued that there were important political struggles to be had over the different populist logics being constructed through opposition to globalization. Further, Part III explored in depth how the activity of these movements generates different and potentially conflictual maps of grievance. Through the discussion of the Caravan in particular I have argued that the ways maps of grievance were constructed had significant effects on the kinds of alliances and identities these movements shaped.

One of the lazy critiques of these movements has been that they mobilize globalized practices through their own conduct and are thus contradictory. This is to miss the point. The geographies of connection they have generated through different conventions, practices and power relations to those that constitute neo liberal globalization constitute actually existing alternatives. These alternatives generate connections between struggles in different places and intervene in the unequal geographies shaped through neo-liberal practices. They do not necessarily offer a 'total' critique or alternative to neo-liberal globalization such as that demanded by Harvey or Hardt and Negri, but rather, one which remains situated and partial, constituting particular networks, particular articulations between different struggles. This diversity and heterogeneity opens up possibilities which transcend the desires of the left for unity in a traditional sense (see De Sousa Santos, 2006; Jain, 2003). These articulations are not smooth, consensual or uncontested. They bring together activists with markedly different positionalities and experiences of neo-liberal globalization, for whom the stakes of organizing can be very different.

This also generates a fraught, ongoing and productive set of negotiations within and between different struggles. These negotiations bear on a significant set of issues over how these movements generate and deal with power relations. The practices through which these are contested and worked through will have important implications for the trajectories of these movements. Firstly, there are important questions about how these transnational forms of mobilization negotiate riven geographies of power themselves. Will they manage to generate forms of transnational organizing that manage to dislocate these riven geographies of power? Secondly, there are questions about the ways in which these movements negotiate geographies of difference and power through their organizing practices. The debates over race and gender raised in relation to the North American global justice movement in chapter 6 throw up important political challenges, the implications of which are still perhaps to be worked through. They raise significant questions about how counter-global networks are generated, and whether they will be generated in ways which treat various forms of difference and subaltern knowledges and experiences seriously. Thirdly, there are a set of questions about how these movements theorize,

contest and engage with the geographies of power produced and reproduced by neo-liberalism. These movements have been productive in localizing and rendering contestable practices of neo-liberal globalization which
too often have been seen as all-powerful and free-floating. There remain,
however, important questions about the extent to which these movements
are engaging with the diffuse power relations and the forms of consent
through which neo-liberalism works.

I have engaged with the diverse and productive maps of grievance
shaped through their activity to intervene in discussions of the relations of
these movements to geographies of power. This necessarily bears on the
contested and multiple ways in which alternative globalizations and futures
are generated through the conduct of counter-globalization movements. In
particular I have attempted to unsettle the status of the local or global as
strategic political panaceas for these movements. As I have demonstrated,
the local and global are frequently set up in oppositional ways through the
political imaginaries mobilized against neo-liberal globalization. These
oppositions are mobilized in different ways by different activists and
theorists. There is a common tendency among some explicitly 'anti-
globalization' activists to fetishize the local against the broader, hostile
forces of the global (see Hines, 2001; Sale, 1993; Starr, 2001). The histories and geographies of the 'motley' struggles of the past discussed in Part
II undermine the dream of opposing neo-liberal globalization with small,
bounded communities characterized by harmonious, 'natural' relations.
There is little space for purity in these traditions of resistance. They suggest
the importance of countering oppressive, hostile power relations through
celebrating the connections and intersections that constituted diverse routes
and traditions of resistance. The inspiration of these struggles suggests the
importance of recognizing connections and exchanges as an integral part
of the political identities produced and deployed through contemporary
struggles.

There is a counter-tendency to advocate the formation of a wholly globalized opposition to neo-liberal globalization through institutions such as
a world parliament (see Monbiot, 2003). This position has been given its
boldest and most eloquent expression in Hardt and Negri's work. They
have insisted that any alternative to neo-liberal globalization must be posed
at the global scale, since adopting strategies of local resistance 'misidentifies
and masks the enemy' (Hardt and Negri, 2000: 45). As I argued in chapter
6, there are tensions with this position. It counterposes space and place,
has a rather dismissive attitude to the actually existing counter-global networks generated through opposition to neo-liberal globalization and doesn't
engage adequately with the different political identities constituted through
these networks. The conduct of the ICC illustrates that the counter-
globalization movement is productive precisely through opening up joint

articulations between different place-based struggles. This activity can make spatially stretched relations of power contestable and localizable. It can also reconfigure place-based political identities.

Constructing a totalizing global resistance, then, is not the most useful or urgent political task. Rather, it is important to find ways of affirming the practices through which opposition to globalization is located at the intersection of routes of resistance. It is also to insist that these geographies can be generative of alternative political imaginaries and practices. This emphasizes that the choice between local or global resistance is both false and destructive of political possibilities. It also masks one of the creative practices that is integral to the activity of counter-globalization movements. That is the construction of situated, partial geographies of connection between different place-based struggles. These geographies of connection are a central part of the actually existing alternatives to neo-liberal globalization generated through the activity of these movements. Such connections can be productive. In particular, crafting connections between different place-located struggles is crucial to opposing exclusionary nationalist oppositions to globalization. These geographies of connection are integral to the formation of transnational political networks defined by open, solidaristic identities.

It is my hope and contention that this can shape a different kind of political common sense. This is a common sense defined by antagonisms over the ways in which globalization is to be generated. It insists that globalization is to be shaped by multiple actors, not something which is only produced by neo-liberal institutions or multinationals. It is based around the assertion that there can be more just, equitable and sustainable ways of ordering the collectives constructed through globalizing practices than the violent, riven, unequal geographies of contemporary neo-liberal globalization. It is a common sense that draws on the actually existing alternatives to neo-liberal globalization shaped through diverse counter-global networks. Finally, it draws on the solidaristic ways in which they have opposed globalization through linking different struggles, rather than creating chauvinistic responses which pit exclusionary versions of the local or national against the global.

This position opens up certain possibilities. It draws on the creative practices formed through ongoing opposition to dominant orderings of globalization. This emphasizes the significance of strategies for resistances to neo-liberal globalization that reject, refuse and transcend exclusionary, particularist identities. These resistances shape solidarities, articulations and political identities that generate new ways of ordering transnational networks and different futures. They speak to political practices which forge new identities and geographies of connection through the ongoing contestation of unequal geographies of power. Through drawing on these multiple histories and geographies of resistance, collective experiments and identities which exceed and oppose the restrictive, limiting tenets of neo-liberalism will continue to be created. They will also continue to shape world-making processes.

Notes

1 From the Public Declaration of the Glasgow event.
2 Edwards (2003: 245): see chapter 1 for a discussion of Edwards's arguments.
3 I use the term 'subaltern' to signal the diverse forms of marginalized groups, including, but not exclusive to, class, gender, ethnicity and race; see Gramsci (1971: 52–5), Guha (1982).
4 In this sense while being sympathetic to the critiques of scalar thinking offered by Marston et al. I think the term flat is unhelpful in its relative occlusion of such contested, fissiparous and uneven relations, see Marston et al. (2005), Jones III et al. (2007).
5 These included the squatting of St George's Hill in Surrey to celebrate the 350th anniversary of the occupation of the land in common by the Diggers, radicals informed by antinomian and egalitarian political philosophies and actions (see Land is Ours, 1999; Hill, 1972). Their story is told in Leon Rosselson's song 'The World Turned Upside Down', see the fine version by Dick Gaughan on his *CD Handful of Earth* Topic 12TS419.

6 There is not the space here to engage with the debates, based on Carretta's discovery of evidence that suggests Equiano was born in South Carolina, about the veracity of Equiano's memoirs (see Carretta, 2005). See the sceptical points raised in Lovejoy (2006) and Rediker (2007: 109, 380n2).
7 This follows a longstanding tendency in the Marxist tradition to denigrate and marginalize the local. Engels, for example, commenting on Irish peasant movements, argued that they were 'local, isolated and can never become a general form of political struggle' (Engels, 1971).
8 These concerns have also been foregrounded by writers like Boaventura De Sousa Santos, who have argued that processes like the World Social Forum constitute a 'counter-hegemonic globalization' (De Sousa Santos, 2006).

9   This discussion of Williams is inevitably partisan. I grew up in the Black Mountains in Wales, though on the Brecon rather than the Abergavenny side, where Williams was from, and was the child of 'blow-ins'. The importance to me of finding a left intellectual from here who had made such a significant contribution cannot be underestimated, though paradoxically this is perhaps the only part of the world where he is best known for his novels.

CHAPTER 2   GEOGRAPHIES OF SOLIDARITIES AND ANTAGONISMS

10   For these solidarities see http://www.labournet.net/docks2/other/update.htm. This discussion draws on conversations with Councillor Steve Munby, Sarah Penny and Dave Williams who were involved in the brigade to El Salvador.
11   The movement of friend-enemy relations between different spatial domains is a tension that haunts Schmitt's discussion. For however strictly Schmitt tries to fix and align the friend-enemy relation to an equivalence with a specific territorial assemblage, the relation moves both beyond and within these alignments. Derrida argues that Schmitt 'at one and the same time, privilege[s] the State (even if he does not reduce the political to it), base[s] the concept of enemy on the possibility of war between states and nevertheless symmetrically align[s] . . . exterior war and civil war as if the enemy were sometimes the foreigner, sometimes the fellow citizen' (Derrida, 1994: 121).

CHAPTER 3   LABOURERS' POLITICS AND MERCANTILE NETWORKS

12   National Archives TS 11/2696 Box 818.
13   See *The Public Advertiser* 9, 16 June, cited by Dobson (1980: 85) and Foote (1778).
14   Taaffe (1767: 19). A 'well born Tipperary Catholic' noted judiciously that they were 'the scum and some of the rabble of three or four baronies' (cited by Donnelly, 1978: 38).
15   For detailed discussion, see Donnelly (1978), Power (1993) and Wall (1973). For theoretical reflections on their forms of activity, see Gibbons (1996: 134–66) and Lloyd (1993).
16   See *Faulkner's Dublin Journal* (hereafter cited as FDJ) 4–8 May, 29 May–1 June 1762; 4–7 May, 5–8 October 1765.
17   *Freeman's Journal,* 17 September 1774; *Waterford Chronicle,* 29 March 1771.
18   *A Short Narrative,* 1762, in Kelly (1989, 22).
19   Ibid., 23.
20   *Gentleman's Magazine,* April 1762.
21   Fortescue (1929: 310–11).
22   Public Record Office of Northern Ireland, Carberry Papers, T 2966/B/3/9–8 March 1762.
23   Ibid., T 2966/B/3/12–30 March 1762.

24 See FDJ 23–27 March, June 1–3 1762.

25 University College Dublin, Folklore Commission Notebook 406: 26–7.

26 See *Gentleman's Magazine*, April 1762; *A Short Narrative*, 1762, in Kelly (1989); FDJ 23–27 March, 6–10 April, 1–4 May, 4–8 May, 3–6 July 1762; 5–8 March, 8–12 March, 12–15 March, 26–29 March, 29 March–2 April 1763; 24–28 September, 1–5 October 1765. For activity in Kilkenny, see FDJ 6–9 April, 9–13 April, 29 September–2 October 1765.

27 See Society for the Propagation of the Gospel (SPG) Ms B6/167/173/ 174/176.

28 SPG Ms B6/174.

29 SPG Ms B6/179.

30 SPG Ms B6/172.

31 National Archives SP/44/14 fos 47–51.

32 See Shelburne Papers, vol. 133: 331–3; Aston (1992: 405–6); *Report of the Grand Committee on Trade* (1780: cxi).

33 See *The Public Advertiser* 9, 16 June, cited by Dobson (1980: 85) and Foote (1778).

34 TS 11/443/1408.

35 TS 11/2696/818.

36 Proceedings, 1768: 244–56. The undertakers were a group of about twenty middlemen, almost all publicans, who 'undertook' to supply Newcastle and other collier ships with gangs of coal heavers to unload their cargo. These undertakers operated systems of networked corruption through interrelations with Newcastle coal dealers (see Featherstone, 2001: 108–9; George, 1927: 234; Wilson, 1995).

37 TS 11/2696/ 818.

38 For the similar forms of action used by the Whiteboys, see Gentleman's Magazine, April, 1762, A Short Narrative: 1762: 22. For accounts of the use of these practices by Journeymen weavers in Dublin and Carrick on Suir, see Donnelly 1983: 314. These rituals were also used in disputes in 1769 by London Irish silk weavers (Linebaugh, 1992: 270, 276).

39 In 1700 London imported 335,000 Chaldrons of coal; by 1768 this had risen to 614,000 (Ashton and Sykes, 1964: 249–50).

40 For the intimidation of coal meters by coal heavers in their disputes of 1768, see National Archives SP/44/142: 102–3.

41 Journal of House of Commons, 39 May 1758.

42 Proceedings, 1768: 244–256.

CHAPTER 4   MAKING DEMOCRATIC SPATIAL PRACTICES

43 This chapter draws heavily from two collections of the papers of the LCS. These are Mary Thale's *Selections from the Papers of the London Corresponding Society, 1792–99* (cited as Selections) and the six-volume edition of *Papers of the London Corresponding Society*, edited by Michael Davis (cited as LCS).

44 British Library Add Mss 27811, folio 4.

45 TS 11/965/3510A No. 93. Letter from the Sheffield Constitutional Society received 19 March 1792.

46 British Library Add Mss 27811, folio 4.

47 Spies like John Groves and George Lynam managed to gain senior positions in the LCS and even succeeded in altering its organizational structure to make it easier to spy on. The infiltration of the LCS by spies is beyond the scope of this chapter. It has been discussed in depth elsewhere; see Barrell (2006: 53), Thale (1983), Thompson (1968).

48 BL Add Mss 27813, fo. 136, 11 September 1795.

49 BL Add Mss 27813, fo. 141, 31 August 1795.

50 TS 11/953.

51 TS 11/965/3510A. On Thelwall, see Thompson (1994a).

52 TS 24/12/2.

53 Lydia Hardy to Thomas Hardy, 2 April 1792, TS 24/12/1.

54 British Library Additional Manuscripts, 27811, folio 12.

55 Wedderburn was also at various times a brothel keeper, raising important questions about the relations between radical subcultures, forms of masculinity and violence against women. See McCalman (1986, 1991).

CHAPTER 5   COUNTER-GLOBAL NETWORKS AND THE MAKING OF SUBALTERN NATIONALISMS

56 National Archives TS 11/914/3164 The King Against John Pollard For Sedition.

57 National Archives Assi 23/9.

58 Quote from the song of mutineers 'All Hail Brother Seamen' from the papers of the *Repulse*, reproduced by Gill (1913: 389).

59 National Archives Adm 1/5346 record of court martial assembled on board HMS *Gladiator* in Portsmouth Harbour, held 8 September to 14th day of September, 1798.

60 See, for the Caribbean, Adm 2/939, Adm 50/ 65; for the Cape of Good Hope, Adm 1/56 and Boucher and Penn (1992: 187); for the Mediterranean fleet, see Adm 1/396.

61 Adm 1/56.

62 *Grampus* Pay Book, Adm 35/738.

63 Adm 1/5340 Court Martial Mutineers of the *Grampus*, July 10th to 12th, 1797.

64 The relationships between the LCS, the United Irishmen and the mutinies still, however, seem to be a matter of scorn for some naval historians. Rodger argues that the Quota Acts, which have been seen as a key source of dissent, were not a source of 'educated trouble-makers', but rather of 'respectable working men in need of employment' (Rodger, 2003: 561). It was precisely 'respectable working men', however, who were members of societies like the LCS and who would have brought their experiences of these organizations to negotiate the harsh life aboard ship.

65 The Defenders were a network of often agrarian Catholic secret societies. Defenderism had 'a chameleon ideology infinitely adaptable to varying local

conditions: now sectarian, now agrarian, always Francophile and anti-ascendancy' (Smyth, 1992: 120; see also Elliott, 1982: 39–46; Quinn, 1998; Wells, 1983: 8–12; Whelan, 1996).

66   National Archives of Ireland 620/31/204.
67   National Archives of Ireland 620/31/138.
68   National Archives of Ireland 620/31/37.
69   Adm 1/5346.
70   *Defiance* Pay Book, ADM 35/469.
71   'An act for more effectually preventing the administering or taking of unlawful oaths', 37 Geo III c. 123.
72   On the use of oaths as aggressive strategies to spread the activity of the movement and as part of practices of intimidation, see A Short Narrative, 1762: 25, FDJ 5th–8th October 1765, *Waterford Chronicle*, 30 April 1771.
73   See Aston (1992: 405–6); Henry (1994: 63); Report of the Grand Committee on Trade (1780).
74   See Shelburne Papers, vol. 133: 331–3.
75   PRO Adm 1/5340 Court Martial Mutineers of the *Grampus* July 10th to 12th, 1797.
76   *Renommée* Pay Book Adm 35/1550.
77   *Renommée* Court Martial, National Archives, Adm 1/5343.
78   National Archives, Adm 1/5343.
79   Adm 1/5346.
80   Adm 1/5347.
81   See Adm 1/5346, Adm 1/5347.
82   Adm 1/5346.
83   Adm 1/5346.
84   Curtin also notes women's participation in oath-bound societies of United Irishwomen (Curtin, 1991: 134).

CHAPTER 6   GEOGRAPHIES OF POWER AND THE COUNTER-GLOBALIZATION MOVEMENT

85   Significantly, they argue in *Empire* that the US is not a central part of the apparatus of Empire, although this position is revised slightly in *Multitude* in the wake of the Second Gulf War.
86   The figuring of space as a passive backdrop to revolutionary political activity also structures Negri's earlier work. See Negri (2003: 21–126), Guattari and Negri (1990: 5).
87   Hardt's account of the 2002 World Social Forum paradoxically points to tensions over national/global sovereignty which are occluded in the concept of multitude (Hardt, 2002: 113–14).
88   This 'solidaristic agriculture' is based on a prioritization of small farms, which is perhaps vulnerable to charges of romanticizing the local and not querying what kind of small farms are to be developed.
89   Though see Thompson's stinging riposte to accusations from Tom Nairn that he articulated forms of 'populist socialism' (Thompson, 1978: iii).

90   ICC discussions, 29/5/99.

91   *Satyagraha*, literally 'exertion for truth', was the term used by Gandhi for non-violent but illegal campaigns. The use of these tactics develops a continuity between New Farmers Movements and Gandhian struggles.

92   Information is drawn from the three ICC newsletters, *Do or Die* (1999) and my own participation.

93   I draw the term 'process geographies' from Routledge (2003).

94   For detailed critiques of the forms of discipline constructed through Gandhian mobilization, see Guha (1997: 100–51), Chatterjee (1984: 153–95).

95   See *The Hindu*, 2 February 2006; *Deccan Herald*, 10 February 2004.

96   In the first meeting I attended there was constant talk of breaking down into groups around particular themes, but this never actually happened (ICC/Discussions/1–24/3/1999).

97   This shortened name was how Nanjundaswamy was known through the networks of the ICC.

98   London Welcoming Committee meeting, ICC/Discussions/6–13/5/1999.

99   ICC/Discussions/6–13/5/1999.

100 As Madsen argues, 'The caravanists . . . represented the middling and biggish farmers, and some of those families who have succeeded in diversifying their economic base, due mainly to the prosperity created by the green revolution' (Madsen, 2001: 3740).

101 ICC/Discussions/24/3/1999.

102 ICC/Discussions/13/5/1999.

103 ICC/Discussions/20/6/1999.

104 ICC/Discussions/27/5/1999.

105 ICC/Discussions/29/5/1999.

106 ICC/Discussions/29/5/1999.

107 Thus, at an action outside the Bayer plant in Leverkusen, an activist from the Indian Karnataka State Farmers Union spoke against the pressure to adopt non-traditional farming methods, methods that she argued imposed a heavy reliance on chemicals, while other Indian speakers spoke against the high prices of the chemical fertilisers produced by Bayer.

108 For an example of the productivist stories of the BKU, see Tikait (1999).

109 ICC/Discussions/19/6/1999.

110 ICC/Discussions/27/10/1999.

CONCLUSION: TOWARDS POLITICIZED GEOGRAPHIES OF CONNECTION

111 Woody Guthrie, radical American singer and songwriter, cited on Dick Gaughan's website, www.dickgaughan.co.uk/main.html; accessed 27 October 2007.

References

Agnew, J. (2004) 'Nationalism', in Duncan, J. S., Johnson, N. and Schein, R. H. (eds) *A Companion to Cultural Geography*, Oxford: Blackwell, 499–521.

Agnew, J. (2003) 'Contemporary political geography: intellectual heterodoxy and its dilemmas', *Political Geography* 22(6), 223–237.

Ainger, K. (2003) 'Life is not business: the intercontinental caravan', in Notes From Nowhere (eds) *We Are Everywhere*, London: Verso, 160–170.

Allen, J. (2003) *Lost Geographies of Power* Oxford: Blackwell.

Amin, A. (2004) 'Regions unbound: towards a new politics of place', *Geografisker Annaler* B 86(1), 33–44.

Amin, A. (2002) 'Spatialities of globalization', *Environment and Planning A* 34(3), 385–399.

Anderson, A. (1998) 'Cosmopolitanism, universalism, and the divided legacies of modernity', in Cheah, P. and Robbins, B. (eds) *Cosmopolitics: Thinking and Feeling Beyond the Nation*, Minnesota: University of Minnesota Press, 265–289.

Anderson, B. (2006) ' "Transcending without transcendence": utopianism and an ethos of hope', *Antipode* 38(4), 691–710.

Anderson, B. (1991) *Imagined Communities: Reflections on the Origins and Spread of Nationalism* 2nd edn London: Verso.

Anderson, P. (2002) 'Internationalism: a breviary', *New Left Review* 14, March–April, 5–25.

Anderson, P. (1980) *Arguments Within English Marxism* London: Verso.

Appiah, K. A. (1998) 'Cosmopolitan patriots', in Cheah, P. and Robbins, B. (eds) *Cosmopolitics: Thinking and Feeling Beyond the Nation*, Minneapolis: Minnesota University Press, 91–114.

Arditi, B. (2005) 'Populism as an internal periphery of democratic politics', in Pannizza, F. (ed.) *Populism and the Mirror of Democracy* London: Verso, 72–98.

Ashman, S. (2004) 'Resistance to neoliberal globalization: a case of militant particularism?', *Politics* 24(2), 143–153.

Ashton, T. S. and Sykes, J. (1964) *The Coal Industry of the Eighteenth Century* Manchester: Manchester University Press.

Assadi, M. (1997) *Peasant Movement in Karnataka* Delhi: Shipra Publications.

Assadi, M. (1996) 'Attack on multinationals: re-enactment of Gandhian violence', *Economic and Political Weekly* May 18, 1184–1186.

Assadi, M. (1995a) 'Dunkelism and peasant protest in Karnataka: a view from within', *Social Action* 45, April–June, 191–205.

Assadi, M. (1995b) ' "Khadi Curtain," "Weak Capitalism" and "Operation Ryot": some ambiguities in farmer's discourse, Karnataka and Maharashtra 1980–93', in Brass, T. (ed.) *New Farmers' Movements in India*, Ilford: Frank Cass, 212–227.

Aston, R. [1763] (1992) 'A charge by Richard Aston', in Lamoine, G. (ed.) *Charges to the Grand Jury, 1689–1803*, London: Offices of the Royal Historical Society, 399–410.

Barnett, C. (2004a) 'Deconstructing radical democracy: articulation, representation, and being with others', *Political Geography* 23(5), 503–528.

Barnett, C. (2004b) 'Media, democracy and representation: disembodying the public', in Barnett, C. and Low, M. (eds) *Spaces of Democracy: Geographical Perspectives on Citizenship, Participation and Representation*, London: Sage, 185–206.

Barnett, C. (2003) *Culture and Democracy: Media, Space and Representation* Edinburgh: Edinburgh University Press.

Barnett, C. and Low, M. (2004) 'Geography and democracy: an introduction', in Barnett, C. and Low, M. (eds) *Spaces of Democracy: Geographical Perspectives on Citizenship, Participation and Representation*, London: Sage, 1–22.

Barrell, J. (2006) *The Spirit of Despotism: Invasions of Privacy in the 1790s* Oxford: Oxford University Press.

Barrell, J. (2003) 'Divided we grow', *London Review of Books*, 5 June, 8–11.

Barrell, J. (2000) *Imagining the King's Death* Oxford: Oxford University Press.

Barry, A. (2001) *Political Machines: Governing a Technological Society* London: Continuum Publications.

Beckett, A. (2002) *Pinochet in Picadilly* London: Faber.

Bell, W. (ed.) (1964–8) *Naval Documents of the American Revolution: Volume 6, 1776* Washington, DC: US Government Printing Office.

Bentall, J. (1996) 'Bharat vs India.' Unpublished Ph.D. thesis, University of Cambridge.

Bentall, J. and Corbridge, S. (1996) 'Urban-rural relations, demand politics and the "new agrarianism" in northwest India: the Bharatiya Kisan Union', *Transactions of the Institute of British Geographers* 21(1), 27–48.

Berlin, I. (1998) *Many Thousands Gone: The First Two Centuries of Slavery in North America* Harvard, MA: Harvard University Press.

Berlin, I. (1996) 'From Creole to African: Atlantic Creoles and the origins of African-American society in mainland North America', *William and Mary Quarterly* 53(2), 251–288.

Bhabha, H. (1994) *The Location of Culture* London: Routledge.

Bijoy, C. R. (2006) 'Kerala's Plachimada struggle: a narrative on water and governance rights', *Economic and Political Weekly* October, 14, 4332–4339.

Binns, J. (1854) *Recollections of the Life of John Binns* Philadelphia.

Bird, S., Georgakas, D. and Shaffer, D. (1987) *Solidarity Forever: An Oral History of the IWW* London: Lawrence and Wishart.

Blackburn, R. (1988) *The Overthrow of Colonial Slavery* London: Verso.

Bohstedt, J. (2000) 'The pragmatic economy, the politics of provisions and the "invention" of the food riot tradition in 1740', in Charlesworth, A. and Randall, A. (eds) *Moral Economy and Popular Protest*, London: Macmillan, 55–92.

Bolster, W. J. (1997) *Black Jacks: African American Seamen in the Age of Sail* Cambridge, MA: Harvard University Press.

Boucher, M. and Penn, N. (1992) *Britain at the Cape, 1795–1803* Houghton: Brenthurst Press.

Bové, J. and Dufour, F. (2001) *The World is Not for Sale* London: Verso.

Branford, S. and Rocha, J. (2002) *Cutting the Wire: The Story of the Landless Movement in Brazil* London: Latin America Bureau.

Brass, T. (2000) 'Moral economists, subalterns, new social movements and the (re)-emergence of a (post-) modernized (middle) peasant', in Chaturvedi, V. (ed.) *Mapping Subaltern Studies and the Postcolonial*, London: Verso, 127–162.

Brass, T. (1995) 'The politics of gender, nature and nation', in Brass, T. (ed.) *New Farmers' Movements in India*, Ilford: Frank Cass, 27–71.

Braun, B. (2005) 'Writing geographies of hope', *Antipode* 37(4), 834–841.

Braun, B. and Disch, L. (2002) 'Radical democracy's "modern constitution"', *Environment and Planning D: Society and Space* 20(5), 505–511.

Brecher, J., Costello, T. and Smith, B. (2000) *Globalization From Below: The Power of Solidarity* Cambridge, MA: South End Press.

Brewer, J. (1994) *The Sinews of Power: War, Money and the English State, 1688–1783* London: Routledge.

Bunnell, T. and Nah, A. (2004) 'Counter-global cases for places: contesting displacement in globalizing Kuala Lumpur Metropolitan Area', *Urban Studies* 41(12), 2447–2467.

Byrne, C. J. (1992) 'The Waterford colony in Newfoundland 1700–1850', in Nolan, W. and Power, T. (eds) *Waterford: History and Society*, Dublin: Geography Publications, 351–372.

Byrne, C. J. (ed.) (1984) *Gentlemen-Bishops and Faction-Fighters: The Letters of Bishops O Donel, Lambert, Scallan and Other Irish Missionaries*, St Johns: Jesperson Press.

Byrne, C. J. (1977) 'Ireland and Newfoundland: the United Irish Rising of 1798 and the Fencible's Mutiny in St John's, 1799–1800.' Paper presented to Newfoundland Historical Society, St John's.

Calhoun, C. (2002) 'The class consciousness of frequent travellers: towards a critique of actually existing cosmopolitanism', in Vertovec, S. and Cohen, R. (eds) *Conceiving Cosmopolitanism: Theory, Context and Practice*, Oxford: Oxford University Press, 86–109.

Callon, M. (1998) 'Introduction: the embeddedness of economic markets in economics', in Callon, M. (ed.) *The Laws of the Markets*, Oxford: Blackwell, 1–57.

Cameron, A. and Palan, R. (2004) *The Imagined Economies of Globalization* London: Sage.

Canovan, M. (1999) 'Trust the people! Populism and the two faces of democracy', *Political Studies*, 47, 2–16.

Carretta, V. (2005) *Equiano the African: Biography of a Self-Made Man* Athens: University of Georgia Press.

Carter, T. (1986) *Shattering Illusions: West Indians in British Politics* London: Lawrence and Wishart.

Castells, M. (1997) *The Rise of the Network Society* Oxford: Blackwell.

Castree, N. (2007a) 'Neoliberalising nature 1: the logics of de- and re-regulation', *Environment and Planning A*, 40(1), 131–152.

Castree, N. (2007b) 'Neoliberalising nature 2: processes, outcomes and effects', *Environment and Planning A*, 40(1), 153–173.

Castree, N. (2006) 'The detour of critical theory', in Castree, N. and Gregory, D. (eds) *David Harvey: A Critical Reader*, Oxford: Blackwell, 247–269.

Castree, N. (2000) 'Geographic scale and grass-roots internationalism: the Liverpool dock dispute, 1995–1998', *Economic Geography* 73(3), 272–292.

Cavanagh, J., Anderson, S. and Hansen-Kuhn, K. (2001) 'Crossborder organizing around alternatives to free trade: lessons from the NAFTA/FTAA experience', in Edwards, M. and Gaventa, J. (eds) *Global Citizen Action*, London: Earthscan, 149–162.

Centre for Science and Environment (2006) 'Soft Drinks Still Unsafe . . .' www.cseindia.org/misc/cola-indepth/cola2006/cola_press2006.htm, accessed 17 July 2007.

Chakrabarty, D. (2000) *Provincializing Europe: Postcolonial Thought and Historical Difference* Princeton, NJ: Princeton University Press.

Chase, M. (1988) *The People's Farm: English Radical Agrarianism* Oxford: Clarendon Press.

Chatterjee, P. (2004) *The Politics of the Governed: Reflections on Popular Politics in Most of the World* Colombia: Colombia University Press.

Chatterjee, P. (1993) *The Nation and Its Fragments: Colonial and Postcolonial Histories* Colombia: Colombia University Press.

Chatterjee, P, (1989) 'Caste and subaltern consciousness', in Guha, R. (ed.) *Subaltern Studies* VI, 169–209.

Chatterjee, P. (1984) 'Gandhi and the critique of civil society', in Guha, R. (ed.) *Subaltern Studies III*, Delhi: Oxford University Press, 153–195.

Christopher, E. (2006) *Slave Ship Sailors and Their Captive Cargoes, 1730–1807* Cambridge: Cambridge University Press.

Claeys, G. (1995) 'Introduction', in Claeys, G. (ed.) *The Politics of English Jacobinism: Writings of John Thelwall*, Philadelphia: Pennsylvannia State University Press, xiii–lviii.

Clark, A. (1996) *The Struggle for the Breeches: Gender and the Making of the British Working Class* London: University of California Press.

Coal Heavers (1764) *The Case of the Coal Heavers* London.

Cockburn, A. and St. Clair, J. (2000) *Five Days That Shook the World: Seattle and Beyond* London: Verso.

Cohen, R. and Rai, S. M. (2000) 'Global social movements: Towards a cosmopolitan politics', in Cohen, R. and Rai, S. M. (eds) *Global Social Movements* London: Athlone Press, 1–17.

Cole, P. (2003) 'Quakertown blues: Philadelphia's longshoremen and the decline of the IWW', *Left History* 8(2), 39–70.

Colley, L. (1992) *Britons: Forging the Nation, 1707–1837* London: Yale University Press.

Colombia Solidarity Campaign (2007) 'It's oil, stupid!: background', www.colombiasolidarity.org.uk/content/view/115/68/, accessed 10 July 2007.

Colquhoun, P. (1800) *Treatise on the Commerce and Police on the River Thames* London.

Connolly, W. E. (1995) *The Ethos of Pluralization* Minneapolis: University of Minnesota Press.

Conway, J. (2004) 'Prefiguring Seattle? Direct action movements of the 1990s as "moments in a possible future"', *Antipode* 36(5), 994–997.

Coombs, B. L. (1939) *These Poor Hands* London: Left Book Club.

Corporate Europe Observer (1999) 'Biotech PR initiative reaps poor harvest', *Corporate Europe Observer*, Issue 5, October.

Cotlar, S. (2005) 'Reading the foreign news, imagining an American public sphere: radical and conservative visions of "the public" in mid-1790s newspapers', in Kamrath, N. and Harris, S. (eds) *Periodical Literature in Eighteenth Century America*, Knoxville: University of Tennessee Press, 307–338.

Cox, K. R. (1998) 'Spaces of dependence, spaces of engagement and the politics of scale, or: looking for local politics', *Political Geography* 17(1), 1–23.

Creighton, M. and Norling, L. (eds) (1996) *Iron Men and Wooden Women: Gender and Seafaring in the Atlantic World, 1700–1920* Baltimore: Johns Hopkins University Press.

Cudjoe, S. (1997) 'C. L. R. James and the Trinidad & Tobago intellectual tradition, or, not learning Shakespeare under a mango tree', *New Left Review* 223, 114–125.

Curtin, N. J. (1991) 'Women and eighteenth-century Irish republicanism', in MacCurtain, M. and O'Dowd, M. (eds) *Women in Early Modern Ireland*, Edinburgh: Edinburgh University Press, 133–145.

Danaher, K. (2001) 'Conclusion', in Danaher, K. (ed.) *Democratizing the Global Economy: The Battle Against the World Bank and the IMF*, Novato, CA: Global Exchange Books, 198–204.

Daniel, P. (2007) 'Is another world possible without the women's perspective?', Open Democracy, 17 January, www.opendemocracy.net/xml/xhtml/articles/4257.html, accessed 6 June 2007.

Davies, A.D. (forthcoming) 'Ethnography, space and politics: interrogating the process of protest in the Tibetan Freedom Movement', *Area*.

Davis, M. T. (2005) 'An evening of pleasure rather than business': songs, subversion and radical cultures in the 1790s', *Journal of the Study of British Cultures* 12(2), 115–126.

De Sousa Santos, B. (2006) *The Rise of the Global Left: The World Social Forum and Beyond* London: Zed Books.

De Sousa Santos, B. (2003) 'The World Social Forum: toward a counter-hegemonic globalization', www.ces.fe.uc.pt/bss/fsm.php, accessed 7 July 2003.

De Sousa Santos, B. (2002) *Toward a New Legal Common Sense*, London: Butterworths, Lexis Nexis.

Deleuze, G. and Guattari, F. (1987) *A Thousand Plateaus* London: Athlone Press.

della Porta, D. (2005) 'Multiple belongings, tolerant identities, and the construction of "another politics": between the European Social Forum and the local social fora', in della Porta, D. and Tarrow, S. (eds) *Transnational Protest and Global Activism*, Lanham, MD: Rowman and Littlefield, 175–202.

della Porta, D. and Mosca, L. (2007) '*In movimento*: "contamination" in action and the Italian global justice movement', *Global Networks* 7(1), 1–27.

Dening, G. (1992) *Mr Bligh's Bad Language: Passion, Power and Theatre on the Bounty* Cambridge: Cambridge University Press.

Derrida, J. (1994) *The Politics of Friendship* London: Verso.

Desmarais, A. (2002) 'The Via Campesina: consolidating an international peasant and farm movement', *Journal of Peasant Studies* 29(2), 91–124.

Di Chiro, G. (1996) 'Nature as community: the convergence of environment and social justice', in Cronon, W. W. (ed.) *Uncommon Ground: Rethinking the Human Place in Nature* 2nd edn. London: W. W. Norton, 298–320.

Dickson, D. (1993) 'Paine and Ireland', in Dickson, D., Keogh, D. and Whelan, K. (eds) *The United Irishmen: Republicanism, Radicalism and Rebellion*, Dublin: Lilliput Press, 135–150.

Dikeç, M. (2007) *The Badlands of the Republic: Space, Politics and Urban Policy*, Oxford: Blackwell.

Dikeç, M. (2005) 'Space, politics, and the political', *Environment and Planning D: Society and Space* 23(2), 171–188.

DN (2001) 'Globalization of Protest', *Economic and Political Weekly* 6 October, 3818–3819.

Dobson, C. R. (1980) *Masters and Journeymen: A Prehistory of Industrial Relations* London: Croom Helm.

Doherty, B. (2002) *Ideas and Actions in the Green Movement* London: Routledge.

Donnelly, Jr, J. S. (1983) 'Irish agrarian rebellion: the Whiteboys of 1769–76', *Proceedings of the Royal Irish Academy*, 83: C: 12, 293–331.

Donnelly, Jr, J. S. (1978) 'The Whiteboy movement, 1761–5', *Irish Historical Studies* 21(81), 20–54.

Do or Die (1999) *Do or Die: Magazine of Earth First in UK* No. 8.

Drescher, S. (1987) *Capitalism and Antislavery: British Mobilization in Comparative Perspective* Oxford: Oxford University Press.

Drew, G. and Levien, M. (2006) 'The opposition to Coca Cola and water privatization: activists in Medhiganj, India rise up', www.zmag.org/content/showarticle.cfm?ItemID=10641, accessed 2 July 2007.

Du Bois, W. E. B. [1929] (1972) 'The AFofL and the Negro', in Walden, D. (ed.) *The Crisis Writings*, Greenwich, CT: Fawcett Publications, 228–233.

Duberman, M. (1996) *Paul Robeson* New York: New Press.

Durey, M. (1997) *Transatlantic Radicals and the Early American Republic* Lawrence: University Press of Kansas.

Edwards, B. H. (2003) *The Practice of Diaspora: Literature, Translation, and the Rise of Black Internationalism* Harvard, MA: Harvard University Press.

Elliott, M. (1989) *Wolf Tone: Prophet of Irish Independence* Yale, CT: Yale University Press.

Elliott, M. (1982) *Partners in Revolution: The United Irishmen and France* Yale, CT: Yale University Press.

Engels, F. [1882] (1971) 'Letter to Eduard Bernstein June 26, 1882', in Marx, K. and Engels, F., *Ireland and the Irish Question*, ed. R. Dixon, London: Lawrence and Wishart, 451–454.

Epstein, J. (2003) *In Practice: Studies in the Language and Culture of Popular Politics in Modern Britain* Stanford, CA: Stanford University Press.

Equiano, O. [1789] (1995) *The Interesting Narrative and Other Writings*, ed. V. Carretta, London: Penguin.

Escobar, A. (2001) 'Culture sits in places: reflections on globalism and subaltern strategies of localization', *Political Geography* 20(2), 139–174.

Evans, N. (1980) 'The South Wales race riots of 1919', *Llafur, the Journal of Welsh Labour History* 3(1), 5–29.

Featherstone, D. J. (2007) 'Skills for heterogeneous associations: the Whiteboys, collective experimentation and subaltern political ecologies', *Environment and Planning D: Society and Space* 25(2), 284–306.

Featherstone, D. J. (2005a) 'Towards the relational construction of militant particularisms: or why the geographies of past struggles matter for resistance to neo-liberal globalization', *Antipode* 37(2), 250–271.

Featherstone, D. J. (2005b) 'Atlantic networks, antagonisms and the formation of subaltern political identities', *Social and Cultural Geography* 6(3), 387–404.

Featherstone, D. J. (2004) 'Spatial relations and the materialities of political conflict: the construction of entangled political identities in the London and Newcastle Port Strikes of 1768', *Geoforum* 35(6), 701–711.

Featherstone, D. J. (2003) 'Spatialities of transnational resistance to neo-liberal globalization: the maps of grievance of the Inter-continental Caravan', *Transactions of the Institute of British Geographers* 28(4), 404–421.

Featherstone, D. J. (2001) *Spatiality, Political Identities and the Environmentalism of the Poor* Ph.D. thesis, Department of Geography, Open University.

Featherstone, D. J. (1997) 'Reimagining the inhuman city: the "Pure Genius" and occupation', *Soundings: A Journal of Politics and Culture* 7, 45–60.

Fernandes, F. M. (2005) 'The land occupation as a form of access to land in Brazil: a theoretical and methodological contribution', in Moyo, S. and Yeros, P. (eds) *Reclaiming the Land: The Resurgence of Rural Movements in Africa, Asia and Latin America*, London: Zed Books, 317–340.

Fischer, S. (2004) *Modernity Disavowed: Haiti and the Cultures of Anti-Slavery* Durham, NC: Duke University Press.

Fletcher, B. and Gapasin, F. (2003) 'The politics of labour and race in the USA', *Socialist Register 2003*, London: Merlin Press, 245–264.

Foote, S. (1778) *The Tailors: A Tragedy for Warm Weather* London.

Fotopoulos, T. and Gezerlis, A. (2002) 'Hardt and Negri's *Empire*: a new Communist Manifesto or a reformist welcome to neoliberal globalization?', *Democracy and Nature* 8(2), 319–330.

Foucault, M. (1980) *Power/Knowledge* London: Harvester Wheatsheaf.

Fortescue, J. (ed.) (1929) *The Papers of King George III, Volume 1* London: Macmillan.

Francis, H. (1984) *Miners Against Fascism: Wales and the Spanish Civil War* London: Lawrence and Wishart.

Francis, H. and Smith, D. (1980) *The Fed: A History of the South Wales Miners in the Twentieth Century* London: Lawrence and Wishart.

Froude, J. A. (1881) *The English in Ireland in the Eighteenth Century*, 3 vols. London: Longman, Green.

Gale Jones, J. (1796) *Sketch of a Political Tour Through Rochester, Chatham, Maidstone, Gravesend &c* London.

Geggus, D. (1982) 'British opinion and the emergence of Haiti', in Walvin, J. (ed.) *Slavery and British Society, 1776–1846*, London: Macmillan, 123–149.

George, D. (1927) 'The London coal heavers: attempts to regulate waterside labour in the eighteenth and nineteenth centuries', *Economic Journal History Supplement* 1, 229–248.

Gibbons, L. (2003) *Edmund Burke and Ireland: Aesthetics, Politics and the Colonial Sublime* Cambridge: Cambridge University Press.

Gibbons, L. (1996) *Transformations in Irish Culture* Cork: Cork University Press.

Gibson-Graham, J. K. (2002) 'Beyond global vs local: economic politics outside the binary frame', in Herod, A. and Wright, M. W. (eds) *Geographies of Power: Placing Scale*, Oxford: Blackwell, 25–60.

Giddens, A. (1998) *The Third Way: The Renewal of Social Democracy* Cambridge: Polity Press.

Gidwani, V. K. (2006) 'Subaltern cosmopolitanism as politics', *Antipode* 38(1), 7–21.

Gill, C. (1913) *The Naval Mutinies of 1797* Manchester: Manchester University Press.

Gill, L. (2006) 'Fighting for justice, dying for hope: on the protest line in Colombia', *North American Dialogue* 9(2), 9–13.

Gilroy, P. (2004) *After Empire* London: Routledge.

Gilroy, P. (1993a) *Small Acts* London: Serpent's Tail.

Gilroy, P. (1993b) *The Black Atlantic* London: Verso.

Gilroy, P. (1992) 'Cultural studies and ethnic absolutism', in Grossberg, L., Nelson, C. and Treichler, P. (eds) *Cultural Studies*, London: Routledge, 187–198.

Gilroy, P. (1987) *There Ain't No Black in the Union Jack: The Cultural Politics of Race and Nation* London: Routledge.

Girard, R. (1987) *Things Hidden Since the Foundation of the World* London: Athlone Press.

Glasco, J. D. (2004) 'The seaman feels him-self a man', *International Labor and Working Class History* 66, 40–56.

Glassman, J. (2001) 'From Seattle (and Ubon) to Bangkok: the scales of resistance to corporate globalization', *Environment and Planning D: Society and Space* 20(5), 513–533.

Graeber, D. (2004) 'The new anarchists', in Mertes, T. (ed.) *A Movement of Movements: Is Another World Really Possible?* London: Verso, 202–218.

Graeber, D. (2002) 'The new anarchists', *New Left Review* 13, 61–73.

Gramsci, A. (1978) *Selections from Political Writings, 1921–26* London: Lawrence and Wishart.

Gramsci, A. (1971) *Selections From Prison Notebooks* London: Lawrence and Wishart.

Greenfield, G. (2005) 'Bandung redux: imperialism and anti-globalization nationalisms in Southeast Asia', *Socialist Register 2005*, London: Merlin, 166–196.

Griggs, L. (1936) *Thomas Clarkson: The Friend of Slaves* London: George Allen and Unwin.

Guattari, F. and Negri, A. (1990) *Communists Like Us: New Spaces of Liberty, New Lines of Alliance* New York: Semiotext(e).

Guha, R. (1997) *Dominance Without Hegemony: History and Power in Colonial India* Harvard, MA: Harvard University Press.

Guha, R. (1983) *Elementary Aspects of Peasant Insurgency* New Delhi: Oxford University Press.

Guha, R. (1982) 'On some aspects of the historiography of colonial India', in Guha, R. (ed.) *Subaltern Studies I*, New Delhi: Oxford University Press, 1–7.

Gupta, A. (1998) *Postcolonial Developments: Agriculture in the Making of Modern India* Oxford: Oxford University Press.

Gupta, D. (1997) *Rivalry and Brotherhood: Politics in the Life of Farmers in Northern India* New Delhi: Oxford University Press.

Gutkind, P. C. W. (1985) 'Trade and labour in early precolonial African history: the canoemen of Southern Ghana', in Coquery-Vidrovitch, C. and Lovejoy, P. E. (eds) *The Workers of African Trade*, London: Sage, 25–50.

Hale, A. and Wills, J. (eds) (2005) *Threads of Labour: Garment Industry Supply Chains from the Workers' Perspective* Oxford: Blackwell.

Hall, C. (2003) 'What is a West-Indian?', in Schwarz, B. (ed.) *West Indian Intellectuals in Britain*, Manchester: Manchester University Press, 31–50.

Hall, C. (2000) 'The rule of difference: gender, class and empire in the making of the 1832 Reform Act', in Blom, I., Hageman, K. and Hall, C. (eds) *Gendered Nations: Nationalisms and Gender Order in the Long Nineteenth Century*, Oxford: Berg, 107–136.

Hall, S. (2002) 'Political belonging in a world of multiple identities', in Vertovec, S. and Cohen, R. (eds) *Conceiving Cosmopolitanism: Theory, Context and Practice*, Oxford: Oxford University Press, 25–31.

Hall, S. (1996) 'Gramsci's relevance for the study of race and ethnicity', in Morley, D. and Chen, K.-H. (eds) *Stuart Hall: Critical Dialogues in Cultural Studies*, London: Routledge, 411–440.

Hall, S. (1992) 'Cultural studies and its theoretical legacies', in Grossberg, L., Nelson, C. and Treichler, P. (eds) *Cultural Studies*, London: Routledge, 277–294.

Hall, S. (1988) *The Hard Road to Renewal: Thatcherism and the Crisis of the Left* London: Verso.

Hall, S. and James, C. L. R. (1996) 'A conversation with C. L. R. James', in Farred, G. (ed.) *Rethinking C. L. R. James*, Oxford: Blackwell, 15–44.

Hall, S. and Schwarz, B. (1998) 'Breaking bread with history: C. L. R. James and the Black Jacobins', *History Workshop Journal* 46, 17–32.

Haraway, D. (1997) *Modest_Witness@Second_Millenium.FemaleMan_Meets_OncoMouse* London: Routledge.

Haraway, D. (1992) 'The promise of monsters: a regenerative politics for inappropriate/d others', in Grossberg, L., Nelson, C. and Treichler, P. (eds) *Cultural Studies*, London: Routledge, 295–337.

Haraway, D. (1991) *Simians, Cyborgs and Women: The Reinvention of Nature* London: Free Association Books.

Hardikar, A. (2006) 'Declaring (incomplete) victory: the Coke campaign, corporate accountability & people of color movements', www.criticalmoment.org/issue15/coke, accessed, 15 June 2007.

Hardt, M. (2002) 'Porto Allegre: today's Bandung?' *New Left Review* 14, 112–118.

Hardt, M. and Negri, A. (2004) *Multitude* New York: Penguin.

Hardt, M. and Negri, A. (2001) *Empire* Harvard, MA: Harvard University Press.

Hardy, T. [1832] (1976) 'Memoir of Thomas Hardy', in Vincent, D. (ed.) *Testaments of Radicalism: Memoirs of Working Class Politicians 1790–1885*, London: Europa, 31–102.

Harvey, D. (2001) *Spaces of Capital: Towards a Critical Geography* Edinburgh: Edinburgh University Press.

Harvey, D. (2000) *Spaces of Hope* Edinburgh: Edinburgh University Press.

Harvey, D. (1996) *Justice Nature and the Geography of Difference* Oxford: Blackwell.

Harvey, D. (1989) *The Condition of Post-Modernity* Oxford: Blackwell.

Harvey, D. and Swyngedouw, E. (1993) 'Industrial restructuring, community disempowerment and grass-roots resistance', in Harvey, D. and Hayter, T. (eds) *The Factory and the City: The Story of the Cowley Automobile Workers*, London: Mansell, 11–25.

Held, D. (1995) *Democracy and Global Order* Cambridge: Polity Press.

Henry, B. (1994) *Dublin Hanged: Crime, Law Enforcement and Punishment in Late Eighteenth-Century Dublin* Dublin: Irish Academic Press.

Herman, P. and Kuper, R. (for the Confédération Paysanne) (2003) *Food for Thought: Towards a Future for Farming*. London: Pluto Press.

Herod, A. (2001) *Labor Geographies* London: Guilford Press.

Herring, R. (2006) 'Why did "Operation Cremate Monsanto" Fail?: Science and Class in India's Great Terminator-Technology Hoax', *Critical Asian Studies* 38(4), 467–493.

Higginbottom, A. (2007) 'Killer Coke', in Dinan, W. and Miller, D. (eds) *Thinker, Faker, Spinner, Spy: Corporate PR and the Assault on Democracy*, London: Pluto Press, 278–294.

Hill, C. (1972) *The World Turned Upside Down: Radical Ideas During the English Revolution* London: Penguin.

Hinchliffe, S. (2001) 'Indeterminacy in-decisions – science, policy and politics in the BSE (Bovine Spongiform Encephalopathy) crisis', *Transactions of the Institute of British Geographers* 26(2), 182–204.

Hinchliffe, S. (2000) 'Entangled humans – specifying powers and their spatialities', in Sharp, J., Philo, C., Paddison, R. and Routledge, P. (eds) *Entanglements of Power: Geographies of Domination/Resistance*, London: Routledge, 219–237.

Hinchliffe, S., Kearnes, M., Degen, M. and Whatmore, S. (2005) 'Urban wild things: a cosmopolitical experiment', *Environment and Planning D: Society and Space* 23(5), 643–658.

Hines, C. (2001) *Localization: A Global Manifesto* London: Earthscan.

Hobsbawm, E. and Ranger, T. (eds) (1983) *The Invention of Tradition* Cambridge: Cambridge University Press.

Hodgson, R. (1768) 'The conduct of Ralph Hodgson, esq; one of His Majesty's justices of the peace for the County of Middlesex, in the affair of the coal-heavers', in Carpenter, K. E. (ed.) *Labour Disputes in the Early Days of the Industrial Revolution: Four Pamphlets 1758–1770*, New York: Arno Press.

Holton, R. J. (2002) 'Cosmopolitanism or cosmopolitanisms? The Universal Races Congress of 1911', *Global Networks* 2(2), 143–170.

Hope, J. (2001) *United Irishman: The Autobiography of James Hope*, ed. J. Newsinger, London: Merlin.

Hume, M. (2006) 'Contesting imagined communities: gender, nation and violence in El Salvador', in Fowler, W. and Lambert, P. (eds) *Political Violence and the Construction of National Identity in Latin America*, Basingstoke: Palgrave, 73–90.

Humphries, J. (1990) 'Enclosures, common rights and women: the proletarianization of families in the late eighteenth and early nineteenth centuries', *Journal of Economic History* 1, 17–42.

Ignatiev, N. (1996) *How the Irish Became White* London: Routledge.

Inter-Continental Caravan for Solidarity and Resistance (1999a) News bulletin issue no. 1, 30 May.

Inter-Continental Caravan for Solidarity and Resistance (1999b) 'Evaluation call' circulated on email networks.

Inter-Continental Caravan for Solidarity and Resistance (1999c) 'Press release', Cologne, 17 June, www.lists.essential.org/mai-intl/msg00103.html, accessed 1 July 2001.

Jain, D. (2003) 'The empire strikes back: a report on the Asian Social Forum', *Economic and Political Weekly*, 11 January, 99–100.

James, C. L. R. [1963] (1994) *Beyond a Boundary* London: Serpents Tail.

James, C. L. R. [1937] (1992) 'The Black Jacobins [script]', in Grimshaw, A. (ed.) *The C. L. R. James Reader*, Oxford: Blackwell, 67–111.

James, C. L. R. [1937] (1989) *The Black Jacobins* London: Allison and Busby.

James, C. L. R. (1980) *Spheres of Existence: Selected Writings* London: Allison and Busby.

James, C. L. R. (1969) 'The West Indian intellectual.' Introduction to Thomas, J. J., *Froudacity*, London: New Beacon Books, 23–48.

James, W. (2003) 'A race outcast from an outcast class: Claude McKay's experience and analysis of Britain', in Schwarz, B. (ed.) *West-Indian Intellectuals in Britain*, Manchester: Manchester University Press, 71–92.

James, W. (1998) *Holding Aloft the Banner of Ethiopia: Caribbean Radicalism in Early Twentieth Century America* London: Verso.

Jepson, W. (2005) 'Spaces of labor activism: Mexican American women and the farm worker movement in Texas's lower Rio Grande valley', *Antipode* 37(4), 679–702.

Johnson, M. P. (2001) 'Denmark Vesey and his co-conspirators', *William and Mary Quarterly* 58(4), 915–976.

Jones, R. and Fowler, C. (2007) 'Placing and scaling the nation', *Environment and Planning D: Society and Space* 25(2), 332–354.

Jones, R. and Phillips, R. (2005) 'Unsettling geographical horizons: premodern and non-European imperialism', *Annals of the Association of American Geographers* 95(1), 141–161.

Jones III, P., Woodward, K. and Marston, S. (2007) 'Situating flatness', *Transactions of the Institute of British Geographers* 32(2), 264–276.

Justice for Colombia (2004) 'Trade union delegation to Colombia', www.tuc.org. uk/international/tuc-9082-f0.pdf, accessed 3 July 2007.

KRRS (1998) 'Monsanto's cremation starts in Karnataka', www.pharm.chula.ac. th/vsuntree/monsan/monsan.htm, accessed 5 June 2001.

Kaldor, M. (2003) *Global Civil Society: An Answer to War* Cambridge: Polity Press.

Kaplan, C. (1998) 'Black heroes/white writers: Toussaint L'Ouverture and the literary imagination', *History Workshop Journal* 46, 33–61.

Karr, D. (2001) 'Thoughts that flash like lightning: Thomas Holcroft, radical theater, and the production of meaning in 1790s London', *Journal of British Studies* 40(3), 324–356.

Kazin, M. (1995) *The Populist Persuasion: An American History* Ithaca, NY: Cornell University Press.

Kelly, J. (1989) 'The Whiteboys in 1762: a contemporary account', *Journal of the Cork Historical and Archaeological Society* 94, 19–26.

Kennedy, W. B. (1990) 'The United Irishmen and the Great Naval Mutiny of 1797', *Eire-Ireland* 25, 7–18.

Kenny, K. (2003) 'Diaspora and comparison: the global Irish as a case study', *Journal of American History* 90(1), 134–162.

Kenny, K. (1998) *Making Sense of the Molly Maguires* Oxford: Oxford University Press.

Klein, N. (2003) 'Cut the strings', *Guardian*, 1 February, www.guardian.co.uk/ comment/story/0,3604,886644,00.html, accessed 1 February 2003.

Klein, N. (2002a) 'Farewell to "the end of history": organization and vision in anti-corporate movements', in Panitch, L. and Leys, C. (eds) *Socialist Register 2002: A World of Contradictions*, London: Merlin Press, 1–14.

Klein, N. (2002b) *Fences and Windows* London: Flamingo.

Kornprobst, M. (2005) 'Episteme, nation-builders and national identity: the reconstruction of Irishness', *Nations and Nationalism* 11(3), 403–421.

Koschnik, A. (2001) 'The Democratic Societies of Philadelphia and the limits of the American public sphere, circa 1793–1795', *William and Mary Quarterly* 58(3), 615–636.

Krishnarajulu, B. (1986) 'The Karnataka peasant movement: it's role in "identity" formation', in Shahasrabudhey, S. (ed.) *The Peasant Movement Today*, New Delhi: Ashish, 30–39.

Laclau, E. (2005a) *On Populist Reason* London: Verso.

Laclau, E. (2005b) 'Populism: what's in a name', in Panizza, F. (ed.) *Populism and the Mirror of Democracy*, London: Verso, 32–49.

Laclau, E. (1996) *Emancipation(s)* London: Verso.

Laclau, E. (1990) *New Reflections on the Revolutions of Our Time* London: Verso.

Laclau, E. (1977) *Politics and Ideology in Marxist Theory* London: New Left Books.

Laclau, E. and Mouffe, C. (1985) *Hegemony and Socialist Strategy* London: Verso.

Lambert, D. (2005) 'The counter-revolutionary Atlantic: white West Indian petitions and proslavery networks', *Social and Cultural Geography* 6(3), 405–420.

Land is Ours (1999) 'Diggers 350', www2.phreak.co.uk/tlio/campaigns/diggers/, accessed 13 June 2003.

Landes, J. B. (1996) 'The performance of citizenship: democracy, gender and difference in the French Revolution', in Benhabib, S. (ed.) *Democracy and Difference: Contesting the Boundaries of the Political*, Princeton, NJ: Princeton University Press, 295–313.

Larner, W., Le Heron, R. and Lewis, N. (2007) 'Co-constituting "after neoliberalism"? Political projects and globalizing governmentalities in Aotearoa New Zealand', in England, K. and Ward, K. (eds) *Neo-liberalization: States, Networks, People*. Oxford: Blackwell, 223–247.

Latour, B. (2004) *Politics of Nature: How to Bring the Sciences into Democracy* Harvard, MA: Harvard University Press.

Latour, B. (1999a) *Pandora's Hope: Essays on the Reality of Science Studies* Harvard, MA: Harvard University Press.

Latour, B. (1999b) 'Ein ding ist ein thing: a (philosophical) platform for a Left (European) party', *Soundings: A Journal of Politics and Culture* 12, 12–25.

Latour, B. (1998) 'To modernise or ecologise: that is the question?', in Castree, N. and Braun, B. (eds) *Remaking Reality: Nature at the Millennium*, London: Routledge, 221–242.

Latour, B. (1994) 'On technical mediation – philosophy, sociology, genealogy', *Common Knowledge* 3, 29–64.

Latour, B. (1993) *We Have Never Been Modern* London: Harvester Wheatsheaf.

Laurier, E. and Philo, C. (1999) 'X-morphizing: review essay of Bruno Latour's Aramis, or the Love of Technology', *Environment and Planning A* 31, 1047–1072.

Law, J. (1994) *Organizing Modernity* Oxford: Blackwell.

Law, J. (1986) 'On the methods of long-distance control vessels navigation and the Portuguese route to India', in Law, J. (ed.) *Power, Action and Belief: A New Sociology of knowledge?* London: Routledge, 234–263.

Law, J. and Mol, A. (2008) 'Globalization in practice: on the politics of boiling pigswill', *Geoforum*, 39:1, 133–143.

Lee, N. and Brown, S. (1994) 'Otherness and the actor network: the undiscovered continent', *American Behavioural Scientist* 37, 772–790.

Leitner, H., Sheppard, E.S., Sziarto, K. and Marniganti, A. (2007) 'Contesting urban futures: decentring neoliberalism', in Leitner, H., Peck, J., and Sheppard, E.S., (eds) *Contesting Neoliberalism: Urban Frontiers* New York: Guilford Press.

Lerche, J. (1999) 'Politics of the poor: agricultural labourers and political transformations in Uttar Pradesh', in Byres, T., Kapadia, K. and Lerche, J. (eds) *Rural Labour Relations in India*, London: Frank Cass, 182–243.

Levenson-Estrada, D. (1994) *Trade Unionists Against Terror: Guatemala City 1954–1985*, Durham, NC: University of North Carolina Press.

Levidow, L. (2001) 'Utilitarian bioethics: market fetishism in the gm crops debate', *New Genetics and Society* 20(1), 75–84.

Lewis, G. C. (1836) *On Local Disturbances in Ireland and on the Irish Church Question* London: B. Fellowes, Ludgate Street.

Ley, D. (2004) 'Transnational spaces and everyday lives', *Transactions of the Institute of British Geographers* 29(2), 151–64

Linebaugh, P. (2003) 'The terror of the petrolarchs: an open letter to brother Perry Anderson', *Counterpunch* 15 March.

Linebaugh, P. (2002) 'Levelling and 9/11', *Counterpunch* 7 September.

Linebaugh, P. (1993) 'A little jubilee? The literacy of Robert Wedderburn in 1817', in Rule, J. and Malcolmson, R. (eds) *Protest and Survival: Essays for E. P. Thompson*, London: Merlin Press, 174–220.

Linebaugh, P. (1992) *The London Hanged* Cambridge: Cambridge University Press.

Linebaugh, P. (1988) 'All the Atlantic mountains shook', in Eley, G. and Hunt, W. (eds) *Reviving the English Revolution*, London: Verso, 193–219.

Linebaugh, P. (1986) 'What if C. L. R. James had met E. P. Thompson in 1792?', in Buhle, P. (ed.) *C. L. R. James: His Life and Work*, London: Allison and Busby, 212–219.

Linebaugh, P. and Rediker, M. (2000) *The Many Headed Hydra: Sailors, Slaves and Commoners and the Hidden History of the Revolutionary Atlantic* London: Verso.

Linebaugh, P. and Rediker, M. (1990) 'The many headed hydra: sailors, slaves and the Atlantic working class', *Journal of Historical Sociology* 3(3), 225–252.

Lloyd, D. (2003) 'Rethinking national Marxism', *Interventions* 5(3), 345–370.

Lloyd, D. (1993) *Anomalous States: The Post-Colonial Moment in Irish Literature* Dublin: Lilliput Press.

London Corresponding Society [1792–9] (2002) *London Corresponding Society, 1792–1799*, 6 vols, ed. M. T. Davis. London: Pickering and Chatto.

Lovejoy, P. (2006) 'Autobiography and memory: Gustavus Vassa, alias Olaudah Equiano, the African', *Slavery and Abolition* 27(3), 317–347.

Low, M. (2004) 'Cities as spaces of democracy: complexity, scale and governance', in Barnett, C. and Low, M. (eds) *Spaces of Democracy: Geographical Perspectives on Citizenship, Participation and Representation*, London: Sage, 128–146.

Lumley, R. (1990) *States of Emergency: Cultures of Revolt in Italy From 1968 to 1978* London: Verso.

McAdam, D., Tarrow, S. and Tilly, C. (2001) *Dynamics of Contention* Cambridge: Cambridge University Press.

McCalman, I. (1991) 'Introduction', in McCalman, I. (ed.) *The Horrors of Slavery and Other Writings by Robert Wedderburn*, Kingston, Jamaica: Ian Randle Publishers, 1–42.

McCalman, I. (1986) *Radical Underworld* Oxford: Oxford University Press.

McDonel Hall Government (2006) 'Resolution regarding Michigan State University's contract with the Coca-Cola Company and further concerning allegations leveled against the Coca-Cola Company', www.killercoke.org/msures0206.htm, accessed 2 July 2007.

McDowell, L. (1999) 'City life and difference', in Allen, J., Massey, D. and Pryke, M., *Unsettling Cities*, London: Routledge, 143–160.

McGirr, L. (1995) 'Black and white longshoremen in the IWW: a history of the Philadelphia Marine Transport Workers Industrial Union Local 8', *Labor History* 36(3), 377–402.

McKay, C. [1935] (1985) *A Long Way From Home: An Autobiography* London: Pluto Press.

McKittrick, K. (2006) *Demonic Grounds: Black Women and the Cartographies of Struggle*, Minnesota: University of Minnesota Press.

Madsen, S. T. (2005) 'Coconut toddy, chewing tobacco and genetically modified cotton: moral choices for a farmer's association in India', *Eastern Anthropologist* 58(3–4), 471–486.

Madsen, S. T. (2001) 'The view from Vevey', *Economic and Political Weekly* 29 September, 3733–3742.

Madsen, S. T. (2000) 'Post festum: the lotus and the mud in an Indo-global context', unpublished paper quoted with kind permission of the author.

Mandelblatt, B. (2007) 'A transatlantic commodity: Irish salt beef in the French Atlantic world', *History Workshop Journal* 63, 18–47.

Mannion, J. (2001) 'Irish migration and settlement in Newfoundland: the formative phase, 1697–1732', *Newfoundland Studies* 17(2), 257–291.

Manwaring, G. E. and Dobree, B. (2004) *The Floating Republic: An Account of the Mutinies at the Spithead and the Nore in 1797* Barnsley: Pen and Sword Military Classics.

Marston, S. A., Jones III, J. P. and Woodward, K. (2005) 'Human geography without scale', *Transactions of the Institute of British Geographers* 30, 416–432.

Martinez, E. B. (2000) 'Where was the color in Seattle?: looking for reasons why the Great Battle was so white', www.arc.org/C_Lines/CLArchive/story3_1_02.html, accessed 6 June 2002.

Martinez-Alier, J. (2002) *The Environmentalism of the Poor: A Study of Ecological Conflicts and Valuation* Cheltenham: Edward Elgar.

Massey, D. (2007a) *World City*, Cambridge: Polity.

Massey, D. (2007b) 'Book review symposium: author's response', *Progress in Human Geography* 31(3), 403–405.

Massey, D. (2005) *For Space* London: Sage.

Massey, D. (2004) 'Geographies of responsibility', *Geografiska Annaler* B 86(1), 5–18.

Massey, D. (2002) 'Don't let's counterpose place and space', *Development* 45(1), 24–25.

Massey, D. (2000) 'Travelling thoughts', in Gilroy, P., Grossberg, L. and McRobbie, A. (eds) *Without Guarantees: In Honour of Stuart Hall*, London: Verso, 225–232.

Massey, D. (1999) *Power-Geometries and the Politics of Space-Time* Heidelberg: Department of Geography, University of Heidelberg.

Massey, D. (1995) 'Thinking radical democracy spatially', *Environment and Planning D: Society and Space* 13(3), 283–288.

Massey, D. (1993) 'Power-geometry and a progressive sense of place', in Bird, J., Curtis, B., Putnam, T., Robertson, G. and Tickner, L. (eds) *Mapping the Future*, London: Routledge, 59–69.

Mawdsley, E. (2006) 'Hindu nationalism, postcolonialism and environmental discourses in India', *Geoforum* 37(3), 380–390.

Mee, J. (2003) 'Rough and respectable Radicalisms', *History Workshop Journal* 56(1), 238–244.

Melville, H. [1924] (1995) *Billy Budd, Sailor* London: Penguin.

Merrifield, A. (2002) 'Seattle, Quebec, Genoa: après le déluge . . . Henri Lefebvre?', *Environment and Planning D: Society and Space* 20, 127–134.

Midgley, C. (1992) *Women Against Slavery: The British Campaigns, 1780–1870* London: Routledge.

Miller, B. (2004) 'Spaces of mobilization: transnational social movements', in Barnett, C. and Low, M. (eds) *Spaces of Democracy: Geographical Perspectives on Citizenship, Participation and Representation*, London: Sage, 224–246.

Miller, B. (2000) *Geography and Social Movements* Minneapolis: University of Minnesota Press.

Mitchell, D. (2002) 'Controlling space, controlling scale: migratory labour, free speech, and regional development in the American West', *Journal of Historical Geography* 28(1), 63–84.

Mitchell, D. (1995) 'The end of public space? People's Park, definitions of the public, and democracy', *Annals of the Association of American Geographers* 85(1), 108–133.

Mitchell, M. (1998) *The Irish in the West of Scotland, 1797–1848* Edinburgh: John Donald.

Mohanty, C. T. (2003) *Feminism Without Borders: Decolonizing Theory, Practicing Solidarity* Durham, NC: Duke University Press.

Mol, A. (1999) 'Ontological politics: a word and some questions', in Law, J. and Hasard, J. (eds) *Actor Network Theory and After*, Oxford: Blackwell, 74–89.

Molesworth, R. (1723) *Some Thoughts and Considerations of Agriculture and Employing the Poor* Dublin.

Monbiot, G. (2003) *The Age of Consent* London: Flamingo.

Monbiot, G. (1998) 'Reclaim the fields and country lanes: the land is ours campaign', in McKay, G. (ed.) *Do It Yourself Culture*, London: Verso, 174–186.

Moore, D. S. (1998) 'Subaltern struggle and the politics of place: remapping resistance in Zimbabwe's Eastern Highlands', *Cultural Anthropology* 13(3), 353–381.

Moore, D. S. (1997) 'Remapping resistance: "ground for struggle" and the politics of place', in Pile, S. and Keith, M. (eds) *Geographies of Resistance*, London: Routledge, 87–106.

Moore III, J. P. (1991) '"The greatest enormity that prevails": direct democracy and workers' self-management in the British naval mutinies of 1797', in Howell, C. and Twomey, R. J. (eds) *Jack Tar in History: Essays in the History of Maritime Life and Labour*, New Brunswick, NJ: Acadiensis Press, 76–104.

Morris-Suzuki, T. (2000) 'For and against NGOs: the politics of the lived world', *New Left Review* 2, 63–84.

Mouffe, C. (2005) *On the Political* London: Routledge.

Mouffe, C. (2000) *The Democratic Paradox* London: Verso.

Mouffe, C. (1999a) 'Introduction: Schmitt's challenge', in Mouffe, C. (ed.) *The Challenge of Carl Schmitt*, London: Verso, 1–6.

Mouffe, C. (1999b) 'Carl Schmitt and the paradox of liberal democracy', in Mouffe, C. (ed.) *The Challenge of Carl Schmitt*, London: Verso, 38–53.

Mouffe, C. (1998) 'The radical centre: a politics without adversary', *Soundings* 10, 11–23.

Mouffe, C. (1993) *The Return of the Political* London: Verso.

Mouffe, C. (1988) 'Hegemony and new political subjects: toward a new concept of democracy', in Grossberg, L. and Nelson, C. (eds) *Marxism and the Interpretation of Culture*, London: Macmillan, 89–104.

Movimento Sem Terra (2005) 'Agriculture', www.mstbrazil.org/ag/, accessed 1 March 2005.

Movimento Sem Terra (2001) 'Fundamental principles for the social and economic transformation of rural Brazil', *Journal of Peasant Studies* 28(2), 153–161.

Mukherji, P. N. (1998) 'The farmers movement in Punjab: politics of pressure groups and the pressure of party politics', *Economic and Political Weekly* 2 May 2, 1043–1049.

Mulligan, A. (2005) 'Absence makes the heart grow fonder: transatlantic Irish nationalism and the 1867 rising', *Social and Cultural Geography* 6(3), 439–454.

Munck, R. (2007) *Globalization and Contestation: The New Great Counter-Movement* London: Routledge.

Murdoch, J. (1998) 'The spaces of actor-network theory', *Geoforum* 29(4), 357–374.

Murdoch, J. (1997) 'Towards a geography of heterogeneous associations', *Progress in Human Geography* 21(3), 321–337.

Mustafa, Z. (2006) 'WSF comes to Pakistan', www.dawn.com/2006/03/15/op.htm, accessed 19 July 2007.

Nagaraj, D. R. (1996) 'Anxious hindu and angry farmer: notes on culture and politics of two responses to globalization in India', in Soares, L. E. (ed.) *Cultural Pluralism, Identity and Globalization*, Rio de Janeiro: UNESCO, 271–293.

Nairn, T. (1997) *Faces of Nationalism* London: Verso.

Nairn, T. (1977) *The Break Up of Britain* London: Verso.

Nanjundaswamy, M. D. (2003) 'Cremating Monsanto: genetically modified fields on fire', in Notes From Nowhere (eds) *We Are Everywhere*, London: Verso, 152–159.

Nanjundaswamy, M. D. (1998) 'Cremate Monsanto!', www.mailbase.ac.uk/lists/crit-geog-forum/1998-11/0117.html, accessed 14 January 2002.

Nash, C. (1998) 'Editorial: mapping emotions', *Environment and Planning D: Society and Space* 16(1), 1–9.

Neeson, J. (1993) *Commoners: Common Right, Enclosure and Social Change in England 1700–1820* Cambridge: Cambridge University Press.

Negri, A. (2005) *Books for Burning: Between Civil War and Democracy in 1970s Italy* London: Verso.

Negri, A. (2003) *Time for Revolution* London: Continuum.

Nicholls, W. J. (2007) 'The geographies of social movements', *Geography Compass* 1(3), 607–622.

Norris, A. (2002) 'Against antagonism', *Constellations* 9(4), 554–573.

North, P. (2007) 'Neoliberalizing Argentina?', in England, K. and Ward, K. (eds) *Neoliberalization: States, Networks, Peoples*, Oxford: Blackwell, 137–162.

Novelli, M. (2004) 'Globalizations, social movement unionism and new internationalisms: the role of strategic learning in the transformation of the Municipal Workers Union of EMCALI1', *Globalization, Societies and Education* 2(2), 161–190.

Nuffield Foundation (1999) *Genetically Modified Crops: The Ethical and Social Implications* London: Nuffield Foundation.

Ogborn, M. (2005) 'Guest editorial: Atlantic geographies', *Social and Cultural Geographies* 6(3), 379–386.

Ogborn, M. (2004) 'Designs on the city: John Gwynn's plans for Georgian London', *Journal of British Studies* 43(1), 15–39.

Ogborn, M. (2002) 'Writing travels: power, knowledge and ritual on the English East India Company's early voyages', *Transactions of the Institute of British Geographers* 27, 155–171.

Ogborn, M. (1998) *Spaces of Modernity: London's Geographies 1680–1780* London: Guilford Press.

Olesen, T. (2005) *International Zapatismo* London: Zed Books.

Omvedt, G. (1998) 'Terminating choice', www.saxakali.com/southasia/iniaenv2. html, accessed 2 December 1998.

Omvedt, G. (1995) '"We want the return for our sweat": the formation of a national agricultural policy', in Brass, T. (ed.) *New Farmers' Movements in India*, Ilford: Frank Cass, 126–164.

Omvedt, G. (1991) 'Shetkari Sanghtana's new direction', *Economic and Political Weekly* 5 October, 2287–2290.

O'Shea, M. J. (1954) *History of Native Irish Cattle* Cork: Cork University Press.

Osava, M. (2001) 'Peasants speak out against food imports', *Third World Network Website*, www.twnside.org.sg/title/peasants.htm, accessed 5 November 2004.

Oza, R. (2001) 'Showcasing India: gender, geography and globalization', *Signs: Journal of Women in Culture* 26(4), 1067–1095.

Palliser, H. (1767a) 'Governor Palliser's order for sending home from Newfoundland men that are useless in the country after the fishing season is over', Shelburne Papers, William L. Clements Library, Volume 65, folios 149–155.

Palliser, H. (1767b) 'Memorandum of Mr Palliser concerning the oppression of the Newfoundland fishermen from their employers', Shelburne Papers, William L. Clements Library, Volume 65, folios 145–147.

Palmer, B. D. (1994) *E. P. Thompson: Objections and Oppositions* London: Verso.

Panelli, L. (2007) 'Time-space geometries of activism and the case of mis/placing gender in Australian agriculture', *Transactions of the Institute of British Geographers* 32(1), 46–65.

Panini, M. (1999) 'Trends in cultural globalization: from agriculture to agribusiness in Karnataka', *Economic and Political Weekly* 31 July 31, 2168–2173.

Panizza, F. (2005) 'Introduction: populism and the mirror of democracy', in Panizza, F. (ed.) *Populism and the Mirror of Democracy*, London: Verso, 1–31.

Patton, P. (2000) *Deleuze and the Political* London: Routledge.

Peck, J. and Tickell, A. (2002) 'Neoliberalizing space', *Antipode* 34(3), 380–404.

Penrose, J. (2002) 'Nations, states and homelands: territory, territoriality in nationalist thought', *Nations and Nationalism* 8(3), 277–297.

People's Global Action Against Free Trade (1999a) 'Inter-Continental Caravan/ ICC99', www.agp.org/agp/en/Calendar/9905caravan.html, accessed 5 November 2000.

People's Global Action Against Free Trade (1999b) 'Report on second PGA gathering in Bangalore', www.agp.org/agp/en/index.html, accessed 5 November 2000.

People's Permanent Tribunal (2007) 'What is the Colombia PPT oil industry hearing?', www.tppcolombia.info/node/53, accessed 10 July 2007.

Phillips, R. (2007) 'Histories of sexuality and imperialism: what's the use?', *History Workshop Journal* 63(1), 136–153.

Pickerill, J. and Chatterton, P. (2006) 'Notes towards autonomous geographies: creation, resistance and self-management as survival tactics', *Progress in Human Geography* 30(5), 1–17.

Pile, S. and Keith, M. (eds) (1997) *Geographies of Resistance* London: Routledge.

Place, F. (1972) *The Autobiography of Francis Place*, ed. M. Thale, Cambridge: Cambridge University Press.

Pollack, A. (forthcoming) 'K'iche' uprising in Totonicapán, 1820: the places and scales of subaltern politics' *Antipode*.

Pope, D. (2003) *The Black Ship* Barnsley: Pen and Sword Military Classics.

Power, T. P. (1993) *Land, Politics and Society in Eighteenth Century Tipperary* Oxford: Clarendon Press.

Preston, T. (1817) *The Life and Opinions of Thomas Preston Patriot and Shoemaker* London.

Pugh, J. (2005) 'The disciplinary effects of communicative planning in Soufriere, St Lucia: governmentality, hegemony and space-time-politics', *Transactions of the Institute of British Geographers* 30(3), 307–321.

Quinn, J. (1998) 'The United Irishmen and social reform', *Irish Historical Studies* 31(122).

Rajah, C. (2001) 'Where was the color at A16?', in Yuen, E., Burton Rose, D. and Katsiaficas, G. (eds) *The Battle of Seattle: The New Challenge to Capitalist Globalization*, New York: Soft Skull Press, 237–240.

Raman, R. (2005) 'Corporate violence, legal nuances and political ecology: cola war in Plachimada', *Economic and Political Weekly* 18 June, 2481–2485.

Rancière, J. (2007) *On the Shores of Politics* London: Verso.

Rane, W. (1993) 'Farmers' rally against GATT proposals', *Economic and Political Weekly* 30 October, 2391.

Rediker, M. (2004) *Villains of All Nations: Atlantic Pirates in the Golden Age* London: Verso.

Rediker, M. (1988a) *Between the Devil and the Deep Blue Sea: Merchant Seamen, Pirates and the Anglo-American Maritime World, 1700–1750* Cambridge: Cambridge University Press.

Rediker, M. (1988b) 'Good hands, stout heart and fast feet: the history and culture of working people in Early America', in Eley, G. and Hunt, W. (eds) *Reviving the English Revolution*, London: Verso, 221–249.

Reid, W. H. (1800) *The Rise and Dissolution of the Infidel Societies in this Metropolis* London.

Report of the Grand Committee on Trade (1780) *Journal of the Irish House of Commons*, cxi–cxviii.

Retort Collective (2003) *Afflicted Powers* London: Verso.

Roach, J. (1996) *Cities of the Dead: Circum-Atlantic Performance* New York: Colombia University Press.

Robinson, J. (1998) 'Spaces of democracy: remapping the apartheid city', *Environment and Planning D: Society and Space* 16(5), 533–548.

Rodger, N. A. M. (2004) *The Command of the Ocean: A Naval History of Britain, 1649–1815* London: Penguin.

Rodger, N. A. M. (2003) 'Mutiny and subversion? Spithead and the Nore', in Bartlett, T., Dickson, D., Keogh, D. and Whelan, K. (eds) *1798: A Bicentenary Perspective*, Dublin: Four Courts Press, 549–564.

Rodgers, N. (2007) *Ireland, Slavery and Anti-Slavery: 1612–1865* Basingstoke: Palgrave, Macmillan.

Rodgers, N. (2000) 'Ireland and the Black Atlantic in the eighteenth century', *Irish Historical Studies* 126, 174–192.

Rodgers, N. (1997) 'Equiano in Belfast: a study of the anti-slavery ethos in a northern town', *Slavery and Abolition* 18(2), 73–89.

Rogers, A., Cohen, S. and Vertovec, S. (2001) 'Editorial statement', *Global Networks* 1(1), 1–3.

Rogers, N. (2003) 'Archipelagic encounters: war, race and labor in American-Caribbean waters', in Nussbaum, F. (ed.) *The Global Eighteenth Century*, Baltimore: Johns Hopkins University Press, 211–225.

Ross, R. (1983) *Cape of Torments: Slavery and Resistance in South Africa* London: Routledge.

Ross, S. (2003) 'Is this what democracy looks like? The politics of the anti-globalization movement in North America', *Socialist Register 2003*, London: Merlin Press, 281–304.

Routledge, P. (2008) 'Acting in the network', *Environment and Planning D: Society and Space* 26(2), 199–217.

Routledge, P. (2003) 'Convergence space: process geographies of grassroots globalization networks', *Transactions of the Institute of British Geographers* 28(3), 333–349.

Routledge, P. (1998) 'Going globile: spatiality, embodiment, and mediation in the Zapatista insurgency', in O Tuathail, G. and Dalby, S. (eds) *Rethinking Geopolitics*, London: Routledge, 240–260.

Routledge, P. (1993) *Terrains of Resistance: Nonviolent Social Movements and the Contestation of Place in India* Westport, CT: Praeger.

Routledge, P., Nativel, C. and Cumbers, A. (2006) 'Entangled logics and grassroots imaginaries of global justice networks', *Environmental Politics* 15(5), 839–859.

Russell, T. (1796) *A Letter to the People of Ireland on the Present Situation of the Country* Belfast: Printed at the Northern Star Office.

Sahai, S. (2000) 'Farmers' rights and food security', *Economic and Political Weekly* 11 March, 878–880.

Sahai, S. (1993) 'Dunkel draft is bad for agriculture', *Economic and Political Weekly* 19 June, 1280–1281.

Said, E. (2004) *Power, Politics and Culture: Interviews with Edward W. Said*, ed. G. Viswanathan, London: Bloomsbury.

Said, E. (1993) *Culture and Imperialism* London: Vintage.

Sale, K. (1993) *Rebels Against the Future* New York: Addison Wesley.

Samuel, R. (1994) *Theatres of Memory: Volume 1* London: Verso.

Schmitt, C. (1976) *The Concept of the Political* New York: Rutgers University Press.

Schwarz, B. (2004) 'Not even past yet', *History Workshop Journal* 57, 101–114.

Schwarz, B. (2003a) 'C. L. R. James and George Lamming: the measure of historical time', *Small Axe* 14, 39–70.

Schwarz, B. (2003b) 'Introduction: crossing the seas', in Schwarz, B. (ed.) *West-Indian Intellectuals in Britain*, Manchester: Manchester University Press, 1–30.

Schwarz, B. (1997) 'The break-up of the Conservative nation', *Soundings* 7, 13–29.

Schwarz, B. (1982) ' "The people" in history: the Communist Party Historians' Group, 1946–56', in Johnson, R., McLennan, G., Schwarz, B. and Sutton, D. (eds) *Making Histories: Studies in History-Writing and Politics*, London: Hutchinson, 44–95.

Scott, D. (2004) *Conscripts of Modernity: The Tragedy of Colonial Enlightenment* Durham, NC: Duke University Press.

Scott, J. (1986) ' "The common wind": currents of Afro-American communication in the era of the Haitian revolution', Ph.D. thesis, Department of History, Duke University.

Sen, J., Anand, A., Escobar, A. and Waterman, P. (eds) (2004) *The World Social Forum: Challenging Empires* New Delhi: Viveka.

Sharp, J. (2007) 'Geography and gender: finding feminist political geographies', *Progress in Human Geography* 31(3), 381–387.

Sharp, J. (2003) 'Decentering political geography: feminist and postcolonial engagements', in Agnew, J., Mitchell, K. and Toal, G. (eds) *The Companion to Political Geography*, Oxford: Blackwell, 59–74.

Sharp, J., Routledge, P., Philo, C. and Paddison, R. (2000) 'Entanglements of power: geographies of domination/resistance', in Sharp et al. (eds) *Entanglements of Power: Geographies of Domination/Resistance*, London: Routledge, 1–42.

Sheldon, R. (1996) 'The London sailors' strike of 1768', in Charlesworth, A., Gilbert, D., Randall, A., Southall, H. and Wrigley, C. (eds) *An Atlas of Industrial Protest in Britain, 1750–1990*, Basingstoke: Macmillan, 12–17.

Shiva, V. (1999) Critique of Inter-Continental Caravan circulated widely on activist email networks. Copy available from author.

Shiva, V., Jafri, A. H., Beli, G. and Holla-Bhar, R. (1997) *The Enclosure and Recovery of the Commons: Biodiversity, Indigeneous Knowledge and Intellectual Property Rights* New Delhi: Research Foundation for Science, Technology and Ecology.

Shotter, J. (1993) *Cultural Politics of Everyday Life: Social Constructionism, Rhetoric and Knowing of the Third Kind* Buckingham: Open University Press.

Singh, J. (2001) 'Resisting global capitalism in India', in Yuen, E., Burton Rose, D. and Katsiaficas, G. (eds) *The Battle of Seattle: The New Challenge to Capitalist Globalization*, New York: Soft Skull Press, 47–52.

Sivanandan, A. (1990) *Communities of Resistance: Writings on Black Struggles for Socialism* London: Verso.

Skelley, J. (ed.) (1976) *The General Strike, 1926* London: Lawrence and Wishart.

Slater, D. (2004) *Geopolitics and the Post-Colonial* Oxford: Blackwell.

Slater, D. (2002) 'Other domains of democratic theory: space, power, and the politics of democratization', *Environment and Planning D: Society and Space* 20(3), 255–276.

Slater, D. (1998) 'Post-colonial questions for global times', *Review of International Political Economy* 5(4), 647–678.

Smith, D. (2005) Comment on BBC Bristol programme *Border Crossing: On Raymond Williams*, directed by Colin Thomas. Broadcast on BBC 4 in February 2005.

Smith, N. (2000) 'Global Seattle', *Environment and Planning D: Society and Space* 18, 1–4.

Smith, N. (1993) 'Homeless/global: scaling places', in Bird, J., Curtis, B., Putnam, T., Robertson, G. and Tickner, L. (eds) *Mapping the Futures: Local Cultures, Global Change*, London: Routledge, 87–119.

Smith, R. (2003) 'World city topologies', *Progress in Human Geography* 27, 561–582.

Smyth, J. (1992) *Men of No Property: Irish Radicals and Popular Politics in the Late Eighteenth Century* Basingstoke: Macmillan.

Smyth, W. J. (1976) 'Estate records and the making of the Irish landscape: an example from Co. Tipperary', *Irish Geography* 9, 29–49.

Snow, D. A., Rochford, J. R., Burke, E., Worden, S. K. and Benford, R. D. (1986) 'Frame alignment processes, micromobilization and movement participation', *American Sociological Review* 51(4), 464–481.

Somerville, R. (2003) 'Presentation' to *Chile and Scotland: 30 Years On* Glasgow Caledonian University: Research Collections Witness Seminar and Open Forum Series,   www.gcal.ac.uk/archives/witness/chile/documents/chiletranscript.pdf Accessed 5th October, 2007.

Sparke, M. (2008) 'Political geographies of globalization III: resistance', *Progress in Human Geography*, 32:(3), 423–440.

Sparke, M. (2005) *In the Space of Theory: Postfoundational Geographies of the Nation State* Minneapolis: University of Minnesota Press.

Sparke, M., Brown, M., Corva, D., Day, H., Faria, C., Sparks, T. and Varg, K. (2005) 'The World Social Forum and the lessons for economic geography', *Economic Geography* 81(4), 359–380.

Spivak, G. C. (1985) 'Subaltern studies: deconstructing historiography', in Guha, R. (ed.) *Subaltern Studies IV*, New Delhi: Oxford University Press, 330–363.

Staeheli, L. A. and Mitchell, D. (2004) 'Spaces of public and private: locating politics', in Barnett, C. and Low, M. (eds) *Spaces of Democracy: Geographical Perspectives on Citizenship, Participation and Representation*, London: Sage, 147–160.

Stallybrass, P. and White, A. (1986) *The Politics and Poetics of Transgression* Ithaca, NY: Cornell University Press.

Starr, A. (2003) 'Is the North American anti-globalization movement racist? Critical reflections', *Socialist Register 2003*, London: Merlin Press, 264–280.

Starr, A. (2000) *Naming the Enemy: Anti-Corporate Movements Confront Globalization* London: Zed Books.

Stedile, J. P. (2004) 'Brazil's landless battalions', in Mertes, T. (ed.) *A Movement of Movements: Is Another World Really Possible?* London: Verso, 17–48.

Stedile, J. P. (1999) 'Popular march arrives at Brasília: interview with João Pedro Stedile, member of the MST national board', circulated on email network of Land is Ours.

Stone, G. D. (2007) 'Agricultural deskilling and the spread of genetically modified cotton in Warrangal', *Current Anthropology* 48(1), 67–103.

Sundberg, J. (2007) 'Reconfiguring North–South solidarity: critical reflections on experiences of transnational resistance', *Antipode* 39(1), 144–166.

Swyngedouw, E. (2007) 'Impossible "sustainability" and the post-political condition', in Gibbs, D. and Krueger, R. (eds) *The Sustainable Development Paradox: Urban Political Economy in the United States and Europe*, New York: Guilford Press.

Swyngedouw, E. (2004) 'Globalization or "glocalisation"? Networks, territories and re-scaling', *Cambridge Review of International Affairs* 17(1), 25–48.

Taaffe, V. (1767) *Observations on affairs in Ireland from the settlement in 1691 to the present time*, 3rd edn, Dublin.

Tarrow, S. (2005) *The New Transnational Activism* Cambridge: Cambridge University Press.

Tarrow, S. (1994) *Power in Movement: Social Movements, Collective Action and Politics* Cambridge: Cambridge University Press.

Tarrow, S. and McAdam, D. (2005) 'Scale shift in transnational contention', in della Porta, D. and Tarrow, S. (eds) *Transnational Protest and Global Activism*, Lanham, MD: Rowman and Littlefield, 121–147.

Taylor, B. (1983) *Eve and the New Jerusalem: Socialism and Feminism in the Nineteenth Century* London: Virago.

Thale, M. (ed.) (1983) *Selections from the Papers of the London Corresponding Society, 1792–99* Cambridge: Cambridge University Press.

Thelwall, J. [1796] (1995) 'The Rights of Nature, Against the Usurption of Establishments', in Claeys, G. (ed.) *The Politics of English Jacobinism: Writings of John Thelwall*, Philadelphia: Pennsylvannia State University Press, 389–501.

Thompson, E. P. (1994a) 'Hunting the Jacobin fox', *Past and Present* 142, 94–140.

Thompson, E. P. (1994b) *Persons and Polemics* London: Merlin Press.

Thompson, E. P. (1991a) 'Ends and histories', in Kaldor, M. (ed.) *Europe From Below: An East-West Dialogue*, London: Verso, 7–26.

Thompson, E. P. (1991b) *Customs in Common: Studies in Traditional Popular Culture* New York: New Press.

Thompson, E. P. (1978) *The Poverty of Theory and Other Essays* London: Merlin Press.

Thompson, E. P. (1968) *The Making of the English Working Class* London: Penguin.

Thompson, G. (2003) 'The age of confusion', www.opendemocracy.net/debates/article-3-33-1499.jsp, accessed 19 November 2003.

Thompson, G. F. (2004) 'Is all the world a complex network?', *Economy and Society* 33(3), 411–424.

Thrift, N. (2000) 'Entanglements of power: shadows?', in Sharp, J., Philo, C., Paddison, R. and Routledge, P. (eds) *Entanglements of Power: Geographies of Domination/Resistance*, London: Routledge, 269–278.

Thrift, N. (1999) 'Steps to an ecology of place', in Allen, J., Massey, D. and Sarre, P. (eds) *Human Geography Today*, Cambridge: Polity Press, 295–322.

Thrift, N. (1996) *Spatial Formations* London: Sage.

Tikait, M. S. (1999) 'Statement by the leader of Bharatiya Kisan Union (BKU)', www.stad.dsl.nl/~caravan/index.htm, accessed 5 November 2000.

Tilly, C. (1995) 'Contentious repertoires in Great Britain, 1758–1834', in Traugott, M. (ed.) *Repertoires and Cycles of Collective Action*, Durham, NC: Duke University Press, 15–42.

Townes, J. (1999) 'Bangin in Banga', www.squall.co.uk/feats.html, acessed 10 January 2000.

Truxes, T. (1988) *Irish-American Trade 1660–1783* Cambridge: Cambridge University Press.

Tuan, Y.F. (1979) *Space and Place: the Perspective of Experience*, London: Arnold.

Tyner, J. (2004) 'Territoriality, social justice and gendered revolutions in the speeches of Malcolm X', *Transactions of the Institute of British Geographers* 29(3), 330–343.

UNISON (2007) 'Colombia', www.unison.org.uk/international/pages_view. asp?did=1453, accessed 19 July 2007.

United Steel Workers Union and the International Labor Rights Fund (2001) 'Coca-Cola (Coke) sued for human rights abuses in Colombia', www.mindfully. org/Industry/Coca-Cola-Human-Rights20jul01.htm, accessed 2 July 2007.

Vanaik, A. (2004) 'Rendezvous at Mumbai', *New Left Review* 26, 53–65.

Vanaik, A. (2001) 'The New Indian Right', *New Left Review* 9, 43–67.

Vertovec, S. and Cohen, R. (2002) 'Introduction: conceiving cosmopolitanism', in Vertovec, S. and Cohen, R. (eds) *Conceiving Cosmopolitanism: Theory, Context and Practice*, Oxford: Oxford University Press, 1–22.

Vidal, J. (1999) 'The seeds of wrath', *Guardian Weekend* 19 June, 10–19.

Visvanathan, S. and Parmar, P. (2002) 'A biotechnology story: notes from India', *Economic and Political Weekly* 6 July, 2714–2724.

Wall, M. (1973) 'Whiteboys', in Williams, T. D. (ed.) *Secret Societies*, Dublin: Gill and MacMillan, 13–25.

Wainwright, J. (2005) 'The geography of political ecology: after Edward Said', *Environment and Planning A* 37, 1033–1043.

Wainwright, J. and Oritz, R. (2006) 'The battles in Miami: the fall of the FTAA/ ALCA and the promise of transnational movements', *Environment and Planning D: Society and Space* 24, 349–366.

Wainwright, J., Prudham, S. and Glassman, J. (2000) 'The battles in Seattle: microgeographies of resistance and the challenge of building alternative futures', *Environment and Planning D: Society and Space* 18(1), 5–13.

War on Want (2006) *Coca Cola: The Alternative Report* London: War on Want.

Waterman, P. (2003) 'World Social Forum: another forum is possible!' www. opendemocracy.net/debates/article-6-91-1293.jsp, accessed 16 July 2003.

Waterman, P. and Wills, J. (eds) (2001) *Place, Space and the New Labour Internationalisms* Oxford: Blackwell.

Waters, J. (2007) ' "Roundabout routes and sanctuary schools": the role of situated educational practices and habitus in the creation of transnational professionals', *Global Networks* 7(4), 477–497.

Watts, M. (2005) 'Left retort', *Antipode* 37(4), 643–653.

Weber, M. (1968) *Economy and Society Volume 1* New York: Bedminster Press.

Wedderburn, R. [1817] (1991) 'The axe laid to the root 1–6', in McCalman, I. (ed.) *The Horrors of Slavery and Other Writings by Robert Wedderburn*, Kingston, Jamaica: Ian Randle Publishers, 81–110.

Wells, R. (1983) *Insurrection: The British Experience 1795–1803* Gloucester: Alan Sutton.

Whatmore, S. (2002) *Hybrid Geographies: Natures Cultures Spaces* London: Sage.

Whelan, K. (2004) 'The Green Atlantic: radical reciprocities between Ireland and America in the long eighteenth century', in Wilson, K. (ed.) *A New Imperial History: Culture, Identity and Modernity in Britain and the Empire*, Cambridge: Cambridge University Press, 216–238.

Whelan, K. (1996) *The Tree of Liberty* Cork: Cork University Press.

Willes, E. [1760] (1990) *The Letters of Lord Chief Baron Edward Willes to the Earl of Warwick 1757–62: An account of Ireland in the Mid-Eighteenth Century*, ed. J. Kelly, Aberystwyth: Boethius Press.

Wills, J. (1998) 'Taking on the cosmocorps: experiments in transnational labor organization', *Economic Geography* 74(2), 111–130.

Williams, C. (2002) *Sugar and Slate* Aberystwyth: Planet.

Williams, R. (2003) *Who Speaks for Wales? Nation, Culture, Identity*, ed. D Williams, Aberystwyth: University of Wales Press.

Williams, R. (1989) *Resources of Hope* London: Verso.

Williams, R. (1983) *Towards 2000* London: Chatto and Windus.

Williams, R. (1979) *Politics and Letters* London: New Left Books.

Williams, R. (1977) *Marxism and Literature* Oxford: Oxford University Press.

Wilson, D. (2005) 'Comment: whiteness and Irish experience in North America', *Journal of British Studies* 44(1), 153–160.

Wilson, D. (1998) *United Irishmen, United States: Immigrant Radicals in the Early Republic* Dublin: Four Courts Press.

Wilson, K. (2003) *The Island Race: Englishness, Empire and Gender in the Eighteenth Century* London: Routledge.

Wilson, K. (1995) *The Sense of the People: Politics, Culture and Imperialism in England, 1717–1785* Cambridge: Cambridge University Press.

Wolford, W. (2005) 'Agrarian moral economies and neoliberalism in Brazil: competing worldviews and the state in the struggle for land', *Environment and Planning A* 37(1), 241–261.

Wolford, W. (2004) 'The land is ours now: spatial imaginaries and the struggle for land in Brazil', *Annals of the Association of American Geographers* 94(2), 409–424.

Wong, K. (2001) 'The showdown before Seattle: race, class, and the framing of a movement', in Yuen, E., Burton Rose, D. and Katsiaficas, G. (eds) *The Battle of Seattle: The New Challenge to Capitalist Globalization*, New York: Soft Skull Press, 215–224.

Woodward, K., Jones III, J. P. and Marston, S. A. (2007) 'The eagle and the flies, a fable for the micro', *Secons Discussion Forum Contribution* No. 12, University of Bonn: SECONS Disussion Forum.

Wynne, B. (1996) 'May the sheep safely graze? A reflexive view of the expert-lay knowledge divide', in Szerszynski, B., Lash, S. and Wynne, B. (eds) *Risk, Environment and Modernity*, London: Sage, 44–83.

Yates, J. (1989) *Mississippi to Madrid: Memoir of a Black American in the Abraham Lincoln Brigade* Seattle: Open Hand.

Young, A. (1892) *Arthur Young's Tour in Ireland 1776–1779*, 2 vols, ed. A. Wollaston Hutton, London: George Bell and Sons.

Young, I. M. (1990) *Justice and the Politics of Difference* Princeton, NJ: Princeton University Press.

Žižek, S. (2005) 'Against the populist temptation', www.lacan.com/zizpopulism. htm, accessed 5 July 2007.

Žižek, S. (1999) 'Carl Schmitt in the age of post-politics', in Mouffe, C. (ed.) *The Challenge of Carl Schmitt*, London: Verso, 18–37.

Index